Patina

Patina

A PROFANE ARCHAEOLOGY

Shannon Lee Dawdy

THE UNIVERSITY OF CHICAGO PRESS

CHICAGO AND LONDON

SHANNON LEE DAWDY is associate professor of anthropology at the University of Chicago. She was awarded a MacArthur Genius Fellowship in 2010.

The University of Chicago Press, Chicago 60637
The University of Chicago Press, Ltd., London
© 2016 by The University of Chicago
All rights reserved. Published 2016.
Printed in the United States of America

25 24 23 22 21 20 19 18 17 16   1 2 3 4 5

ISBN-13: 978–0-226–35105–6 (cloth)
ISBN-13: 978–0-226–35119–3 (paper)
ISBN-13: 978–0-226–35122–3 (e-book)

DOI: 10.7208/chicago/9780226351223.001.0001

Library of Congress Cataloging-in-Publication Data

Names: Dawdy, Shannon Lee, 1967– author.
Title: Patina : a profane archaeology / Shannon Lee Dawdy.
Description: Chicago ; London : The University of Chicago Press, 2016. | Includes
    bibliographical references and index.
Identifiers: LCCN 2015042386 | ISBN 9780226351056 (cloth : alk. paper) | ISBN
    9780226351193 (pbk. : alk. paper) | ISBN 9780226351223 (e-book)
Subjects: LCSH: New Orleans (La.)—Antiquities. | Material culture—Social aspects—
    Louisiana—New Orleans. | Antiques—Social aspects—Louisiana—New Orleans. |
    Historic districts—Social aspects—Louisiana—New Orleans. | Historic buildings—Social
    aspects—Louisiana—New Orleans. | Historic preservation—Social aspects—Louisiana—
    New Orleans. | Archaeology and history—Louisiana—New Orleans. | Excavations
    (Archaeology)—Louisiana—New Orleans.
Classification: LCC F379.N547 D39 2016 | DDC 976.3/35—dc23 LC record available
    at http://lccn.loc.gov/2015042386

♾ This paper meets the requirements of ANSI/NISO Z39.48–1992
(Permanence of Paper).

To Patrick and Lydia. You are here.

Time—He's waiting in the wings
He speaks of senseless things
His script is you and me boys

Time—He flexes like a whore

DAVID BOWIE, lyrics to "Time," written
in New Orleans, November 1972

CONTENTS

ACKNOWLEDGMENTS

If I were a Kula trader, I'd be a very bad one, as I've received a lot of gifts and accumulated a lot of debt that I can probably never repay. If I were a riverboat gambler, I'd be a very dandy one, as I have been outrageously lucky in my career.

Before I begin a very long thank-you list, it may be helpful to trace the historical circuit of my debts. My interest in the aesthetic and affective complex of New Orleans comes in part from living there, off and on, since 1994. And in part from working there. Between 1995 and 1998, I was director of the Greater New Orleans Archaeology Program at the University of New Orleans, which led to the opportunities to excavate at Madame John's Legacy (a National Historic Landmark located in the French Quarter) and the Maginnis Cotton Mill (in the Warehouse District). After completing my dissertation and starting my post at the University of Chicago in 2004, I recommenced archaeological fieldwork in the city, first at the Pitot House in the Bayou St. John neighborhood and then, in 2005, at the Rising Sun Hotel Site in the French Quarter. I finished this last excavation just before Hurricane Katrina hit. In 2008, I began collaborating with the Catholic Cultural Heritage Center of the Archdiocese of New Orleans to research and restore the hurricane-damaged garden behind St. Louis Cathedral locally known as St. Anthony's Garden. This collaboration led to two seasons of fieldwork at the garden (2008 and 2009), followed by another project at an even older church property, Ursuline Convent, in 2011. Years of laboratory work then followed these intensive excavations. As the projects are introduced, notes will refer the reader to the available technical reports as well as previously published articles that offer greater detail about the methods and results.

Due to my background in public archaeology, I became part of a network of colleagues who work in historic preservation, cultural tourism, and public advocacy. When Katrina hit, I found myself pulled back into this network, from which I had drifted in my academic pursuits. I was called upon to serve as a liaison between the Federal Emergency Management Agency (FEMA) and the Louisiana Historic Preservation Office to help assess damage to historic sites in New Orleans and come up with strategies to deal with the scale of the event. I served three months in this capacity in late 2005 that involved, among other things, a block-by-block windshield survey of nearly every street of every historic neighborhood in New Orleans. In the FEMA offices and over candlelit dinners with friends (by necessity, not romance), I had many conversations about the rationales of historic preservation and what counts as old. We talked about whether the city would ever come back and, if it did, whether its unique character would be lost along with so much rotted wood.

This experience and conversations with residents during the early years of recovery led me to develop a more formal program of ethnographic interviews that I conducted between 2008 and 2011. I sought out individuals involved in preservation, in tourism, in the antiques market, and in the collecting of local things. Friends of friends led to more referrals. Nine individuals whose voices are transcribed in the following pages were known to me before the storm. Twenty-three other people I met for the first time through the haphazard pathmaking of ethnographic fieldwork. I have protected their identities through pseudonyms and so cannot thank them by name, but I am deeply grateful for their patience and time.

In Louisiana, I have been the recipient of incredible kindness and real help throughout my career, and especially since Katrina. I am particularly indebted to the late Msgr. Crosby Kern, Dr. Alfred Lemmon, Dr. Chip McGimsey, the late Bettie Pendley, and Steven Schwartz. Staff members at the Office of the Archives of the Archdiocese of New Orleans, the Southeastern Architecture Archives of Tulane University, the Historic New Orleans Collection, and the Louisiana Division of the New Orleans Public Library have been a tremendous resource and help over the years.

I am also grateful for the funding, logistical support, and general tolerance of muddy archaeological work supported by the Louisiana State Museum (for Madame John's Legacy), Historic Restoration, Inc. (for the Maginnis Cotton Mill), the Louisiana Landmarks Society (for the Pitot House), the Historic New Orleans Collection (for the Rising Sun Hotel site), the Getty Foundation (for St. Anthony's Garden), and the Archdiocese of New Orleans (for St. Anthony's Garden and Ursuline Convent). In addition, the work at St. Anthony's Garden and Ursuline Convent, plus three years of comparative and collaborative analysis, was supported by grants from the National Science Foundation (Archaeology Division, Award #0917736) and the National Endowment for the Humanities (Award #RZ-50992–09). The latter institution requests that I make it clear that nothing stated in this book necessarily reflects the views of the NEH. My research and writing were also materially assisted by the Lichtstern Fund of the Department of Anthropology at the University of Chicago and the John D. and Catherine T. MacArthur Foundation.

Archaeology is absurdly labor-intensive and always a team effort. Although I use the convention of the project director to talk about these projects as "mine," they are really "ours." At this point, hundreds of students and volunteers have helped me on-site or in the lab. I wish I could name them all. I want to single out some of the University of Chicago students who made especially important contributions and with whom I feel a bond of sweat, laughs, and tears: Adela Amaral, Joe Bonni, Claire Bowman, Zachary Chase, Geneviève Godbout, Rebecca Graff, Sarah Kautz, Jason Ramsey, and Matt Reilly. In this group, exceptional gratitude goes to D. Ryan Gray and Lauren Zych for years of collaboration and generosity with the results of their own research. In addition to their work in the field and lab, Chris Grant and Theo Kassebaum helped me pull together the photos and images for the book under a tight deadline, and I am grateful for their efforts to make me look good. Although their results do not appear in these pages, I am also grateful for the insight, good cheer, and assistance of my professional collaborators on projects undertaken since 2005: Drs. Susan deFrance, Gayle Fritz, and Kristen Gremillion, as well as Clarissa Cagnato.

Now to get to the densest part of this list—those who have been kindly asking after the health of this book for some years now. Among these are many friends who were exposed to early or fragmentary versions of these chapters. Some exchanges were simply through conversation or collaboration on other projects but contributed to my thought process in some way. Some colleagues invited me to speak at their institutions or events, helping push chapters along. A few just suggested something to read or gave me words of encouragement when I needed them. They include Anna Agbe-Davies, Kevin Anzzolin, Jeremy David Bendik-Kramer, Lauren Berlant, Iris Bernblum, Matthew Briones, Bill Brown, El Casella, Jean Comaroff, John Comaroff, Zoe Crossland, Mickey Dietler, Judy Farquhar, Andrew Ferrell, Sev Fowles, Chris Garces, Alexandra Hartnett, Kate Ingold, Christopher N. Matthews, Yael Navaro-Yashin, Stephan Palmié, Lawrence Powell, Danilyn Rutherford, Ken Sassaman, Elizabeth Scott, Rebecca Scott, Julie Skurski, Adam Smith, Nick Spitzer, Dell Upton, Daniel Usner, Barb Voss, and Norm Yoffee. Some people who belong on this list have also been there for me personally and rescued me in little ways that I will always be grateful for: Hussein Agrama, Jessica Cattelino, François Richard, Seth Richardson, Anwen Tormey, and Mary Weismantel. A very special thanks goes to Nancy Munn for tea, for conversations that went to the heart of the matter here, and for pointing out my bad habit of loading up single words with multiple meanings.

Although I can't list them all, I know that I have benefited from gentle challenges by many other colleagues at forums hosted by the following institutions: Anthropology Department of Cornell University; Archaeology Seminar, University of Manchester; Bard Graduate Center; Cambridge University; New York Academy of Sciences / Wenner Gren Foundation seminar; Institute for Fine Arts, New York University; Department of Anthropology, Columbia University; Department of Anthropology, University of California–Santa Cruz; Harvard University; University of Massachusetts–Boston; Tulane University; Louisiana State University; University of Florida; and more than one session each at the annual meetings of the North American Theoretical Archaeology Group, the Conference on Historical Archaeology in Theory, and the American Anthropological Association.

I am also grateful for the intellectual environment and support of the Department of Anthropology at the University of Chicago. Staff members Anne Chien and Sandra Hagen have helped me out in many pinches over the years. Colleagues at the University of Chicago's Center for Contemporary Theory were especially helpful with feedback and encouragement in the late stages. Students enrolled in the following graduate seminars were marvelous teachers and interlocutors: Time and Temporality, Anthropology of Louisiana, and Archaeology of the Contemporary. I also want to thank Owen Kohl, an amazing coteacher who helped free me up so I could finish this.

One of my recent great strokes of luck was running into my talented editor, Priya Nelson, in the gym and talking books. I am grateful to her and to Ellen Kladky, Lois Crum, and the anonymous reviewers for their advice and timely responses. It was a delightfully stress-free process.

Writing this book has kept me going. More importantly, some people have. I want to thank my California family—Arletta Dawdy, Jess and Kim Dawdy and Allie—for their tolerance and understanding. My mom is an inspiration. I hope that I am aging as gracefully as she is. While I have always felt a family connection to New Orleans, in recent years this has come to feel like one with tensile strength. I send out a virtual embrace to all the extended Rogan clan, and especially to sisters Alcena, Alicia, Amanda, and Jessica. Other New Orleans friends I hold dear have contributed to this project, either directly or indirectly: Jimbo Crouch, Juana Ibáñez, Benjamin Maygarden, and Ruben and Louise Saenz. In Chicago, my flesh and blood, Asa McNaughton, offers comic relief and thoughtful companionship that exceed my expectations for motherhood. I am grateful to his father, Dan McNaughton, for helping raise a fine young man and for his goodwill in working around my erratic schedule. My friend Jane Baxter deserves some kind of trophy I am still trying to fashion in my head for her creative outings, warm wisdom, and artisan whiskey. She has helped me through several winters.

For last, I have saved my deepest gratitude for two individuals who bravely ventured into the messiest underbrush of the manuscript and gave generously of their time and thoughts, reading it cover to cover. I dared not ask such a massive favor from two brilliant people who were not also among my closest peeps, so there's more to thank them for than heavy edits. So double scotch thanks to Alison Kohn for making me dance and to William Mazzarella for shared mana.

CHAPTER 1

Introduction: Katrina, Nostalgia, Profanity

> It generally happens that people's surroundings reflect more or less accurately their minds and dispositions. —Andrew Lang, *The Green Fairy Book*

For several weeks after Hurricane Katrina's slow-blooming devastation, New Orleans was horribly quiet. But by the end of October 2005, dump trucks, chain saws, and the familiar strains of self-deprecating irony began to fill the air. An irreverent sense of humor marked by pain and politics is one of the enduring qualities of the city's residents. It often takes material form, such as in satiric Mardi Gras floats. Or, after the levee breaks, as refrigerators ruined by rotted food, set out on the street and tagged with graffiti messages such as "Loot this!" or "Stinky Cheese: Return to France!" Local wit also paraded in new linguistic inventions. A slang developed among residents struggling to cope with the continuing disaster. They complained about "Katrina brain" and described the uncanny place where they lived as "K-ville." The new vocabulary gestured to the foggy confusion of posttraumatic stress and the shrunken, redundantly scarred landscape. One particularly redolent phrase, "Katrina Patina," referred to the multihued encrustation that water and mold left in horizontal strata upon houses, possessions, and even the people sullied by the hard work of cleanup. The term mocks New Orleans's vanity about its status as a well-preserved "antique city." More seriously, it is a phrase used to describe any visible mark of the storm that evokes epic stories of evacuation, abandonment, rescue, and despair.

In my interview with a clock collector and antique dealer I'll call Tom, our conversation moved quickly from why he prefers clocks that haven't been "spiffed up" too much, that retain a bit of dirt and what he professionally calls *patina*, to his experiences during and after the storm:

> Talking about patina. When my son and I snuck in here . . . and we came in and nothing was stirring, just some soldiers walking by, they stopped and

talked to us. We didn't see anything moving. Maybe a car now and then. It was like the end of the world. Everything was grey. *That's* a patina. We had a patina after the storm. It was grey and desolate. . . . [Now] everything's *before* and *after* Katrina.[1]

In the rebuilding process, some residents were careful to preserve one section of unpainted wall on their houses that bears Katrina patina, as a material archive of their historical experience. Another visible sign ubiquitous on any street-level tour of the city, even many years after the storm, is the spray-painted "X" symbol left by rescue and recovery teams on every one of New Orleans's buildings (fig. 1.1). So every building, whether affected directly by storm damage and the levee failures or not, was still damaged—was marked—by the disaster. The same could be said of the city's residents. Some whitewashed over the marks as one of their first acts upon return to the city. Others do not have the means to repaint or have not returned. And some are purposefully preserving the graffiti as a form of memorial. These markers and the varied human responses to them underscore how New Orleans is an especially archaeological place. Residents are keenly aware of dirt and debris, of the processes of decay, burial, demolition, and the creation of new landscapes. Survivors understand their lives stratigraphically. Referring to the rupture of an event still difficult to comprehend, the new slang divides time into "Pre-K" New Orleans and "Post-K" New Orleans.

Pre-K patina was also very much a concern—and a point of contention—among historic preservationists, urban planners, and the purveyors of modular homes. While there are several new housing designs now offered on the market that quote historic New Orleans styles, many residents find something lacking: "What everyone wants to avoid . . . [is] more stage-set re-creations of vernacular architecture . . . and blocks of traditional houses in period costume." Local architect Robert Cangelosi warned, "We're homogenizing the city very quickly. If we aren't careful, we will lose our greatest economic engine, which is our gumbo culture. That's why people come here. It's not Disneyland, and it's not Anywhere USA."[2] Others argued that the Disneyfication of New Orleans was already complete in the French Quarter and that after the storm it would simply creep further into the neighborhoods. Although Walt Disney admired New Orleans, once saying, "Where else can you find iniquity and antiquity so close together?," it was precisely these qualities that he sanitized out of his one-half-scale version of a "cleaner, shinier" French Quarter at Disneyland. He erased the patina—the peeling paint of exterior walls and the lacquer of cigarette smoke and fry grease clinging to interior walls. Patina told a

FIGURE 1.1. Post-Katrina house. Photo by the author.

story inappropriate to Disneyland—a story of iniquity perhaps, but also of inequality, multiple layers of colonialism, the cyclical disasters of capitalism, and an orientalism that has long fed a different form of fantasy consumption. There also seemed to be something uncomfortably intimate about New Orleans. Perhaps something that shouldn't, or couldn't, be sold.[3]

Katrina patina does not just cover buildings. It coats small objects. In a CNN interview at the Jackson Barracks Museum, a complex dating to the 1820s situated in the Lower Ninth Ward, the reporter described the scene: "Nearly 9,000 military artifacts, dating from colonial times to today, are strewn about the museum. Many are laid out on drying pads like wounded troops. The mannequin of a buffalo soldier, mud-soaked epilets [epaulets], a priceless pre–Civil War knapsack. From tea cups to field radios, the items in this room date throughout Louisiana's history in battle. When the levees broke, the water rose up over my hand. Everything in here was submerged and floating in water, along with the identifying tags on each item." The reporter then turned to interview Harmon Fischer, a member of the National Guard's Restoration Unit, who offered: "It's very tedious, but very worthwhile once you get through with the process. When I look at all of it, I look at it as history with a little more history tacked onto it. Still going to be the same item. Just a little more history. It went through

Katrina." An off-camera voice piped in: "I guess they have a Katrina patina to them now, those artifacts."[4]

Lori Gordon is a visual artist who lives on the Mississippi Gulf Coast. She lost her home, her studio, and her entire beachfront community to the storm surge. When she returned, she began to gather objects of Katrina debris from her house site and those of others, finding beauty in their battered skins. She made use of objects bearing what she, too, called "Katrina Patina." Patina seems to be simultaneously a thing of beauty, a residue of history, and a marker of social belonging in the present.[5]

Beyond the storm, the word *patina* encompasses an aesthetic sensibility that defines much of cultural and material life in New Orleans, from the connoisseurship of traditional jazz, to the facades of the French Quarter, to recipes for Creole turtle soup and the dandified consumption of "the Green Fairy" (absinthe) in ornamented bars. Why are New Orleanians so fixated on old things? What does patina do for them?

For this book, the word *patina* summons a triangular relationship between time, materiality, and the social imaginary that I will explore at different scales and from various angles. In the case of New Orleans, a local aesthetic embraces the look of age with overtones of romanticism, death, and the erotic. New Orleans brands itself as an antique city. Locals seem particularly alert to the complex space-time of their environment and map the city through a knowledge of the past, both deep and recent.

Although there are some peculiarities to the New Orleans story, it shares the antique aesthetic with places like Kyoto, Venice, Cairo, Rome, and Havana. Globally, the appeal such cities have for tourism derives in part from their contrast with the clean lines of modernism and the linear time of modernity. They are often perceived as slow zones and remnants of a way of life that has been lost or is in danger of extinction. But this perception risks misunderstanding antique cities as static dioramas and ignoring their vitality in the present. They also tend to be places where the imagined community of the city is quite declarative. Ultimately, I will argue that the patina aesthetic has social effects of a totemic kind.[6]

While patina undoubtedly drives an economy of heritage tourism and provincial sentimentality, it also dangles keys to understanding the sociology of the city. My drive to understand New Orleans as a package of self-reinforcing representations and practices has risen out of a struggle with a puzzle. It is not so difficult to comprehend what divides the city by race, class, religion, and ethnicity. Such tensions have been the subjects of many studies, and more are surely needed with the city's sudden leap from desolation to gentrification.[7] What is more baffling, and less explored, is what holds it together *despite* these divides. As will become evident in the interviews dispersed throughout the chapters, New Orleanians insist there *is* something that holds them together. Although some have a hard time putting their finger on it, others are not hesitant to call it a kind of love.

In a peculiar demographic counterpoint, by one measure New Orleans is the most visited city in the United States, and by another it is home to one of the most stable, multigenerational urban populations in the country.[8] Before Katrina, everyone visited and natives rarely moved on. The economy of New Orleans has long been oriented toward the passer-through: the *coureur de bois*, the Irish smuggler, the deployed soldier, the Kaintuck, the Mexican sailor, the slave trader, the cotton merchant, the Storyville john, and the Texas tourist. This demographic oddity is paralleled by a material one. From its early colonial days, the city has been depicted as "ancient" and well-preserved, although it was actually destroyed and rebuilt several times prior to Katrina. Locals imagine so-called Creole culture as stable, traditional, even conservative, and built upon the bedrock of a French colonial past, although only a tiny number of residents could actually claim biological descent from this population, and even though materially there is almost nothing left from this period. The French Quarter is not even French. With the exception of a single building (Ursuline Convent), all of the standing structures the visitor sees today were built in the later Spanish (1769–1803) or American (post–1804) periods. Residents insist that the materiality of the city (its distinctive food, architecture, gardens, and Creole interiors) have deep roots fiercely preserved by a strong sense of tradition. However, a closer scrutiny of the archaeological and archival records shows that these material realms have undergone major renovations, revolutions, and episodes of invention. One way, then, to understand patina is as a medium of aesthetic value *perceived* to have accumulated through time that represents the social palimpsest of New Orleans.

This book is a sum of diverse parts: archaeology, ethnography, the eighteenth century, Hurricane Katrina, literature, phenomenology, critical theory, Durkheim's mana, and Freud's fetish. My hope is that this work will find an audience as diverse as its sources and methods. The questions I pursue demand different forms of evidence and a wide range of engagements. The project has emerged from a deep immersion in New Orleans, but it is ultimately about how things that happen there illuminate questions far beyond the city's limits. I am committed to the belief that New Orleans may be extreme, but not exceptional. Stated broadly, I want to better understand the intimate relationships that can develop between old objects and humans, both as a historical accumulation and as a dynamic in the present.

CRITICAL NOSTALGIA

Before Weber theorized the "disenchantment of the world" wrought by capitalism, there were already moves afoot to reenchant it through aesthetic and affective practices under the patina effect: a value for old, quaint things. These social-aesthetic movements include romanticism, nostalgia, orientalism, and the picturesque, and they began as early as the mid-eighteenth century. While Marx argued that the commodity was enchanted through the false magic of fetishization (more on this in chapter 5), like Weber and Durkheim, he worried that this was a distraction from the growing forces of alienation and anomie, an impersonalization of humans' relations with one another and with their physical environment. Later theorists of commodity aesthetics came to recognize that urbanism and the commodity form emanated their own kind of modernist enchantment promising a future full of possibility. At the same time, they produced dialectical reactions in the form of antimodern utopian movements and the fetishization of objects seen to have an aura that set them apart from the store-bought. Such objects included those that were handmade, pre-industrial, or "primitive."[9]

In New Orleans, these retro reactions to capitalist modernity became particularly well developed in the nineteenth century. Perhaps more surprising, they intensified in the twentieth, when aesthetic modernism was reshaping other "old" cities such as New York, Paris, and Mexico City.[10] Instead, New Orleans came to be a place invested in what I call *critical nostalgia*. One way to refute capitalism and its temporality is to reject its accompanying aesthetic of "the new." This move is not simply a retreat into the past. Svetlana Boym distinguished two types of nostalgia—the *restorative*, which aims to naturalize power structures and inequalities, and the *reflective*, which selectively values past lifeways and old objects as a form of protest against the present.[11] Restorative nostalgia invents traditions, maintains buildings in like-new condition, and serves nationalist agendas through heritage programs. It consists of efforts to *erase* the passage of time rather than valorize it. In contrast, reflective nostalgia emphasizes the look of age and the contrasts between past and present. It engages with history as a resource for utopian alternatives to the present. Aesthetically, it is a funky, unrepaired type associated with an ironic Gemeinschaft, in contrast to restorative nostalgia's cleanliness and serious demeanor (think Williamsburg or Prague). Anyone having a passing familiarity with New Orleans will recognize it as the American ideal of Boym's reflective type. But I am not quite satisfied with the label. I have chosen to add my own neologism, *critical nostalgia*, because "reflective" sounds too passive to adequately convey what I see at work in New Orleans. While Boym identifies nostalgia as primarily an idea existing in the heads of actors and the words of writers, I am interested in nostalgic *practices* and material *things* as world-making. Patina is not only a political aesthetic but a political *force* flowing through alternative circuits of value that are both moral and material.

New Orleans has often been depicted as insular, self-indulgent, and frozen in time, but behind the veil of heritage, the city and its people have constantly adapted to new conditions and often posed a challenge to the prevailing values of its reluctant host nation. It is one of those places (and there are others) where capitalist ideology is given a hard time. Some of the reasons for this are quite local and contingent, but telling. They include a Creole backlash against an onslaught of entrepreneurial Americans following the Louisiana Purchase; the contradictions of slavery in which the peculiar rationality of valuing humans as commodities was exposed in extremis in New Orleans's slave markets in the nineteenth century; and the ways in which New Orleans has been repeatedly abandoned by major capital following World War II, the civil rights movement, and, most recently, Hurricane Katrina. It is a place that has suffered more busts than booms in capitalist cycles, making local residents wary of modernity's promises, if not outright rejecting its ideology of progress. Admittedly, New Orleans has had a particularly disruptive history, not all of which can be blamed on capitalism, from the wars between the French and their American Indian neighbors,[12] to two subsequent imperial invasions by the Spanish and the Americans, and a seemingly relentless parade of human and natural disasters. The city has experienced wild pendulum swings since the 1720s, not uncommonly seeing its population double in a decade or decline just as fast. Despite (or because of?) all this, New Orleans today does not hesitate to fashion itself as a heterotopia that offers a form of old-timey enchantment. Its success in tourism suggests that many consumers buy into their own alienation, coming to find something they are convinced is missing from their lives elsewhere.

The effort to understand local nostalgic practices plunged me into the domains of historic preservation, intimate hospitality, ghost stories, heirlooming, antique and junk collecting, perfumes, gardening, and Mardi Gras. Some of these practices are inflected with an auto-orientalism encouraged by tourism, but I came to see that they are also deeply affective modes that have collective social effects, a realization that encouraged a return to venerable anthropological ideas like mana, totem, and fetish. My informants led the way down this unexpected path by resorting to an anthropological vernacular about "mana" and "tribal information" when I asked them why they liked old things. Their responses described an intimate relationship to old objects that at times ventured into mysticism. They frequently slid from a fact-filled narrative history into a more fumbling expression of the presence of pastness all around them. For some, this took the form of a haunting; old houses and objects are mediums for the spirits of the dead. This disposition toward the uncanny seems closely related to a more general phenomenological orientation of New Orleanians to their surroundings that can best be described as heterotemporal, comprised of multiple pasts, presents, and futures. Such heterotemporal sensitivity resonated with my archaeological knowledge of the city and its cycles of buildup and rupture. The past is both spectral and real in New Orleans. The city's traditions cannot in any simple way be said to be either invented or inherited. The dead are a creative force in ongoing life. If we understand a city as a churning assemblage of human and nonhuman elements undergoing processes of accumulation, demolition, decay, and rebirth (which I argue we *should*, and in chapter 2 I give it a name: *social stratigraphy*), then the New Orleans habit of granting recognition to old things seems entirely warranted, if unusually alert. Patina represents generations of social formation.

PROFANE ARCHAEOLOGY

Results of archaeological excavations I have conducted in New Orleans over the past twenty years anchor each chapter and provide the time-depth necessary to witness how patina develops. My encounters in post-Katrina New Orleans with residents who saved, lost, or recovered artifacts from their ruined house sites also inform this project, as do their arguments about preservation and authenticity in the rebuilding process. The results of thirty-two ethnographic interviews conducted between 2008 and 2011 help make sense of the archaeology of both past and present, as do forays into the city's literary and bureaucratic archives.[13]

The "Profane Archaeology" of the book's title cites several themes of both content and form. In terms of method, this project is a kind of archaeology, but one that may offend the mainstream of the discipline—a kind of profanity. I use my archaeological research to provide temporal depth and problematic examples of phenomena strewn across time. I do not deploy archaeological data as empirical forensics. My approach is unapologetically humanist. Sometimes the archaeology presents a productive question but the answer might be pursued by other means.[14] Without the archaeology, the questions would have been more predictable. Above all, excavation should disturb the surface of things. Although I would not object to having this work classified with the emerging field of the archaeology of the contemporary, that label might give a false impression that I privilege the *now*. I am more interested in working back and forth across my field site's period of documented occupation, from about 1715 until the day this book was completed in 2015, just a few days after the ten-year anniversary of the storm.[15]

Secondly, this work is an experiment in Benjaminian archaeology, and so "profane archaeology" also refers to Walter Benjamin's "profane illumination." The poet-philosopher often imagined himself as a kind of archaeologist. *The Arcades Project* has even been called "an urban archaeology of the recent past" for its attention to mundane artifacts, streetscapes, and temporal processes such as discard and abandonment.[16] Benjamin was as interested in the conditions of consumption as in the conditions of production. He strove to see how material culture pulses with meaning long after the labor of production within an ongoing web of social relations. Benjamin used the phrase *profane illumination* to refer to a "materialist, anthropological inspiration" that surrealism, hashish smoking, and solitary contemplation (or *distraction*) can induce.[17] I am not necessarily advocating these as the methods of a new archaeology, but I am suggesting that the insights Benjamin arrived at are useful, particularly those regarding the profoundly muddled relations between objects and subjects, in both psychoanalytic and Marxian terms. He models a way of understanding everyday objects that takes into account their shifting meanings over time and the way in which they can suddenly activate currents from the past that alter the present.

I propose that Benjamin's approach to "dialectical images" be extended to *dialectical objects*. In his terms, dialectical seeing means attending to the multiple temporal frames that can endow an image (an object) with meaning and make it politically active. He sought out experiences in which the past seemed to flash into the present, revealing contradictory conditions and nonteleological histories. He distinguishes this method both from hermeneutics (reading intentionally encoded messages) and from phenomenology (sensing the immediacy of the present). Instead, looking for the dialectical is akin to provoking Proust's "involuntary memories." When applied to the multiple relations between objects and people, these flashes of lost time highlight moments of desire, routine use, or breakdown. Archaeology, both the dirty kind and the thought experiment, is a deliberate attempt to induce these moments of illumination—the past shining a troubled light on the present.[18]

Aura, another word borrowed from Benjamin, links to the final allusion contained in *profane archaeology*. Although the political significance of aura appears to have changed over the course of Benjamin's work, it consistently indexed an aspect of images, individuals, art objects, and the beauty of natural landscapes that exceeds their concreteness. Aura is "an elusive phenomenal substance, ether, or halo that surrounds a person or object of perception, encapsulating its individuality and authenticity."[19] The best-known deployment of this idea is in Benjamin's piece on artwork in the age of mechanical reproduction, in which he forecasts that art will lose its aura. But in other passages, aura emanates from everyday objects that have been intimately modified by human use and touch—what he calls the "aura of the habitual." Aura is not always seen or recognized, but in certain modes of perception, "experience of the aura . . . arises from the transposition of a response characteristic *of* human society to the relationship of the inanimate or nature *with* human beings. . . . To experience the aura of a phenomenon we look at means to invest it with the ability to look back at us."[20] If this sounds like a theory verging on theosophy, that would not be a wrong impression. Benjamin felt cautiously drawn to spiritual and cabalistic thinkers. If this sounds like a theory verging on totemism, then you begin to follow where I am going. Benjamin's *aura* sounds a lot like Durkheim's *mana*.

The "profane" in the book's subtitle is thus also meant to irreverently reference the sacred-profane dichotomy that Durkheim pursued in *Elementary Forms of Religious Life*. I feel that Durkheim was right about the social effects of certain *mana*-full objects but that the formalities of ritual, taboo, and religion simply delineate extreme forms (sacred forms) of a more generalized way of being with the world. *Mana* is a word from Polynesia and Melanesia that has excited the field of comparative religion since the Victorian era. Sir James Frazer, E. B. Tylor, R. R. Marett, and Marcel Mauss all postulated generalized theories of mana, although among the Austronesian cultures from which it is borrowed, its meaning varied from simply a force of nature (like lightning or wind), to the charismatic power of an individual (that could be used for good or evil), to an impersonal, unseen force that characterized those objects/people/animals that are set aside as sacred. Durkheim went with this last conception and interpreted it as the general principle behind all religious practices, from animism to monotheism. He then argued that the various strategies employed to channel *mana* are collective representations of society itself and that the affect surrounding them promotes solidarity. He fully recognized the role of material objects in these practices. The totem relates to mana as "the tangible form in which that intangible substance is represented in the imagination." Further, any old object would do: "The most insignificant objects, even the most commonplace ones, can play this role."[21]

Although *Elementary Forms of Religious Life* still carries a profound load for anthropology and sociology today, Durkheim has been criticized for depending overmuch on two polarities. The sacred and the profane may be harder to separate than he hoped. Mary Douglas's work *Purity and Danger* showed how the same objects can move back and forth across this line (which is precisely what makes them dangerous), and Edmund Leach argued in favor of a graduated spectrum of objects and practices ranging from the sacred to the profane.[22] The second duality that preoccupied Durkheim's generation was that between the primitive and the modern. In Durkheim's case, he worried that modern capitalist society was losing its religion—fewer and fewer things were sacred—and thus it was losing its ability to form social bonds. In the short historical perspective, writing on the eve of World War I, his existential anxieties seem well founded. However, in the long view, as Benjamin discovered, certain objects colloquially understood as plain, everyday "profane" things can have "the aura of the habitual." And this aura, this nonsacred sense of historical connection, can do its own work of citing something that transcends the isolation of the individual. Perhaps patina is aura made curiously concrete. It is, after all, also known as the golden stain.

A BRIEF HISTORY OF PATINA

In contemporary English, patina has three definitions: (1) "a surface appearance of something grown beautiful esp. with age or use"; (2) "an appearance or aura that is derived from association, habit, or established character," and (3) "a superficial covering or exterior."[23] Patina thus has an aesthetic quality with connotations of age, is a signifier of certain social habits, and can be artificially created, or faked. I find conceptual power in the idea of patina precisely because it has these three meanings that together imply some ambivalence. These definitions are of relatively recent origin, dating to the middle of the eighteenth century, when both architectural romanticism and the authentication of antiquity emerged as preoccupations in the West—trends that grew stronger and more philosophically articulated in the nineteenth century.

The word *patina* itself derives from the Greek and Latin term for a shallow dish. In the medieval period, "paten" referred to a flat metal serving dish that carried the Eucharist during Communion. Perhaps this dish, usually made from a precious metal such as silver, was lovingly polished, since the term then gets picked up by Italian cobblers in the Renaissance to refer to the gloss they give shoes (thus giving us "patent leather"). By

1681, an entry for "patina" appears in Filippo Baldinucci's dictionary of art as a slang term used by painters to refer to "the darkening that time makes on pictures." He says they also call this effect the *skin* of a painting, layers that darken in the sun and crack with age.[24] Although the term as we know it dates to the Renaissance, recognition of this aesthetic effect has a deeper history. Apelles of Kos was a classical Greek painter of the fourth century whom Pliny praises for his many innovations in the art, including a closely guarded recipe for a black varnish, called *atramentum,* which served both to preserve and to soften the paint's colors. Our earliest known reference to patina was thus to a kind that was artificially applied.[25]

Today most scholarly references to patina occur in art history and conservation, referring either to the buildup on old paintings or to various natural and artificial surface effects on metal objects. The so-called conservation wars have raged since the middle of the nineteenth century. A controversy continues over whether it is a good idea to "clean" the accumulated patinas on paintings, particularly those of the Old Dutch Masters, and venerated landmarks such as Michelangelo's painting of the Sistine Chapel.[26] Matters of both taste and interpretation are at stake. Would the paintings still look like authentic *old* masters if the "yellowing of time" was removed? Or is it desirable to restore the once-fresh colors, thus returning the works to an original state? Complicating these controversies is the fact that many painters either intentionally darkened their paintings, much as Apelles did, or painted with the forethought that young colors would mellow with age. In the latter case, their intention was to produce a color composition as it would appear several years after the paint had dried.

Fluctuations in the fashion for patina in the Western art world are clearly tied to social and political dynamics. Anthropologist Grant McCracken is one of the few scholars to have addressed the phenomenon of patina, although his understanding differs significantly from my own. He argues that the look of age accrued on family heirlooms and houses in medieval and early modern Europe became an icon (in Charles Sanders Peirce's sense) of the family's social status in a system based on aristocratic birth privilege.[27] He avers that antique objects provided a way to authenticate claims made to privilege, as their patina would have been difficult to fake— they acquired their sheen only by being passed down through rooted generations. According to McCracken, this political aesthetic breaks down in the mid-eighteenth century when a new aesthetic novelty arrived on the revolutionary scene, allowing the nouveaux riches to set different aesthetic terms for distinction, based on knowledge and connoisseurship rather than on simple inheritance of antiquated things. He opposes ancien régime patina to the fashions of modernity. However, patina in fact *can* be faked, and it was being faked extensively in the early modern period. Perhaps more troubling, the significance of patina appears to be quite a bit less obvious, stable, or universal than "icon" would suggest. Different groups impute different meanings to it, for different purposes. Finally, opposing ancien régime patina to modern fashion creates a false dichotomy and overstates a historical trajectory. Patina is still very much with us. And in some places, like New Orleans, it grows like mold. As an aesthetic it comes and goes, spiraling around in reaction to whatever counts as "the new." What counts as "the old" is, of course, an ever-growing pile of possibilities.

In the eighteenth century, a taste for patina did inform a collecting craze for classical, Renaissance, and Old Dutch Master art among the West's old and new elites. Collectors would decline to buy pieces that failed to exhibit the requisite crust and haze of time, either finding such items less aesthetically pleasing or fearing they were forgeries. Ironically, these buyers may have been duped, as the patina itself could be the sign of a fake. In this period, many painters accelerated the patina look by adding a final coat of yellow lacquer or by blowing tobacco smoke onto the canvas, a practice parodied in an etching by Hogarth (fig. 1.2).[28]

In Europe, the appeal of patina declined in the late eighteenth century. The art trends popularized by the American and French revolutions valorized neoclassical styles with simple, egalitarian lines and themes, as well as bold, fresh colors. Popular democracy had no need for patina, no need for art to validate the roots and educated tastes of elites. But even this fad faded with time, and the romantic era of the mid-to-late nineteenth century heralded a return to patina simultaneous with the hardening of Victorian class hierarchies and the spread of the new imperialism across Asia and Africa. During this period, the craze for patina expanded into larger media, encrusting architecture and entire landscapes. John Ruskin, the well-known British romantic art critic, valorized patina in his work *The Seven Lamps of Architecture*. Specifically, patina is a quality of his Lamp of Memory: "The greatest glory of a building is not in its stones, nor in its gold. Its glory is in its Age. . . . It is in [the walls'] lasting witness against men, in their quiet contrast with the transitional character of all things. . . . [It] connects forgotten and following ages with each other, and half constitutes the identity, as it concentrates the sympathy, of nations: It is in that golden stain of time."[29]

Ruskin also asserted that the new architecture of his day should "be made historical," or constructed with an eye toward its future past. He advocated preservation, but not restoration, which he called "the worst manner of destruction" because it removed the finish and "some sweetness in the gentle lines which rain and sun had wrought."[30] Ruskin's project

FIGURE 1.2. Etching by William Hogarth, *The Time Smoking a Picture.*

was not only to illuminate what he felt were important principles for aesthetically evaluating architecture, but to argue that architecture is full of
morality—that in describing the proper relationship between the "body
and soul" of architecture, one is at the same time describing the proper
relationship between the body and soul of society. According to Ruskin, a
proper social body must respect its forebears and age gracefully, refusing
mawkish modern fads. His ideas may now seem like a quaint reflection

of the romantic era, but they are not without analytic validity. Edmund Leach asserted that "logically, aesthetics and ethics are identical. If we are to understand the ethical rules of a society, it is aesthetics that we must study."[31] The romantic patina *ethic* became commonplace by the late nineteenth century in the works of travel writers, journalists, poets, and early historic preservationists. Strains of it are still present today in the same genres, as well as in the principles applied through the driest preservation laws and archaeology contracts.

Alois Riegl, a young Austrian contemporary of Ruskin's, was more a formalist than a moralist. He also believed buildings should be allowed to naturally decay and to show their "age value."[32] Riegl's philosophy might be thought of as a sort of ethical phenomenology that has been revived within cultural studies among those disaffected with modernism. While Madalina Diaconu includes an aura of "nobility" in the associations of patina, she also recognizes more general aspects of patina in that it "exemplifies the aesthetic (i.e. positive) value of time. Patina records the passage of an object through time, whether continuous or homogenous or violent and discontinuous; it stores history—the object's story within the life-world—and saves the past from oblivion."[33] She also recognizes that there is something peculiarly agentive and vulnerable about patinated material—a polished metal door handle or a well-worn book bear the signs of reacting to human touch.

The art world and archaeology come together in a common interest in the type of patina that appears on metal sculptures and artifacts, such as the verdigris of bronze. Many archaeologists have benefited from the electrochemical metal conservation processes developed by the Metropolitan Museum of Art in the 1920s to remove and halt corrosion. In one of the earliest how-to reports of this process, the conservators note that natural patinas have a stratigraphy. They result from multiple layers of oils and environmental agents encountered during stages in the artifact's life course. This otherwise dry technical brief exudes a Ruskin-like language of beauty and morality. Patina is not a neutral substance. It is either good or malignant:

> This corrosion is so slow that years pass before it attains perfection. It is probable that the best patinas owe much of their beauty to a slight impregnation by oily substances coming from handlings and polishing. These oils or greases fill the pores and, though minute in quantity, affect the luster and to a lesser degree the color. Such a patina protects the bronze and the attractive color, texture and luster add much to its beauty.

> There is another kind of patina, corrosive in its nature and unattractive in appearance, which not only is undesirable but must be eliminated whenever it is present. This . . . [is] the malignant patina or bronze disease.[34]

The writers insist that nonmalignant patinas should be preserved, as they give the object the desirable appearance of antiquity. But the report also describes the manner in which objects, at the end of their treatment, should be artificially repatinated. Thus, the final step of the conservation process is to fake patina.[35] This ambivalence about patina highlights that it is a process of both accumulation and decay that must be kept in a cared-for balance.

Yuriko Saito draws a parallel between the British tradition of the picturesque and the Japanese principle of *wabi* as aesthetic systems that share a value for the look of age. Her thinking derives not from art history but from environmental philosophy's engagement with landscape aesthetics and a search for the sublime in nature.[36] She moves from there into what she calls "everyday aesthetics" that govern the relationships between people and the materials of their quotidian life, such as meals, gardens, and household interiors. In Japan, the aesthetic criteria applied to these domains include neatness and clutter and ideas of what is natural and proper. She argues that for everyday objects we need an approach different from the predominating art-centered theories, because the latter are predicated on the experience of contemplation (perhaps *the* core idea of Kantian aesthetics). Everyday objects, however pretty they may be, rarely trigger long contemplative moments. Instead, they activate taken-for-granted standards of sensual pleasure at the same time that they define what is socially acceptable in quick moments of consumption, socializing, work, and flânerie. This is a mode of attention that Walter Benjamin called *distraction*. "Distraction and concentration form polar opposites which may be stated as follows: A man who concentrates before a work of art is absorbed by it. . . . In contrast, the distracted mass absorbs the work of art. This is most obvious with regard to buildings."[37]

Saito's identification of certain valued qualities in Japanese everyday aesthetics also has a kinship with Nancy Munn's work in which she deployed Peirce's idea of the *qualisign*. *Qualia* refers to sensual aspects of a sign (such as color, texture, shape) that provoke an intuitive "feeling" that is its referent. Whereas McCracken favored Peirce's *icon* to understand patina as an emblem of social privilege, the latter's idea of qualisign may be a better fit for the "golden stain of time," which tends to be a fairly unstable and underarticulated signifier. When I could get people to articulate what they liked about old things, they talked more freely about how such objects made them feel than about what made the objects beautiful.[38]

Terry Eagleton locates the aesthetic faculty in the body as well as the mind. Aesthetics are what organizes "the whole of our sensate life together—the business of affections and aversions, of how the world strikes the body on its sensory surfaces, of that which takes roots in the gaze and the guts and all that arises from our most banal, biological insertion into the world."[39] The everyday aesthetics of an old coat or a kitchen garden are neither entirely outside symbolic thought, nor are they entirely determined by it. In this slippery relation between *the ways things feel* and *what things mean*, Eagleton recognizes the potential for everyday aesthetics to serve two political masters: that of bourgeois distinction *and* that of utopian critique.[40] When everyday aesthetics have been studied in the social sciences, the tendency has been to emphasize the former to the neglect of the latter. This is an imbalance that New Orleans insists we address.

WHAT FOLLOWS

In the chapters that follow, I use the dialectical objects and landscapes revealed by archaeology as openers for each thematic foray into the relationship between the patina aesthetic, temporal experience, and social life. Along the way, I make several subarguments.

Chapter 2, "Ruins and Heterogeneous Time," opens with an example of how urban archaeology heaves the past back into view, demanding engagement and revision. Ruins and the visible palimpsest of the urban landscape shape experiences of time. In this chapter, I lay out my approach to temporality via three ideas: *heterogeneous time, the social relativity of time,* and *social stratigraphy.* While doing so, I begin to explain how New Orleans became old and to demonstrate the complex ways in which New Orleanians sense and talk about the time-space continuum.

The third chapter, "A Haunted House Society," begins with an account of facts and fictions surrounding the National Historic Landmark site Madame John's Legacy. The connoisseurship of New Orleans's architecture, the cultivation of tourism, and the politics of historic preservation are all key to understanding the aesthetics and social life of old buildings. Patina in the city has built up through a combination of nostalgic forces from both within and without. It stokes the passions of tourism but also incorporates newcomers and totemically connects residents. Locals say their houses have a kind of *mana.* And they talk about ghosts a lot. I argue that New Orleans is something like a "house society" in Lévi-Strauss's words—a community in which kinship is calculated through architecture rather than blood.

In "French Things" (chapter 4), attention turns to small objects such as faience rouge pots, French wine bottles, and perfume bottles. The materialized "Frenchness" of New Orleans is entangled with its perceived antiquity and eroticism. In the early colonial period, New Orleans served as a nostalgic destination for French soldiers and sailors homesick for a familiar sensorium. The hospitality industry that rose up in response helped conserve a version of French culture experienced through a gauze of time and a longing across space. In the nineteenth and twentieth centuries, this Frenchness graded into "Creolité" and took on new connotations for Anglophone travelers and immigrants who experienced the city not as familiar and comforting, but as exotic and sexually charged—an orientalist perception that contributed to the rise of New Orleans's famous red-light district, Storyville. As Frenchness came to mean less a shared language and more a set of embodied and materialized practices, it came serve two masters: fictive ancestry and the market for something different.

The focus of chapter 5, "The Antique Fetish," turns to habits of collecting objects such as souvenirs, Mardi Gras throws, heirlooms, and antiques. Archaeology shows that several elite colonial households in New Orleans curated American Indian pottery. Collecting old things is an old habit. Interviews with Katrina survivors then reveal what archaeology cannot—the intense intimacy many residents feel with certain objects. Other sources highlight the complex temporality of these objects, many of which have highly singular biographies. Nearly all of them are ensconced in a local system of value in critical tension with commodity logic. I focus particularly on patterns of circulation and narration. In doing so, I develop a theory of the "antique fetish" that brings together threads from commodity studies, psychoanalysis, and comparative religion to explain why some objects in our cluttered lives are set aside for their emotionally charged associations—or for their stronger aura.

The concluding chapter, "Patina, Chronotopia, Mana," reviews the facets of the patina aesthetic and its related nostalgic practices while expanding on what it *does*. I argue that patina does two important things. It critiques the present in general and capitalism in particular, by creating a heterotopia of an "other time." And it helps bind people together by providing an everyday sign of fictive ancestry and collective affect—a profane kind of mana.

When I began writing, I had no idea where I was going to end up. My ideas have developed in a recursive, indirect process, going back and forth through field notes, artifacts, maps, novels, theory, and conversations with thoughtful friends. Although I have tried to discipline this process in the editing stage, some traces of it remain in the final form. I imagine the argument unfolding like an artichoke. To eat a whole, steamed artichoke, you have to peel it leaf by leaf in a spiral pattern, tooth-scraping each petal of the flower and discarding it. The petals become softer and meatier as you go, until you make your way down to the heart, with an indescribable flavor. If you've never eaten a whole artichoke, it's never too late to try. My granddad, a dustbowl cowboy, tried one for the first time at age seventy-three with an expression of new delight that I can still see in my mind's eye.

CHAPTER 2

Ruins and Heterogeneous Time

In a part of town now known as the Warehouse District, the shadow of the Greater New Orleans Bridge falls over several large late-nineteenth-century industrial buildings interspersed with surviving townhouses and tenements. One of these brick buildings squats over two city squares and bears the name Cotton Mill Condominiums. When this megalith of a building was erected in 1882, it was called the Maginnis Cotton Mill, a star attraction in Gilded Age New Orleans (fig. 2.1). Newspaper articles covering its opening and the first few years of its operation boasted that the factory housed state-of-the art machinery, from a giant twenty-foot Corliss Steam engine that had just debuted at the Paris World Fair, to block-long rooms with twenty-foot ceilings stacked with perfectly oiled, synchronized machines for combing, threading, and weaving cotton. In these accounts, the hundreds of "hands," or female and child laborers who operated the machinery, virtually disappear.[1]

This little-known chapter of New Orleans's history jars with popular narratives that depict the post–Civil War South as a region bereft of capital and industrial labor. In fact, the mill stayed busy up through World War II, when a decline in the American textile industry shifted manufacturing overseas. From the 1940s through the 1980s, the mill building was chopped into commercial rental properties for a drycleaner and a clothing distributor that specialized in men's ties. During the urban desuetude of the 1980s and early 1990s, the building sat abandoned by all but homeless men and cats. In 1996, however, machines powered up again as a real estate development company named Historic Restoration Inc. moved to convert the sturdy shell to upscale condominiums.

Perhaps because this era of New Orleans's history and this type of historic architecture is not the usual nostalgic fare of the city, the developer agreed to subsidize archaeological excavations in the open courtyard areas of the complex. The public-relations and marketing office of the company hoped we would uncover historical facts and artifacts that would help lend

FIGURE 2.1. Maginnis Cotton Mill exterior during construction. Photo by the author.

interest to the property for potential buyers. Our research design focused on the industrial phase of the site, an understudied topic in the city. The site supervisor gave us permission to dig in a tiny corner courtyard that made up less than 10 percent of the open area of the complex, because construction activities were scheduled there last. Men in hard hats paced back and forth overhead on catwalks while we worked to lift the hundred-year-old courtyard brick.

After carefully removing the brick from a 1 × 1 meter area, we found a bed of yellow sand containing nothing but a few wire nails and nondiagnostic pieces of glass. We kept going and came into a loose black fill of industrial slag, mainly clinker from expired coal and bagasse from burned sugar cane used to fire the steam engines. Other than the occasional liquor bottle, we had little more to go on to understand the evolution of the building or the daily work life of the mill. Newspaper articles celebrating the expansion of the mill in the 1890s lauded it as a paragon of cleanliness and discipline, and this indeed seemed to be true, frustrating the archaeologist in search of trash. After going two feet below surface into the nearly sterile slag and beginning to despair, we encountered a thin, muddy clay lens that quickly turned red with brick dust. We soon found that the dust came from a second floor of soft "plantation brick" that lay intact, in a herringbone pattern, across the base of our units. As we continued to open and extend our units, we began to encounter other brick features, includ-

FIGURE 2.2. Floor of Duplessis (later, Duplantier) Plantation house. Photo by the author.

ing the lower courses of walls, pillars, and a cistern platform. What we had found was an intentionally buried, well-preserved architectural fossil of a substantial old house (fig. 2.2), sheared off near its base and covered over with slag fill. The French colonial past suddenly surged into view. We made the evening news.

Archaeological evidence eventually demonstrated that in 1881 mill developers had effected a massive demolition effort to make way for their enterprise. Archival research clarified that working-class tenement housing, a lumber mill, corner grocery stores, and a French colonial plantation house dating to 1762 had been razed to the ground. Our brick fossil originated from this last component. The former indigo plantation itself attests to the long agro-industrial history of New Orleans, although experiments with this tropical crop never yielded noticeable exports.[2]

The plantation did not turn a large profit, but it remained in the possession of the Duplessis-Duplantier family for several generations. As the new American sector of the city encroached upon the area, financial pressures caused them to sell off the lands surrounding the manor house in the early 1800s. Although it must have appeared increasingly anachronistic in the city's fast-changing landscape, the building still commanded some architectural gravitas, as evidenced by Thomas Jefferson's choice of this house as the seat of the American convoy sent to oversee the Louisiana transfer

FIGURE 2.3. *The Seat of Mr. Duplantier near New Orleans.* . . . Engraving by G. Birch, ca. 1808. Courtesy of Historic New Orleans Collection.

in 1806 (fig. 2.3). By that time, the house violated the new street grid of the surrounding subdivisions and sat akimbo a corner of the block looking toward the receding river. It refused to conform to the new urban plan (fig. 2.4). By the steamboat era of the 1820s, the house began to acquire an antique air. The old plantation house accrued new meaning and value as it stood out against a backdrop of speculative obsolescence. The family maintained it as a large country-style townhouse up through the early antebellum era, as the neighborhood transitioned to a middle-class suburb. By the 1840s, the neighborhood was transitioning once again. Proximity to the river's wharves and the bustling fruit and cotton factor buildings spreading from Canal Street pushed the boundary of elite retreat upriver into the Garden District, making way for the pragmatic structures of commerce and working-class labor. The manor house remained, becoming first a school for girls and then a brewery run by newly arrived German immigrants. Census data for the neighborhood, however, shows that surrounding residents were predominantly Irish and poor. The brewery served as the final chapter of the old house's life before it was knocked flat by the arrival of the Maginnis Cotton Mill.

While preparing the background research for the project, I had talked to local historians enough to know about the mill being in the general vicinity of the Duplessis plantation. But their common sense said no trace of the

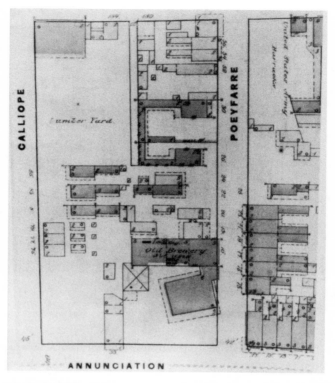

FIGURE 2.4. Sanborn Fire Insurance map, ca. 1876. The Duplessis Plantation house, in lower center, defies the new urban grid. Courtesy of Southeastern Architectural Archive, Tulane University.

plantation structures would remain below the bulky building. Popular perception generally holds that large modern structures obliterate past traces. Thus many people were taken aback by the time capsule we uncovered. The past flashed into view and demanded an engagement and a revision. The material stratigraphy of the city rarely tells a smooth story of progress and erasure of earlier forms. It speaks more consistently to the heterotemporal experience of urban life, from persistent structures laid down in earlier days (much of today's street grid still follows old plantation property lines) to dramatic episodes of catastrophic change.

The site of the Maginnis Cotton Mill illuminates the city's waves of uneven development, but more generally, it helps open up the history of space to focus on elements of *time*—of anachronism, preservation, dereliction, and demolition.

ON TIME

One of Walter Benjamin's most salient interventions was his insistence that the "newness" of modernity is largely an illusion. He arrived at this conclusion through his observations of the materials and spaces of the European metropolis. The ideology of modernity that insists upon invention and progress covers up the persistence and repurposing of old ideas and materials. Rejecting the social evolutionism of Marx and Engels, Benjamin understood temporality as the past and the present constructing each other in an ongoing dialectic. Time for him was not a series of linear strings laid end to end, but a twisted knot. He believed that the source material for a utopian imagination came from the relicts of the past. Benjamin saw a truth-value in archaeology's potential to uncover the ways in which one generation inherits the aspirational objects of earlier ones, as well as the ways in which past experiences were multiple and contradictory and not easy to read into the present. He also appreciated the counterhistory offered by detritus, ruins, and obsolete objects as corrections to the hubris of historical writing.

In sympathy with Benjamin's resistance to what he called the historian's empty, homogeneous time, this chapter explores the nature of *heterogeneous* time. Ruins and patinated objects have a special capacity for inducing different temporal states. I am concerned here with understanding the human experience of pastness in two distinct ways, the first a largely slow, structural one (*social stratigraphy*) and the other an effervescent mode that occurs in flashes and uneven tempos (*social relativity of time*). In neither case do these senses of pastness have the linear, teleological character of most historical narratives.

Philosophers of history now generally consider the possibility of an objective purchase on the past a quaint idea. Contradictory witnesses, ambiguous evidence, and the sheer infinitude of past material conditions, contingent encounters, lost routines, and forgotten moments mean that no account has the privilege of a universal eye. The past is impossible to know in any but the most impoverished way. This is why, as our knowledge builds through digging in archives or dirt, or as we destroy traces and forget events, the past appears to shift. The material out of which we construct histories and memories—the *knowable* past—is an unstable entity subject to taphonomy, or what archaeologists call the formation processes of deposition, burial, decay, disturbance, preservation, and resurrection.[3]

I use *pastness* to mean a quality that is sensed (not narrated, not remembered) about things and experiences filtered through the flux of time. It refers to the sensation of being in the presence of a lifeworld that existed prior to the present. It could feel like a familiar, intimate one with relevance for today, or it could feel like a strange, lost world. When it feels like both at the same time, we experience the uncanny. We may have trouble articulating why it feels like pastness (thus it is not history), and it may refer to something far outside our experience (thus it is not memory). Nor can it be, of course, a reliving of the totality of the past (even access to a time machine would limit us to one place and one perspective). Pastness is spectral. It is a sensation actively cultivated by nostalgic practices, but it can also be provoked by accidents and involuntary relations. Encounters with old objects are among the most common provocations and the type that interests me.

Patinated objects, ruins, and anything with an aura of the antique can evoke many different things. Their meanings are rarely stable or even articulated, and when they are, significance is often contested. An analytic that approaches them like texts would risk both overfixing their meaning and missing something unutterable. As will be seen in the following chapters, antiques, heirlooms, ruins, and old buildings definitely play a role in triggering narration. But they do not produce very predictable stories. In Peircean terms, they seem to work most like indexes, not so much meaning something as pointing to something. And like the famous example of the weather vane, they can spin in the wind of social currents.[4] Of course, they are often taken to point toward the past or toward a present-day preoccupation with heritage.

In practice, heritage refers to collective memories represented and reinforced by tangible things (landscapes, landmarks, archaeological ruins) and intangible practices (music, dance, language). Pierre Nora's work on *lieux de mémoire* identifies landmarks and certain worshipped objects as repositories for collective (primarily national) memory that substitute, in an anxious way, for the loss of a more organic *milieu de mémoire,* in a recapitulation of the romantic opposition of tradition versus modernity.[5] Hobsbawm and Ranger, in their highly influential volume *The Invention of Tradition,* also focus on national identity and rely upon a particularly confident contrast between customary and modern societies.

> "Invented tradition" is taken to mean a set of practices, normally governed by overtly or tacitly accepted rules and of a ritual or symbolic nature, which seek to inculcate certain values and norms of behaviour by repetition, which automatically implies continuity with a suitable historic past. . . . Insofar as there is such reference to a historic past, the peculiarity of "invented" tradi-

tions is that the continuity with it is largely factitious. In short, they are responses to novel situations which take the form of reference to old situations, or which establish their own past by quasi-obligatory repetition.⁶

They draw a line between the invented traditions of modern societies and the customs of preindustrial societies. The former are imagined to be rigid and institutionalized, compensating for social alienation in mass society, whereas the latter are informal and flexible, allowing for change and adaptation in a face-to-face society. Examples of invented traditions include the introduction of the "Scottish kilt" by an Englishman in the 1730s and the gothic architecture of the British parliament building. Modern traditions invented through moments of preservation may involve heavy doses of faked patina and fairy-tale narration, actions that invite local debate about histories and heritage. The argument is that invented traditions are ameliorative reactions to the alienation of modernity's large-scale urbanism, displacement, and industrialization. These traditions have a flashback type of temporality that references the past without drawing a line of continuity into the present. The scholar deploying the invention-of-tradition argument inherently fosters some skepticism about the reality of the past in the present. Consequently, it can lead to a cul-de-sac of evaluating practices in terms of authenticity, an activity that has more to do with the judgment of taste than social analysis.

Nostalgic practices in New Orleans, such as Creole cooking, historic preservation, or Mardi Gras celebrations, do not easily fit with the dichotomies favored by mainstream heritage studies. Their reference to the past is not factitious, nor is their form and symbolic content inflexible. In fact, creolization in New Orleans works by inducing a shared sense of pastness through processes of repetition, fetishization, and playful resignification of inherited elements. And transfer of knowledge between the generations, and between native and newcomer, *is* largely carried out in face-to-face social settings. Further, the group to which heritage and tradition is addressed derives not from nationality, ethnicity, or kinship but from the shared space of what is supposed to be problematic for customary societies: the city. And while *locals* will participate in conversations over authenticity—voiced as "now that's *real* New Orleans" (or not)—the criteria can be learned and are often eagerly taught. Tradition discourse often acts to distinguish touristic New Orleans from "real" New Orleans (in some areas there is a thin line that, indeed, requires explication), but locals do not generally use it against new settlers as an act of exclusion or an assertion of autochthonous privilege. New Orleans's heritage can be adopted.

David Lowenthal, in a lasting work that launched heritage studies in the early 1980s, famously proclaimed that the past is a foreign country. It hasn't always been so. He argues that during the Enlightenment, "Europeans began to conceive of the past as a different realm." They perceived change in their material, social, and political lives as occurring at a faster and faster rate since the eighteenth century and thus whole lifeworlds were slipping away, generation by generation. It is difficult to untangle how much of this perception is due to everyday experiences of social and technological change and how much is due to the ideology of progress's *command* that the past be different.[7] Most plausibly, both are at work. Yet despite preoccupations with fast-tempo time, pastness surrounds us and fills us, in ways of which we may not be aware and in ways that can suddenly take over the present. "A foreign country" is too distant a metaphor to capture these moments. The phrase does not, and was not meant to, capture all of our experience of pastness. Rather, Lowenthal highlights the way interpretations of the past get narrated and mummified (through museums and historic preservation) as heritage. The process of heritage-making can bring the past artificially close, as something to be contemplated, but while doing so, it makes it seem quaint and distant—or foreign. The ways in which people relate to old things that I am focusing on in this book overlap with heritage-making in some nostalgic practices such as historic preservation, but they tap deeper roots than pride of place. I am concerned with a connection rather than a disconnection, one that is felt more often than talked about. We inhabit the past and it inhabits us in ways that *cannot* be foreign. In fact, they animate a sense of *home*, or as Heidegger called it, dwelling. The materiality all around us, even our personalities, is composed of layers laid down in past moments. Everything we are and everything we experience is a kind of unpredictable inheritance. We dwell in pastness. As Hannah Arendt says: "The reality and reliability of the human world rest primarily on the fact that we are surrounded by things more permanent than the activity by which they were produced, and potentially even more permanent than the lives of their authors. Human life, in so far as it is world-building, is engaged in a constant process of reification."[8] There's a tremendous amount of materiality, habitus, and social force that bears down on us with a weight and thickness accumulated through time. And we can feel it. Some venerate it. Some feel spooked by its uncanny tension between the familiar and the strange. To understand how we relate to old things as part of a *home* country, and as elements of a largely unnarrated experience, it is helpful to draw out some ideas about time and temporality that get us outside the heritage loop and the invention-of-tradition thesis that can be so presentist, they deny the autonomy of the past or its presence within us.

Scholars have explored many approaches to temporality, or the different ways we perceive and organize time. The philosophical tradition most relevant here is the twentieth-century phenomenological one through Heidegger and Husserl. Husserl argued that time understood as a steady sequence of linear events is a highly abstracted representation of what our consciousness experiences as a sensual flux of echoes, cycles, and retentions, akin to multipart music. In the phenomenological view, the content of experience matters more than the form of timekeeping (seconds, days, years). The phenomenological intervention of the early twentieth century marked a radical break with Western beliefs in objective and progressive time, or what Walter Benjamin called empty, homogeneous time. Phenomenology acknowledges and embraces what we can term heterogeneous time. Such time is not only multifold but full of a content that defines it—of affect, social relations, and dialectical tensions.[9]

Anthropologists have also struggled with time. They used to get bogged down in a dualistic scheme of historical versus mythical time, or linear versus circular time. Western moderns were supposed to have historical, linear time, and non-Western peoples were thought to be caught in either an unchanging time-warp or a kind of mythical time that tamed the present by understanding it as a variation on a very old theme. Mythical time was either diffuse and changeless, or cyclical. These simple dyads started to break down in the 1980s as anthropologists turned to more ethnographically focused studies of temporality and began to explore the fruitful intersection of history and anthropology. Nancy Farriss demonstrated that circular and linear temporalities in colonial Mexico were not mutually exclusive. They can coexist as forms of time-reckoning between which people code-switch. These time-reckoning systems may also pertain to different domains (religion, agriculture, politics) and thus never come into great conflict. Historian Thomas Allen studied nineteenth-century American practices and concluded that even in the Victorian era, known for its strident faith in progress and train schedules, life continued to be structured according to both circular and linear temporalities without much dissonance.[10]

Nancy Munn's influential integration of a phenomenological approach into anthropology brought a fine-grained resolution to how the space-time continuum is experienced through small acts. Not only can time not be separated from space—an important precept of my own approach here—but it cannot be abstracted from social relations, aesthetic qualities, or estimations of value. Time, in whatever pattern (linear, circular, spiral, or an unchanging block) and according to whatever tempo (fast, slow, steady, sudden, decelerating), is not so much preconceived as lived. Munn's work suggests that we focus on how people experience time qualitatively and not try to quantify it according to a unidimensional, objective concept of time that in any case has now been rejected by both philosophy and theoretical physics.[1]

In recent years, some archaeologists have also radically rethought memory, temporality, and "the past in the past." An archaeological preoccupation with chronology has given way to time perspectivism, an orientation recognizing that "time is multi-layered; change and events happen at different scales or over varied periods of time and, more importantly, the very constitution of objects is determined by this temporality." Some of this work embraces the philosophical break with objectivist historicism, which means recognizing that when archaeology decides what the past is, it engages significantly with efforts to shape the present or even that "the past is a phenomenon of the present."[12] Another move has been to consider heterotemporality, in which different patterns of temporal relation and experience can coexist and be explored archaeologically (from micro events of an individual throwing away a peach pit to dynastic shifts and the slow structural time of a building's decay). The world around us is a living, moving palimpsest, not with layers forever erased or covered over, but dense with potentials for echoes and continuities into the present. Sometimes certain layers laid down in the past are activated by current events and come into the foreground—a retention, in Husserl's terms. Other times they recede or are forgotten again. My sensibilities align with this movement toward heterotemporality, although *profane archaeology* as I practice it here deals as much with historical records and ethnography as with the material remains of past events.[13]

In contemporary consumer society, we may *narrate* time in a linear fashion, but we *experience* it in multiform ways. For example, we can experience time as a thick ether or fog, where nothing much changes and time is not so much what happens to us as what we swim through. When we experience time in this temporality, it is actually the present that feels the most ephemeral; it seems to recede into an ever-accumulating sameness. Another way of experiencing time is what I think of as "bubble time," although Proust called it *mémoire involuntaire*.[14] This occurs when a moment of the past opens up for an actor and, like a reader immersed in a novel, the person loses himself or herself "elsewhere." The present recedes and some other world bubbles up into the mind, shaping affect, thoughts, and possibly actions. In this temporality, the past suddenly lives again, like a haunting. This experience is not unrelated to Walter Benjamin's "flash" time, but it is characterized more by reverie and reminiscence than the shock of new meaning. In the flash (referring to the flash of a camera bulb), on the other hand, "*what has been* comes together in a flash with *the now* to form a constellation" (emphasis added).[15] In this confrontation between the past and the present, a sudden realization about both occurs.

Finally, another temporality important to my story is rupture. An experience of rupture occurs when what we have been experiencing as continuity (a progressive linearity or a foglike unchanging duration) suddenly feels shattered. The tempo of experience speeds up so dramatically that our capacity to narrate the connection between past and present breaks down. Ruptures occur with disaster, war, economic collapse, social upheaval, and more personal traumas. A rupture can feel like an end-time, apocalyptic. Like a hurricane.

THE SOCIAL RELATIVITY OF TIME, OR HOW NEW ORLEANS BECAME OLD

> The cities of the New World have one characteristic in common: that they pass from first youth to decrepitude with no intermediary stage. —Claude Lévi-Strauss, *Tristes Tropiques*

The perception that a particular landscape is old is more a measure of radical social change and cultural dispositions than a measure of actual chronological years. With major events such as disasters, immigration influxes, and economic depressions, a gap opens up between the architecture of the builders and the lived experience of current residents. Time appears to speed up during periods of social rupture, and this rapid aging takes the form of patina. We can call this a theory of *social* relativity. To extend an application of Einstein's physics, observers in motion relative to one another (i.e., occupying different phenomenological space-times) will perceive time differently.

The perception of something as antique, ancient, or retro is a cultural judgment. So when and why did New Orleans become old and quaint? Patina has a long history in New Orleans. It defined Pre-K New Orleans as much as it does Post-K New Orleans. The city has been figured as old, stained, and charming for a very long time. Within ten years of its founding, colonial writers were depicting its buildings as shoddy and decaying, its political economy corrupt, and its moral life devoted more to pleasure than to the civilizing process.[16] In the eighteenth century, New Orleans was old but not yet quaint. Some writers were seduced by the hospitality and good times already brewing on a regular basis in this port town. They noted the regularity of its streets and the pretty, clean white stucco of its walls. More critical writers throughout the city's first eighty years reported it was "old" and deteriorated, even when the buildings had been built scarcely ten years earlier. They noted the presence of a malignant patina: the mold and wood-rot of a town neglected by its imperial patrons and the scabs of its syphilitic morality on the very walls of its buildings, nowhere better represented than in the state of its church buildings, a favorite subject. The British spy Pittman described the town in 1770 with scorn and no hint of romance: "in the back part of the square is the church dedicated to St. Louis, a very poor building, framed with wood; it is in so ruinous a condition that divine service has not been performed in it since the year 1766. . . . The capuchins . . . had a very handsome and commodious brick house, which is totally deserted and gone to ruin."[17] These are ruins, but they are not yet romantic. In 1802, on the eve of the Louisiana Purchase, promotional writer Pitot hoped that another natural disaster would hit the city, which had already been devastated three times by hurricanes and fires: "New Orleans has 1,000 to 1,200 buildings, of which 700 to 800 houses are still of frame construction, in poor condition and very old, where the owner or occupant awaits, with a kind of resignation, another conflagration. Such a disaster, always dreaded and always alarming in its terrible effects, could someday, if one were forewarned, become a sort of benefit in that part of New Orleans, for the buildings there are deteriorating rapidly from lack of care."[18] Remarkably, and rather callously, Pitot wrote this only eight years after a major fire in the French Quarter had wiped out at least one-fourth of the buildings that had been rebuilt following the even larger fire of 1788 (80% of the town's buildings were lost), a disaster he was old enough to remember.

For social critics of the eighteenth century, New Orleans was materially old and decaying within a few decades of its founding in 1718, but it did not yet possess any patina of the charming sort. This attitude, however, changed as the city began to bulge and spread with the arrival of new immigrants following the Louisiana Purchase of 1804.

Benjamin Latrobe, the well-known Anglo-American architect of Washington, DC, spent the last several months of his life in New Orleans and left behind a journal that describes his impressions of the city. In Latrobe's journal entries of 1819–20, we find testimony of the exotic charm the city presented to the flood of English-speaking men. Latrobe describes the arrival scene as his ship emerged out of a deep fog to moor along the levee: "Every thing had an *odd* [original emphasis] look. For 25 Years I have been a traveller . . . and I confess that I felt myself in some degree, again a Cockney, for it was impossible not to stare, at a sight wholly new even to one who has travelled much in Europe and America."[19]

Latrobe was a keen observer of the built environment. As an architect, he admired New Orleans, but unlike earlier admirers, it was not for its neatness and rational design. In fact, his predictions for the architectural effects of Americanization resonate with post-Katrina anxieties nearly two hundred years later: "Altho' the sort of house built here by the French, is not the best specimen of French arrangement, yet it is infinitely in my opinion superior to that arrangement which we have inherited from the English." In the mode of what Renato Rosaldo calls *imperialist nostalgia* for that which you are destroying, Latrobe goes on to say that "the suburb St. Mary, the American suburb, already exhibits the flat, dull, dingy character of Market street in Philadelphia, instead of the motley and picturesque effect of the Stuccoed french buildings of the city. We [the Americans] shall introduce many grave and profitable improvements, but they will take the place of much elegance, ease, and some convenience." He did, though, observe that for the time being the town preserved its "old character" in the backstreets away from the waterfront.[20]

Latrobe gives us the first citation of New Orleans's "good" patina—an aesthetic appreciation of the city's "look of age" and charmingly foreign aspects. It is a foreignness imported as much from the past as from overseas. Patina represents the old Creole, or native-born, population as distinct from the brash, shiny American newcomers who arrived with a strident form of capitalism and cookie-cutter architecture. Latrobe articulates his aesthetic appreciation of patina quite clearly, but he is also aware that it is somewhat of an illusion. In describing the church, he says, "It is extremely discolored, and looks *venerable* [original emphasis] beyond its Years, which are only 25."[21] In fact, due to the rebuilding that occurred following the devastating fires of 1788 and 1794, the vast majority of the architecture in the city's center was no more than thirty-one years old at the time of his visit. He was viewing a heavily scarred and scored landscape. Philadelphia, Baltimore, and New York (other cities that Latrobe knew well) possessed larger cores of older building stock than New Orleans. Yet the architect perceived New Orleans as old and charming and these other cities as drably new. Interest

In the case of St. Louis Cathedral, as with many other buildings in New Orleans, environmental effects in southeast Louisiana have contributed to the city's premature aging. The damp climate nurtures termites, makes foundations sag, and encourages colorful molds to grow on fresh paint. But there are also social causes for the acknowledgment and valuation of patina that Latrobe evoked in 1819. Fifteen years earlier, the Louisiana Purchase had ushered in such a sudden demographic explosion that New Orleans more than doubled in population. It is not unreasonable to imagine the Purchase as instigating a rupture in the local space-time continuum, simultaneously transforming the social and the physical landscape. While not all ruptures are commensurable along the cracks they open up or the type of trauma they induce, the Purchase, like Katrina, altered time. Such a large-scale event made thirty years earlier (the period during which most of the buildings Latrobe witnessed were built) seem like a very long time ago indeed. Mapping patina became a way to remember the older city and mark the event of the American invasion. Perhaps even to apologize for it.

Architecture, when understood as a kind of vertical archaeology, can also reveal dialectical tensions transforming urban fabric. St. Louis Cathedral now distinguishes itself as the oldest continually operating cathedral in the United States. But the building that houses this institution has not been a static landmark. In 1819 Latrobe himself undertook the addition of a central tower with a bell and a clock. By the 1830s the congregation had outgrown the building, which showed signs of structural stress in addition to the patina that Latrobe had described. Designs for a major renovation and expansion were not realized until 1849. By this time, some reverence adhered to the architectural fabric of the building, and the renovators made efforts to preserve the sidewalls and three towers while expanding the church's length. But during construction, the sidewalls and Latrobe's tower collapsed. In the end, most of the building was replaced. Although now the cathedral appears much as it did after this larger-than-intended 1850 renovation (fig. 2.5), its preservation has faced many challenges. In the spring of 1909, suspected Italian anarchists set off a dynamite bomb inside the cathedral, doing significant damage to the interior. Archaeologically, we could see the blast pattern in a scatter of stained glass shards across the back of the site, which at first puzzled us until we cut an unconventional path through the newspaper archives and rediscovered this incident. The 1909 damage spurred another round of renovation and a new set of stained glass windows, many of them donated by the Spanish consulate in its rivalry with France to claim New Orleans as its own American heritage. The structure had barely recovered when a major hurricane struck in 1915 and damaged the steeple. Ninety years later, Hurricane Katrina opened a hole in the roof and water poured into the pipe organ. All of the major trees on the property fell over, upturning large chunks of soil, causing its forgotten chapters to erupt into view in the form of colonial bricks and artifacts. Although proclaiming itself an emblem of foglike unchanging time in New Orleans, the cathedral is, in fact, a survivor of one rupture after another.[22]

FIGURE 2.5. St. Louis Cathedral. Photo taken for the author by Christopher Grant.

During our 2008 and 2009 excavations in the cathedral's green space (called St. Anthony's Garden), we uncovered evidence of each of the afore-mentioned episodes of damage and repair. In addition to the stained glass blown out by the anarchist bomb, we stumbled upon the shallow, well-preserved chain wall foundation for the long-forgotten 1915 Hurricane Chapel, a large temporary structure built over much of the garden to serve the parishioners during the repair of the main building. Although invisible below the sod, this episode in the site's history, as well as that of a refugee camp for victims of the 1788 fire, have surged to view for the first time in generations, imbued with new relevance for the post-Katrina era. Some efforts to engage these flashes from the past are quite deliberate. The landscape designers used our archaeo-botanical findings on the type of trees and plants that once thrived in the space as inspiration for its contemporary redesign.

In the case of St. Louis Cathedral and its garden, episodes of destruction and reconstruction have been cyclical and as much the result of natural forces as human ones. This compounded temporality sits in tension with the church's public image as the most venerable and stable landmark of New Orleans. Its iconic value remains unchallenged. The cathedral is, bar none, the most reproduced image of the city, and it plays a key role in urban branding. Yet below the surface churns a constantly shifting ground of conflict and reinvention. Structures and traces of past events echo down to the present or lie dormant with the potential to erupt into view at any time.

Talking to residents, one can hear a parallel contradiction between timelessness and change expressed. Peter lives adjacent to St. Anthony's Garden and the cathedral, just down the alley from the landmark Jackson Square. I asked him why he chooses to live in the sometimes noisy and inconvenient French Quarter:

> Peter: If you study the history of the quarter, it had periods when it was rough. It was seedy. Probably now, much more civilized than it was 30 or 40 years ago. The value of property has gone up. The renovations people have done. . . . You can go see the rector at the St. Louis Cathedral or any number of merchants up and down the street. . . . And it's a time warp. If you're here today and you know the people and you come back five years from now, then you come back ten years from now, the subject of the conversation hasn't changed very much. About the same.

Things have changed. The Quarter has been renovated and "civilized" (which some might interpret as *whitened*); yet, he asserts, it is a time warp—a romantic fog—where nothing much changes. Peter's brief response captures the temporal complexities of perception. He lives in a neighborhood that has both changed and not changed. If we accept the principle of heterogeneous time, there is no contradiction. In Peter's view, some realms (those of property and demography) have changed dramatically over the past generation while others (conversation and modes of sociality) have not.

Peggy, who lived by the lake before the storm and moved to the French Quarter in her retirement, suggests that New Orleanians have a keen sense of living "*in* history" as she says—not so much stuck in it, like a warp, but highly conscious of its lurches and loops and always at the ready to narrate them. Knowing that I am a historical archaeologist, she talks about a non-local friend who expressed disinterest in what I do.

> Peggy: [He] said you know when you're digging in New Orleans, you're finding ceramics, and glass and metal from 1718 on up to the present day. But if you go to Greece or Rome and Egypt, then you're finding really *old* objects. And so that's what he was more interested in—it's the old objects. But history is history. And history's fascinating. I mean, to live through Katrina—I mean that disaster—you just knew you were in history and then when you talk about Katrina—it's anybody's realm to talk about it.

Peggy moves quickly from archaeology to Katrina to make the point that what one finds historical is relative to one's experience of space and events. And she is quite conscious that ruptures like Katrina are those most likely to alter the way history gets told. She seems vitalized by knowing that she was part of a transformative event. Her voice quakes and her tiny hand hits the café table emphatically. The past in New Orleans is not necessarily old, but it is very much *present*. My many conversations with Peggy have ranged over a long acquaintance. I witnessed her interact with others and speak with evangelical zeal about New Orleans's past and all the things we might do to engage it (historic preservation, archaeology, research in the archives, public history with disadvantaged youth). This is not a foreign country but a palpable lifeworld all around her, ready to be engaged. Peggy loves living in New Orleans because she is surrounded by a pastness that excites her, and she wants others to share in it. It makes her bubbly.

My focus on heterogeneous time is not an entirely unique approach, but I do want to emphasize the perceptions of New Orleanians exemplified in these interview excerpts. Locals seem to share a particularly well-developed folk phenomenology of the space-time continuum.[23] On the one hand they have a hyperalert sense of living *in* history (being aware of changes over time), and on the other they positively value continuities wherever they can find them.

The second part of the social-relativity-of-time hypothesis recognizes that not only are temporalities diverse in their content as well as their form, the two are interdependent. To paraphrase Nancy Munn, social practices do not simply go on *in* or *through* time and space, they *constitute* space-time.[24] This dimension of the social relativity of space-time does not escape local observers either. Peter's description of the French Quarter emphasizes the peculiar, overlapping temporalities encouraged by its public space.

> Peter: If you watch the square at night—the square has many faces—in the morning, it's the artists setting up . . . and during the day you have a flow of traffic, the tourists and the artists. About 5 o'clock it starts to change. The artists are gone. The seediness surfaces, but there's fewer people. And usually they are parked on the benches. At night, you see the people going to dinner. And late at night, it becomes an encampment if the police don't come through.

In the local perception of space-time, these diurnal-nocturnal fluctuations of Jackson Square are marked not by heat, light, and shadow but by the movement and practices of different types of social bodies. This landscape does not exist as a stable space over which clock time simply passes. Rather, it becomes a different place with each shift. It is best understood as a space-time defined by social content—an art market, a tourist attraction, a nightlife zone, an encampment. Peter later adds that the larger space-time of the French Quarter goes through seasonal cycles. There are two types of vagrants: the truly homeless "who don't bother anybody" and these "young kids" (commonly referred to as "street rats") who arrive with Mardi Gras in the spring and leave at the end of summer, panhandling on the sidewalks with their dogs during the day and camping out with their smokes and bottles at night. These seasonal residents present a pierced and tattooed variation on the skin trader and hobo circuit that cycled through New Orleans in the flatboat and steam eras.

These and other space-times popped up archaeologically in St. Anthony's Garden. During our work, we conducted intensive surface collections across the site, picking up and bagging every artifact we could see lying on the ground and bagging them according to the ten-meter square in which they were found. We mapped evidence of both the nocturnal-diurnal fluctuations that Peter sketched and some seasonal ones. A scatter of probable daytime snack wrappers, toys, and small litter items related to religious services concentrated in the center of the garden, indicating that those who left them had access to the entire space through the back doors of the cathedral for special events. Another, denser concentration of artifacts associated with drinking (liquor bottles, plastic hurricane and grenade cups) and smoking (hundreds of cigarette butts, cigar wrappers) lined the areas by the iron fence, indicating they were litter tossed in, probably under the cover of dark, by passersby (fig. 2.6). Some artifacts that could, without great speculation, be associated with illicit activity included needles, con-

FIGURE 2.6. Surface artifacts from St. Anthony's Garden.

doms, a wallet, and a driver's license (likely stolen). Other artifacts are associated with daytime tourism (brochures, convention souvenirs) and some with a particular season, such as Mardi Gras (beads). With a heterotemporal approach, we can think of the garden not as a single site with multiple uses but as several distinct, overlapping space-times. Conventionally, our surface collection would be interpreted as a stratum of the present (probably two to three years of accumulation), but looked at in this light, it can be understood to represent several distinct space-times operating at different tempos and cycles (daily, seasonal, sporadic) that likely have corresponding strata (of illicit nighttime activities, of older Mardi Gras seasons) further below the surface.[25]

Mardi Gras, in fact, serves as a dazzling example of the social relativity of time. For locals, anticipation begins during the quiet lull of Christmas. The season kicks off when the first king cakes become available on Twelfth

Night (January 6). The weather alternates between gloomy cold snaps and promises of a hot, colorful spring. The season of balls, parades, and parties does not end until Mardi Gras day itself, anywhere from twenty-eight to sixty-two days later. The carnival season moves around so much because Mardi Gras is tied to Easter, which is determined by the lunar and solar calendars, not the fixed Gregorian one. Easter falls on the first Sunday after the first full moon after the spring equinox (as does Passover). The beginning of carnival is thus determined by one time-reckoning system (January 6th of the Gregorian calendar) and its end by another (sun and moon cycles). While not all locals are aware of the deep history underlying the Mardi Gras cycle, they do know that carnival is a season of fluctuating duration that makes each year unique (Will there be a Valentine's day parade? Will it be warm or cold on the night of the ball? What flowers will be in bloom? Will the season be so rushed there are events every day? When can we expect houseguests, and for how long?). In contrast, tourists tend to perceive Mardi Gras in one of two quite different ways (and easily at the same time). That is, as a single, once-a-year day when New Orleans hosts the world's biggest party, *or* as a continuous space-time in which the distinction between Mardi Gras the event and New Orleans the place collapses. For visitors filled with images and marketing suggestions, their trip to New Orleans amounts to their own private Mardi Gras. It is, in fact, now possible to find "Mardi Gras beads" (once only thrown from parade floats) sold year-round in tourist shops and given away as convention bling.[26] These, too, made their appearance in the trash accumulated around the periphery of St. Anthony's Garden.

SOCIAL STRATIGRAPHY

I have thus far focused primarily on conscious perceptions of time, but a sense of pastness also comes from structural inheritances that we take for granted, both material and social. We may be able to feel but only dimly articulate the accumulation of what Malinowski called the imponderabilia of everyday life. *Stratigraphy* or "writing in the ground" is the term archaeologists use for the layers and physical features they uncover as they excavate. Of course, the oldest layers are usually on the bottom, but sometimes more recent pits and trenches intrude, or layers get heaved up by frost and roots. And sometimes features, such as walls and roads laid down during the earliest occupation of a site, not only are still visible on the surface but determine how present-day occupants negotiate the space. Ruins provide a good metonymic figure for the other temporal dimension I want to enunciate here: the agency of things from the past in constituting our everyday lives in the present. I call this idea *social stratigraphy*. Let us take a detour to this notion through another archaeological site.

In December 2004, the Historic New Orleans Collection, a nonprofit archive and museum located in the French Quarter, was planning new construction for a climate-controlled archive facility. At first, all we knew was that the site hosted an existing early-twentieth-century single-story garage, but a quick survey of the archives revealed that the lot has been home to, among other things, a French colonial garden, a boarding house, a coffeehouse, and a hotel and tavern that had operated under the name Rising Sun Hotel between 1821 and 1822. It seemed like a good place to dig.[27]

An article in the local newspaper during our excavations in early 2005 unleashed a wave of global press coverage and curiosity, the main impulse of which was to identify the site as a brothel and the physical source of the well-known folk song "House of the Rising Sun," popularly interpreted as the lament of a fallen woman who surrendered to fate in a New Orleans bawdy house. This is a case of a beloved old story in search of a material home—of the satisfying verification provided by tactility. It was a yearning shared by many of my archaeological colleagues, who were disappointed with my hesitancy to authenticate the site as *the* House of the Rising Sun. I could not physically reconstruct the rickety frame structure that housed the Rising Sun Hotel, the molten remains of which we found strewn across the site. However, after all the excavations and laboratory analysis were done and I was writing up the report, I had a moment of recognition while trying to explain the complex stratigraphy of the site. As I examined the otherwise routine site map that traced the outlines of the surface features and the placement of our units, a ghostly image of a long-dead building came into view. A large rectangular depression extended across two-thirds of the parking-lot floor, causing identical layers of dirt and fill to sink down, occurring at quite different depths in the center of the site compared to its periphery (fig. 2.7).

Going back to the terse verbal descriptions of the two-story wood frame building that had housed the Rising Sun hotel and tavern, as well as more complete descriptions of the substantial brick hotel that replaced it, I realized that the tavern building haunted its successors down to the present day. The collapse of the fire-damaged building in which two men died, and the gradual decay of its materials, created a moving surface into which subsequent buildings had sunk. Once settled, the regular outline of the building reasserted itself. In the site's incarnation as a twentieth-century parking garage, the subsidence of the old hotel caused drivers to avoid the center of the lot, where standing water accumulated.

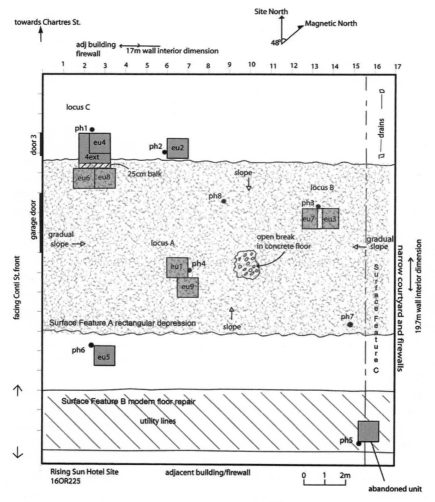

FIGURE 2.7. Field map of Rising Sun Hotel site, showing depression corresponding to burned ruin of 1822 hotel and excavations units.

Although the archives do not contain any maps, plans, or detailed descriptions of the Rising Sun Hotel structure, three taphonomic facts help tie this rectangular depression to the structure. Throughout New Orleans, and especially in the French Quarter, residents frequently filled in their lots in order to elevate them and improve drainage, resurfacing as frequently as every ten or twenty years in order to keep up with the streets and sidewalks, which were themselves being continually resurfaced. On-site episodes of demolition and renovation provided opportunities and materials for this infilling. Thus, the decision by the 1820s developers to leave the debris from the Rising Sun structure in place and spread it across the lot as a new building surface would have been consistent with local practice.

However, when this urban fill contains large amounts of organic materials and/or heavy materials such as brick, the ground surface eventually subsides. Voids created by decayed and compressed wood collapse, or the weight of heavy materials such as brick compact the naturally loose alluvial soils. In either case, the ground surface eventually begins to subside, a process that at the Rising Sun Hotel site had continued up to the time of our excavation (thus observable as a surface depression in 2005). The third taphonomic clue was that identical strata occurred at deeper levels inside the depression than outside it, down to the fire levels of the Rising Sun Hotel. Below the burn levels, the equivalent strata evened out in depth. This means that the rotting in-fill that created the depression dated no earlier than the 1822 fire.

Another look at the archival record confirms this reading of the dirt. In the 1820s, such a valuable piece of real estate was not allowed to rest idle for long. Just a few years after the fire, the more substantial and upscale Richardson Hotel (described as a "gentleman's hotel" in newspaper advertisements) had replaced the old sailor's tavern on the lot. However, as elegant as its builders had intended it to be, only twelve years after its construction, the building was in such bad shape that the proprietor-tenant placed a complaint in the local paper declaring it "uninhabitable." The hotel closed between 1838 and 1840 to make substantial repairs. Given the youth of the building, but also the great weight of its four stories of brick, we can infer that the building suffered considerable subsidence due to the instability of the rotting Rising Sun Hotel debris and the soft soils upon which it was built. This would have led to sloping floors, bent door and window frames, and cracking plaster, among other problems.

Today, the site that bears the physical imprint of the Rising Sun Hotel is once again hidden from view. In 2005–6, the Historic New Orleans Collection removed the parking garage that had replaced the Richardson hotel in the early twentieth century and built a near replica of the benighted gentleman's hotel (fig. 2.8). Whether this building, too, will eventually succumb to the legacy of the Rising Sun Hotel's decay, only time will tell. In other ways, however, the stratigraphy of the site is now more visible than it has been since the antebellum era. Because of our excavations and the publicity surrounding them, some French Quarter tour guides now mention the site as one of the possible locales of the original House of the Rising Sun of folk-song lore. For this distinction it competes with two operating hotels, albeit those have an even thinner archival thread.

FIGURE 2.8. Replica of Richardson Hotel, built for Historic New Orleans Collection. Photo taken for the author by Christopher Grant.

I have described the material taphonomy here to emphasize that the same reality affects human actions down to the present and that such pro-cesses have their connected social formations of stubborn continuities and periodic shifts. The Rising Sun Hotel exemplifies the fact that the city's history as a port town heavily invested in the hospitality trades has been a continuity down to today, as has the material reality of the city's sinking landfill. The types of hospitality offered have shifted over time, accommo-dating first fur traders and sailors, then slave traders and cotton merchants, and now tourists and convention-goers. Struggles over the socioeconomic profile of the French Quarter and its businesses reflect the constant rein-vention of the site, precipitated as much by fires and decay as by bursts of real estate speculation and new kinds of traffic. This stratigraphic dialectic of economic and ecological forces erupted into view with our discovery of the curious past of the Rising Sun Hotel, one that was, in fact, quite a bit more curious than the predictable fallen-woman trope of the folk song.

New Orleanians seem less concerned with authenticating a single House of the Rising Sun than do visitors. It is a landmark of the imagination, but it does not figure much in their day-to-day social geography. Local media coverage did not dwell on this possible identification, nor have there been many follow-up queries from residents, in stark contrast to the interest of the international press and e-mail queries received from places as far away as India and Greece for years after the excavation. As will be seen in the next chapter, historic places laminated with layers of social life rather than those brushed by essentialized myth are what residents value—those places where patina accrues through repetitive handling and occupation. The Rising Sun Hotel at 535 Conti Street may have had this sort of patina as a homey, smoky tavern, but the fire of 1822 wiped it clean of such social associations. The process may have started anew with the Richardson Hotel, but it too eventually died, disappearing around the turn of the twentieth century (replaced by a garage) before reappearing in the twenty-first. Since no one today can live in the replica Richardson Hotel (it is a cold storage facility for rare books and manuscripts), much less the Rising Sun Hotel, the site possesses little patina to rub off on the living. The ruins of the Rising Sun Hotel, like those of most archaeological sites, lie buried and invisible and do not contribute to the phenomenological experience of the cityscape. However, they did for many years contribute to the physical legacy of the site, and now to its public legend.

By *social stratigraphy*, I mean two things. First, human and nonhuman elements of the urban landscape are coformed, layered, and deep. And second, the social present is constructed out of inherited materials, taphonomically transformed and with high variability in retentions and effects. To think this way breaks with the current dominant anthropological belief, in which the deep past is rejected as irrelevant to understanding the present, except rather cynically as a resource to be mined for tacitly inauthentic claims (thus the literature on heritage and uses of the past). But this is not to slide into a recidivist embrace of unchanging tradition. I offer a third alternative. What I am suggesting is that deep layers exist in localities that create a series of grooves into which it is difficult not to fall—like subsiding into the underground ruins of an old hotel.

An all-too-obvious example of what it means to take deep social history seriously is the legacy of racial slavery in the U.S. South. Today's forms of racism and socioeconomic inequalities exist in a quite different legal and political context and cast quite different shadows on popular culture and discourse. Still, for generations, the majority of African Americans in New Orleans have been limited to low-paying service and labor jobs because the social landscape makes it exceedingly difficult for them to do anything else. Post-Katrina rebuilding has done little to change this pattern. The foundations of inequality laid during the colonial and antebellum periods are still settling and shifting. One could call these the social ruins of the past in which we dwell. Social stratigraphy signifies not so much a spoken-about tradition as a hard-to-shed quiet legacy that encompasses socioeconomic structures perpetuated through inheritance and an attitudinal habitus. In fact, taking Bourdieu's idea of habitus seriously means taking the power of the past seriously.[28]

A more positive example comes from the famous hospitality of New Orleans, a major economic sector since the city's founding. Residents mythically associate this element of local culture with the city's "French" heritage (addressed in chapter 4), but African Americans and descendants of more recent Sicilian immigrants are also held up as exemplary practitioners. The deeply ingrained habitus of offering food and drink to anyone who enters your home, organizing large family meals, and flirting with strangers is not ordained (people rarely complain about a bad host), but they are habits that have been modeled as a rewarding way to be-in-the-world for so many generations that rooted New Orleanians cannot imagine going about things any other way. That, too, is social stratigraphy. We might be tempted to call these practices ingrained rather than invented traditions, but the timeless folkloric connotation of tradition within anthropology is troublesome. What I am drawing attention to here is time-*full* practices rather than timeless traditions. We usually understand tradition as something that locals not only talk about but celebrate. Social stratigraphy involves practices that may not be verbalized, much less celebrated. The actions of past generations continue to reverberate down to the present in ways that direct us and in ways that we may sense but can rarely articulate. Social stratigraphy is accumulated habitus, or what Durkheim called *congealed forces*: "We speak a language we did not create; we use instruments we did not invent; we claim rights we did not establish; each generation inherits a treasury of knowledge it did not itself amass."[29] While we may not always be able to put this sense of pastness into words, an awareness of these congealed forces is stimulated by interactions with the inherited or adopted landscape, and by aesthetic encounters with patina. Sometimes this sense of pastness takes the form of a ghost.

• • •

Many years after Katrina, it is still not difficult to find, in the northern and eastern edges of the city, abandoned tract houses with faded curtains blowing in glassless windows and weeds and rot slowly softening the architectural fabric. These ruinous images of the landscape are not romantic. There has been perhaps too much written about ruins through a romantic lens that blurs their agency in constituting a space-time experience. While ancient ruins may indeed evoke a mode of timelessness—a fog—other ruins may provoke a bubble of reminiscence, or the sudden surge of a past reality into our present. Others, such as Katrina ruins, highlight rupture. These are all temporal modes of pastness, but beyond that lie their *moods*—their potential affects.

Recent ruins do not simply evoke a memory of rupture. Through their slow state of decay they *sustain* a rupture of space-time in the present until they can be folded into the landscape as something old, comfortable, and homey—once they have acquired patina. Contemporary ruins shape possible futures. Katrina ruins are considered eyesores, signs of failure or abject neglect. They transitively *ruin* property values and discourage redevelopment. In neighborhoods that moved more vigorously in rebuilding after the storm, ruins were demolished relatively quickly, creating rows of vacant lots. In addition to the economic rationalizations, such erasure can be motivated by a desire to destroy the ruin's power to produce certain affects. Ruins from a foreign country may elicit a kind of orientalist erotics or a dreamy nostalgia for something once familiar, but the ruins of one's own home do something quite different. They reproduce trauma.

The intensification of trauma and blight since Katrina has produced new ghost stories—from burger joints to abandoned public housing units and vacant schools. Before Katrina, New Orleans had a reputation for being America's most haunted city, inspired in no small part, as will be seen in chapter 3, by the patina of its buildings and the emanation of congealed forces. After Katrina, this reputation has only grown, as has its population of ghosts. The new ghosts, however, lurk around new ruins and sites where attempts at renovation have not erased the sense of rupture in local space-time.

CHAPTER 3

A Haunted House Society

Inner as well as outer landscapes seemed increasingly ghostlike.
—T. J. Jackson Lears, *No Place of Grace*

Madame John's Legacy is the name of a house in New Orleans's French Quarter that bears a large bronze historical plaque with the designation "National Historic Landmark" (fig. 3.1). The raised wooden building features prominently on tourist maps and walking tours of the city, being the only extant example of a typical house type from the French colonial period. It stands out anachronistically among the brick townhouses and iron balconies of the Vieux Carré. Although the original structure (built circa 1730) was badly damaged in the fire of 1788, the owners had a replica immediately rebuilt, in the form known by architects as the West Indies Style. The name of the property comes not from a former owner identified in the property records, but from an 1879 short story by George Washington Cable, who used the house—already old and mysterious in his day—as inspiration for one of his best-known tales in *Old Creole Days*. The old house constitutes the inheritance of a free woman of color called "Madame John," after the affectionate fashion in French New Orleans in which a wife would be nicknamed by adding "Madame" to her husband's first name. The Madame John of the story had borne a child by her white common-law husband. Her "legacy" refers simultaneously to her beautiful daughter, who is fair enough to pass into white society, and to the facade of the noble old house, which is respectable enough to pass them into the class of gentlemen and ladies. Cable's tale, while sympathetic to a common experience of free people of color in antebellum New Orleans, highlights the complex truths and intimate inequalities lying behind the veneer—the exaggerated patina—of Creole elegance. It also speaks to the ways in which class and culture can blur color in New Orleans.[1]

When I researched the property history of the site, I found no trace of occupants who could plausibly be tied to the story. Cable either romanticized a case history drawn from some other property or decided to fictionalize a well-known pathway to emancipation and property-holding in New Orleans. The house's notarial archive, however, rivals Cable's imagination

FIGURE 3.1. Madame John's Legacy. Photo taken for the author by Christopher Grant.

in its romantic realism. In the eighteenth century, the house's builder and long-term owner was a woman named Elizabeth Real Pascal Marin. She immigrated as a teenager to the early French colony in the 1710s and survived two husbands, both of them ship captains and smugglers. While they were at sea, Madame Real occupied herself by running an inn out of the house, a business that she conducted for more than fifty years. After her death, the property passed into the hands of another family of smugglers, then to the captain of the Spanish regiment and the family of the first American governor before being chopped up into apartments to house the Sicilian and African American families who crowded into the Lower Quarter after the Civil War.[2]

During excavations undertaken in 1997, we uncovered a trash pit in the rear courtyard dating to the cleanup after the catastrophic Good Friday fire of 1788 that destroyed 80 percent of the city. The taphonomy of the artifacts suggests that Elizabeth Real's house did not burn to the ground. A large set of creamware dishes was smoke-stained but not burned, and animal carcasses from the pantry were nearly whole. Dozens of bone buttons were all that remained from smoke-damaged clothes added to the pit. Architectural historians are convinced that the house was entirely rebuilt, despite its French colonial appearance, based on the existence of a building contract written less than a month after the fire. However, surviving and datable archaeological features indicate that the contract simply fails to mention the survival of a portion of the house that was used in its reconstruction and may have structured the unusual choice of the owner, the commander of the Spanish garrison, to reconstruct the building according to the old French style. In other words, enough of the old house survived to renovate rather than start over from scratch. In the aftermath of the disaster, most residents in the French Quarter opted for more Caribbean-style cottages or brick townhouses. So the survival of the old walls suggests why Cable selected this house for his story. Even older than the eighty-year old structures that dominated the cityscape in his time, the facade of the Dumaine Street house had an age and a patina appropriate to his story in *Old Creole Days.*

As a part of this public archaeology project at Madame John's Legacy, we held an open house. Tourists repeatedly asked: "Who was the 'Madame'?" and "What are the dates for the bordello?" Many of their questions were symptomatic of a confusion not only about the linguistic and social history of New Orleans, but its geography. They assumed the city's notorious red-light district of Storyville mapped onto the French Quarter, no doubt confused by the cultivated seediness of Bourbon Street.

Another memorable encounter during the open house involved a local enthusiast of New Orleans's fabled pirate history. At the end of my tour, he asked why I had failed to mention that the house had been home to the famous smuggler and privateer René Beluche, one of Jean Laffite's Baratarians (and an ancestor of his). I knew that Beluche had been born at the house, but he was only three years old when the family sold the property, so I had figured his archaeological imprint was probably not very significant. This fact did not mollify my interlocutor. For him, the association of the site with a man whose activities helped give New Orleans its crusty charm *mattered*. The residue of Beluche's history had accrued to the house. In both of these encounters, I initially chafed at being put in the conservative role of debunking the myths of New Orleans's commercialized history of hedonism and piracy. However, these moments also illuminated how representations and bits of material patina come together in place-making and attempts to satisfy a hunger for an exotic past.

This chapter takes another step toward understanding the nostalgic practices that have gone into making New Orleans "old," particularly through its preoccupation with architecture. At the level of description, I will show how houses are aged primarily through processes of narration (both literary and oral) and the politics of historic preservation. However, like Cable's story, these are not inventions unrelated to particular histories and singular materialities. Old objects coauthor the past with the dead. Ethnographic interviews demonstrate that nostalgia for tourists and nostalgia for locals as evoked by the city's old houses are romantically entwined but separately experienced. All this builds to the main argument. With some apology to Lévi-Strauss, I argue that New Orleans is a "house society" through which genealogy is created more by habitation than blood. This genealogy can gradually integrate willing newcomers, but not the short-term, ill-informed visitor. While the evaluation of authenticity would be a perilous mode of analysis for the anthropologist, it is a form of play and performance that New Orleanians frequently enjoy. And this play involves a kind of double move, in which they exoticize the city's past and orientalize themselves as latter-day Creoles at the same time that they render the city as homey and familiar. One can, in fact, map two quite distinct old towns, one for locals and one for visitors. Both are occupied by ghosts. In the public version, they are well-known characters in oft-told stories. But in the local town, they are often unnamed and uncanny relations. The nostalgic practices surrounding old houses serve, but also exceed, political revisionism and marketing allure—they create an unreal city that emanates a kind of profane *mana.*

A LONG SABBATH OF DECAY, OR HOW NEW ORLEANS BECAME OLD, PART 2

Before New Orleans could be preserved, it had to be antiqued. The romantic gaze cast upon New Orleans fits within a broader, longer romantic movement, dating from the late eighteenth through the early twentieth century, that valorized the picturesque and preindustrial life. Some of the intellectual and artistic impulses within this genealogy were passively melancholy about the supposed loss of vitality, intimacy, and a slow pace to the cold speed of capitalism, secularization, and the "chromo civilization" of the modern city. Other aspects of this cultural response took an active political form, such as the Arts and Crafts Movement and the many utopian communities established in the late nineteenth century in the United Kingdom and the United States. T. J. Jackson Lears argues that "far from being the nostalgic flutterings of a 'dying elite,' as historians have claimed, antimodernism was a complex blend of accommodation and protest." Tourism offered a form of accommodation, while historic preservation, in its most idealist mode, enacted a form of protest. New Orleans was (and is) one of many locations where antimodernism thrived. Over the long nineteenth century, other nodes included Japan, the Scottish highlands, Venice, and the French countryside. The romantic gaze of the Orientalists toward the whole of the Near East, which Edward Said rightly associated with imperialism, could also be understood as a critical glance back home. All these places were favorite haunts of those in search of something thought to be disappearing from their home worlds. They became destinations for a kind of time travel that was itself not immune from the opportunistic entrepreneurialism of capital. Stops on the Grand Tour in the eighteenth century morphed into the developed sites of consumer tourism in the twentieth.[4]

It is not surprising, then, that the travel writers who followed Latrobe in the antebellum period soon echoed his characterization of romantic exoticism.[5] What stands out in the New Orleans case is the extent to which this idiom came to be appropriated by locals. Some fetishized the city's "Frenchness" while others focused on its racial hues or its multilingual rainbow that defied simple categorization. After the Civil War, a new generation of prolific writers, led by Lafcadio Hearn and George Washington Cable, created a dense literary tradition that weaves together folklore, social critique, and historical narrative. With Cable and Hearn, New Orleans became redundantly figured as old, quaint, and charming. They filled in the cityscape with poetic reminders of a social world of Creole privilege and slave hardship now passing into memory.

This literature is remarkably anchored in materiality. Houses and objects play key roles in reimagining the social landscape of postbellum New Orleans (fig. 3.2). In its literary and social impact, Cable's *Old Creole Days*, the source for the name and legend of Madame John's Legacy, holds a prominent place. As the title suggests, Cable intended to recount a past lifeworld, albeit one within his living memory. It is a world of luxury and chauvinism that he wants to write into obsolescence. He forcefully transforms the recent past into a "foreign country." Every entry in this collection of short stories opens with the description of a building or cross-street where the action will take place. The author claimed to have collected his stories from archives and street gossip. His description of the physical setting establishes the tone of each story and foreshadows its moral cast. The opening of the first story reads:

> You turn, instead, into the quiet, narrow way which a lover of Creole antiquity, in fondness for a romantic past, is still prone to call the Rue Royale. . . . You find yourself in a region of architectural decrepitude, where an ancient and foreign-seeming domestic life in second stories, overhangs the ruins of a former commercial prosperity, and . . . upon every thing has settled down a long sabbath of decay. . . . Many of the humid arches and alleys which characterize the older Franco-Spanish piles of stuccoed brick betray a squalor almost oriental.[6]

FIGURE 3.2. Illustration of Creole cottage housing a well-known café, from Cable's *Old Creole Days.*

As he continues, Cable deftly sketches the architecture and the people with the same strokes: "The faces of the inmates are in keeping; of the passengers in the street a sad proportion are dingy and shabby; but just when these are putting you off your guard, there will pass you a woman—more likely two or three—of patrician beauty."[7] The public image of New Orleans in the eyes of the Victorians had all the elements that Edward Said noted in contemporary picturesques painted of the Middle East by imperialist scholars: quaint antiquity, tempting sexuality, exotic smells and tastes, and an inept native population. Even the local elites were unenlightened in their attachment to old ways.[8] Cable chides the Creoles for being lovers of their own antiquity, while at the same time perpetuating it himself in his architectural poetry.

Hearn, for his part, wrote hundreds of short descriptive pieces on New Orleans for the national press, in which he was unabashedly smitten with patina. In 1877 he wrote: "I find much to gratify an artist's eye in this quaint, curious, crooked French Quarter, with its narrow streets and its houses painted in light tints of yellow, green, and sometimes even blue . . . but there are a great many buildings that cannot have been painted for years, and which look neglected and dilapidated as well as antiquated."

Remarkably, Hearn's imagination twists the rigid right angles of the French Quarter's orthogonal grid in his effort to make the city appear oriental and serpentine (something Walt Disney accomplished materially in the Old World curves of his "New Orleans Square"). He speaks of buildings constructed "Frenchily," now "picturesque and quaint." He recommends New Orleans to future travelers as having some of the "oldest-looking structures one could wish to see." In a quest to ameliorate the anxieties of modernity, Hearn, Cable, and fellow Victorians searched restlessly for antiquity and the exotic (and Hearn later found more in Japan, the other site of his writing). In America, the Victorians found it in New Orleans. For these authors enthralled by imperialist nostalgia, patina is a sign of beauty and the sad decline of an Other world.[9]

Writers of tour guides and collectors of folklore soon joined Cable and Hearn, each adding another layer to the literary patina of New Orleans. In his 1895 publication *New Orleans as It Was*, local writer Castellanos precisely dates the "antiquity" of New Orleans to the period before 1860. He describes his project, saying, "A peculiar feature of the work is the descriptive history of the city's buildings, monuments and customs since its foundation to within a short time before the year 1860. . . . I have drawn many of my facts not only from old records and disused archives, but from oral recitals and traditions."[10] He recounts the quirks of Napoleonic exiles, bungled executions of burglars, and the secret-yet-fabled practices of voodoo—each in its physical setting, such as a popular candy store, the parish prison, or a strip of green field along the St. Bernard Canal. With Castellanos, the status of New Orleans and its landmarks rises from literary to mythic proportions. The Civil War, like the Louisiana Purchase and Katrina for other generations, represented a major rupture in the lives of these Victorian writers. This is why Castellanos dates the "antiquity" of New Orleans to the period before 1860. He himself was born in the city in the 1820s, so by his own account he is one of the ancients of New Orleans. And he stakes some of his authority upon his own memory of even older characters. The peculiar temporality of his project underscores that the designation of antiquity does not measure chronological age so much as it marks off a time before a major social rupture. Castellanos and his contemporaries wrote with romantic longing for a past they felt helpless to recover. But after World War I, writers began to be more proactive in collaborative efforts to stop time and commodify pastness.

TOURISM AND HISTORIC PRESERVATION

Blue is a native New Orleanian and a cabbie who has seen a lot of tourists come through town. I asked him why they like to come here.

> Blue: Well, from what I've seen, from the different people that I've picked up in my taxi, it's the spirit of New Orleans and, especially coming into the French Quarter . . . but you've got all these different cultures here down in the French Quarter. And from what people have said to me, they would rather come here than a place like Las Vegas. You know, Las Vegas has got a lot to offer but it's got no soul. And I think New Orleans has that.

> SD: What gives it soul?

> Blue: I think basically the suffering of the people. Not just black people [Blue is black]. It's just—sometimes it feels like it's almost as if it's a part of the United States. But it's not. You can tell by the way that it responded from Katrina and from all the other things that have happened. It's always been a slow go. Everybody said we're a backward people down here. It's slow and it's got that Napoleonic code versus anywhere else. So things are done a little bit differently. Besides that the French Quarter, this is one of the places that I know of, besides Savannah, Georgia that still has its historic buildings and they try to keep things like that, you know?

> SD: Do you think they keep it just for the tourists?

> Blue: *No* [emphatic]. No, cause you can get outside the French Quarter and look at it and people can buy new stuff but they don't. They always keep that old style and they just fix 'em up. I like it.

Three strands of the city's history are intimately entwined in its space-time—literary-oral narratives (a fine line up through World War II), the built environment, and tourism.[11] Early-twentieth-century local writers such as Harnett Kane, Grace King, Lyle Saxon, and Robert Tallant took the further step toward preserving the material embodiment of New Orleans's antiquity, especially the buildings and gardens of the French Quarter, by becoming active proponents of the historic preservation movement.[12] All the while, they added to the concretions of ghost stories, gentleman duels, and voodoo lore. The city's picturesque landscape also attracted nonnative writers, and a bohemian community began to flourish in the

French Quarter, attracting the likes of Tennessee Williams, William Faulkner, and Sherwood Anderson. Their writing disseminated literary postcards of New Orleans's peeling paint and bougainvillea ever wider, colored with accounts of the city's porous moral boundaries. Through these artistic representations, New Orleans became a foil for the rest of the nation, an imaginary island of colonial dissipation within a country relentlessly committed to moral and material progress. The patina aesthetic became a sign of an alternative way of life.[13]

Many American visitors remarked on the city's foreignness, embodied in its multihued human parade that struck visitors such as Frederick Law Olmstead or its "Frenchness" that inspired one writer to claim in 1901, "To live in this quarter, to know its houses, its streets, its stories, is like reading Balzac."[14] Visitors and residents still cite the city's evocative Frenchness today. When I asked Peter why he lives in the Quarter, he replied:

> I enjoy Paris and this is as close as you can get to a European lifestyle in the
> United States. . . . You look at the architecture. You look at the streets. You
> listen to the bells.

In the early twentieth century, tourism marketers deliberately enhanced these associations by attempting to brand New Orleans as "the American Paris." They made their claims on material grounds: the ambience of the French Quarter, with its quiet cottages and private townhouses, exuded Frenchness. These projections succeeded even though any architectural aficionado who took a close look at the buildings would be hard-pressed to find a postcard from France that looked much like the French Quarter. Much more recognizable citations would be San Juan, Puerto Rico, or the small houses of the Haitian countryside.[15]

Historic preservation in New Orleans at first focused almost exclusively on the French Quarter. The effort began by organizing around major landmarks and demolition cases, such as the French Opera House. Historian Anthony Stanonis argues, "From preservationists' point of view, the decay of the structures within the district came to symbolize the ruins of a gracious French culture, a society to which prominent New Orleanians sought to tie themselves via genealogy or the preservation movement."[16] This characterization is complicated by the fact that bohemian transplants and writers such as Sherwood Anderson also sided with historic preservation. When businessmen threatened to tear down dilapidated French Quarter structures to build a new downtown area with modern skyscrapers, Anderson wrote a scathing satire for *Vanity Fair* in 1926 in which one character put his finger on the cause for the city's architectural patina and the cynicism with which many looked upon capitalist progress: The city "aint never been boomed none." The message that Anderson metaphorically identified with the cracking walls of the Vieux Carré was that economic progress was a mirage. His writing exemplifies a *critical nostalgia*.[17]

In fact, for the early generation of preservationists who colonized the Quarter, the patina aesthetic seems to have had more to do with imagined bohemian individualism of the 1920s and 1930s than with the defense of displaced privilege. Many were well-off women establishing their own space, away from their husbands' uptown businesses and family homes. They boosted the emergent literary life of the Quarter by holding literary teas or by becoming writers, painters, and potters themselves.[18] This atelier culture may help explain why the highly educated preservation coalition so stubbornly refused to see the Spanish and early American qualities of the architecture itself. Instead, they chose to mystify the French Quarter as French, finding small survivals in architectural details such as window frames or even invisible elements such as colombage (brick and wood-beam construction). In the modernist imagination, there exists no more bohemian place than Paris, accounting for the desire to exaggerate a resemblance to the city's grand, distant cousin.

Interwar preservation groups were dominated by women who had come of age in the suffragist and temperance movements. Some sought to enhance their prestige through events such as the Spring Fiesta, when they dressed up in antebellum costumes and opened restored houses and courtyards to the public. Despite their avowed interest in maintaining French cultural traditions such as the Le Petit Salon and Le Petit Theatre, most of these women had Anglo-American roots from outside Louisiana. They came from very different walks of life than the male architects, artists, and writers with whom they collaborated in the preservation movement. William Faulkner rather scathingly captures this odd group marriage in *Mosquitoes*, his early novel of bohemian life in 1920s New Orleans. When not on a boat in Lake Pontchartrain, the physical setting for the cast of ne'er-do-well, high-witted sculptors, writers, and their aging groupies lies among decrepit French Quarter townhouses littered with antique junk. Along with the ubiquitous but unnamed mosquitoes that pester the characters from scene to scene, the lax antiquity of New Orleans supplies a major trope of the novel.[19]

In the midcentury, the French Quarter and its neighborhood organizations such as the Vieux Carré Property Owners and Associates served as command headquarters for historic preservation political action. Far from being bastions of old family oligarchies, the groups were constantly infused with blood from newcomers, albeit largely white. As historian Mark Souther says, after World War II, "unlike the waves of immigrants, drifters, and bohemians who had washed into the Quarter before them, these preservationists were self-conscious urban pioneers who sought antiquity at a time when upwardly mobile Americans were increasingly flooding into new suburbs in an effort to sate their hunger for a more pastoral lifestyle. In short, the choice of place for primarily aesthetic reasons."[20] Many arrived as casual visitors but returned to stay and settle, a pattern that has repeated post-Katrina.

A major watershed in the preservation movement, not only in New Orleans but in the United States writ large, was the establishment of the Vieux Carré Commission (VCC) in 1924. The founding state legislation strove to preserve the whole of the Vieux Carré rather than just isolated landmarks. The conservative architectural review guidelines of the VCC aim as much to preserve the look of age of the Quarter as to prevent buildings from collapsing into total ruin. In other words, the regulations are intended to preserve both the buildings *and* their aestheticized decay.[21] Enforcement did not (and does not) go smoothly among all Quarter residents. Historic preservation is a political act to transform the landscape. Its sudden imposition took the residents of the lower Quarter by surprise. Rosie grew up in the Quarter in the mid-twentieth century.

> Rosie: I'll tell you a funny story about my grandpa Cirio. . . . We owned the building on the corner of Chartres and Governor Nicholls . . . and my grandfather decided he wanted to paint the building and first of all the Vieux Carré Commission said you need a permit. Well, he ignored that completely. He was very hard headed. The second thing is that you could only paint it the colors they told you. He decided he wanted that building to be purple and white. . . . He painted it, they came in, they arrested him, they put him in jail for 24 hours and then he had to go back out and buy all the paint they told him he had to buy.

Although her cantankerous grandfather resisted, Rosie is now quite the VCC advocate. She doesn't like to see buildings too "spiffed up." She speaks fondly of the Quarter's patina, saying that people, "want to see the old city and it's here. And some of it is still in its original shape [laughs] or worse, the wear and tear is worse and worse [laughs again]."

The dirty element of patina could provoke ambivalent reactions. The VCC's regulated aesthetic created an illusion of time travel that writers and tour guides were quick to accent with calligraphic flourish. In the 1950s, one local writer, preservationist, and tour guide offered a dramatic narration: "It is a few moments before the Present dies away on a balcony, an iron grill, the delicate modeling of an upper façade. Something comes over you—the spirit of an older world."[22] While preservationists valued the evocative look of age, they were aware of the subtle perceptual shift between the qualisign of an antique glow and the potential referent of moral decay. A drive to halt prostitution, drinking, and other vices in the Quarter was also intrinsic to the agenda of early preservationists. These goals put them at odds with business owners who recognized that many tourists were drawn as much to the iniquity as to the antiquity of the French Quarter. The argument has been made that the "benign neglect" of this cityscape simply became a convenient commodity for rising tourism entrepreneurs. In this view, marketing "wrapped urban poverty and decay in the cosmetic glow of nostalgia and exoticism."[23] However, to cynically flatten out patina in this way misses some of the deeper roots of aesthetic valuation and the work it performs locally.

In the twentieth century, tourism was a major force in shaping the cityscape in a dialectical relationship with the national imaginary. This economic push, however, cannot be isolated from the city's literary and material patina. Randall Kenan writes: "New Orleans existed, like only a few other American cities, in a realm of mythology and fantasy and history and romance that made it more than a real city. . . . It is a center against which America defines itself. . . . In New Orleans's romantic decay, it is possible to project, and isolate, those antidotes to rectitude Americans want to have."[24] This exotic dance with the nation remains a major engine of tourism, but it should not be misunderstood as a soulless con job. Locally, sociologist Kevin Fox Gotham argues, tourism "helps frame the *habitus* of social life."[25] A key part of this habitus involves the care of architecture, from the regulation of aesthetics to the labor of renovation, and maintaining the story lines of old buildings. City boosters have learned to market the evocative decay of New Orleans quite effectively. But to the extent that tourism and historic preservation have shaped the architectural fabric of New Orleans, they have also shaped the experience of being a New Orleanian.

In an interview with Jack, an out-of-state transplant and now longtime resident, I asked why he chose to live in the French Quarter. He responded as we sat on his iron balcony overlooking a street where our conversation was frequently interrupted by drunken tourists and the loud engines of novelty vehicles promoting new alcoholic products:

Jack: It's one of these things I think about. I go through periods where I think about it. I'm probably thinking about it a lot right now [gesturing sardonically to the street sounds]. But, honestly, I just love the physical environment here so much. . . . This is really one of the great physical environments in America, if not the world. You know, basically, to get something like this I would either have to move to Havana, Cartagena in South America, or somewhere in Europe.

SD: When you say, "something like this," what do those places have in common?

Jack: A very dense street grid. By American standards, very uniform, cohesive urban fabric. And, also it's just very well preserved mainly because of the efforts of the Vieux Carré Commission and the other neighborhood associations that the Vieux Carré Commission grew out of. And, honestly, it's a neighborhood where if you're not a preservationist, well, there's really kind of not much point to living here, if you're not interested in historic preservation or history at some level.

The basis for Jack's attachment to the French Quarter is, above all, informed. He knows the history of preservation that helped create the landscape he lives in, and he frames it as a common cause that unites residents. However it gets marketed, historic preservation corresponds to a strongly felt aesthetic and ethical disposition to place that residents use to shape the present. We should be careful not to overdraw the link between historic preservation and tourism.

In fact, bitter fights have pitted historic preservationists *against* tourism, from large hotel owners to small souvenir shopkeepers, making it clear that one is not in the service of the other.[26] Further, the touristic and preserved landscapes are far from coterminous. The tourist zones of the French Quarter and the Garden District are only two among twenty-three National Register Historic Districts located in New Orleans. Since the 1960s, New Orleanians have been nominating their neighborhoods for this designation, and most can easily identify the district in which they live. The honored neighborhoods represent the full breadth of the city's economic and racial diversity. The age and integrity of a neighborhood's housing stock are the primary criteria. As shown in figure 3.3, there are more areas of New Orleans encompassed by historic districts than not, and they outline large areas where tourists are unlikely to venture.

Historic preservation in New Orleans is suffused with an ethic of critical nostalgia aimed at the present. The resulting effect does not so much preserve a specific history or memory, but evokes a foggy sense of pastness. The architecture of the Quarter dates primarily to the time when New Or-

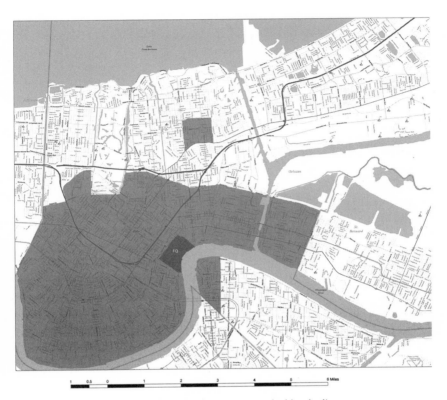

FIGURE 3.3. Historic districts of New Orleans are marked by shading.

leans was defined by the domestic slave market, between 1780 and 1860. And while carriage tours and praline sellers will reference this past (somewhat dubiously explaining that Creoles generally treated their slaves better than Americans did), the historical facts provided to tourists are often quite hazy. Unlike Williamsburg, Virginia, which is carefully groomed to call up a specific period of the nation's history (1699–1780) with references to famous founding fathers and key political struggles that every American high school student learns about, New Orleans is simply *evocative*—of something old, romantic, and somewhat exotic.

A HOUSE SOCIETY

The lengths to which New Orleanians have gone to mark their little-visited, intimate city neighborhoods, both rich and poor, black and white, is remarkable. Local residents find patina value everywhere. As interviewee Eliza recounted, when she told friends in New Jersey during the 1940s that she wanted to go back home and get an old house, "they said: 'you mean a *used* house? A *used house?*!' . . . a different culture! And we love old houses. We love shotguns. We love camelbacks and gingerbread." She went on to emphasize that architecturally beautiful houses could be found all over the city, in poor and rich neighborhoods alike.

The effort to preserve New Orleans's historic landscape has involved an obsessive amount of study and documentation. Through the work and publications of local architects, historians, and preservationists, a clear typology of New Orleans and Louisiana house types had emerged among professionals by the 1930s.[27] By the 1970s, this classificatory language had been adopted into the common vernacular of residents, real estate agents, and tour guides. The names for the most unique and well known forms— Creole Cottage, Creole Townhouse, American Townhouse, Centerhall, Sidehall, West Indies, Shotgun, Camelback—elicit as much the social history and spatial development of the city as aesthetic particulars. Getting this vocabulary right marks cultural fluency.

In the French Quarter, one of the most important documentary efforts goes far beyond architectural typology. The Vieux Carré Survey was created in 1966. This multivolume open archive provides a detailed file on every single address within the Vieux Carré Commission's purview, some 120 city squares and more than two thousand properties. The Vieux Carré Survey's basic form reads like a kinship chart of linear descent, with the current owner added to the top of the list. Deaths, foreclosures, sales, and mortgages appear as events in house biographies, with family names and sometimes personal details attached.[28]

Although it was originally intended to be a tool of enforcement, residents frequently access the survey out of curiosity about the history of their buildings. Sharing this knowledge with friends and neighbors allows New Orleanians to conduct a kind of genealogy. Although few natives with roots to the first generation of settlers live within the French Quarter, the extent to which current residents not only know their long-term genealogies, but can connect them to specific addresses within the city, is remarkable. While it is tempting to see such efforts as a sort of claims-staking, the tone of conversations around house histories does not generally feel proprietary. Rather, the conversations often ramble cordially into strings of connections to other families (funny cousins you didn't know you had, bachelor uncles, and eccentric aunts) with still more physical connections to other sites and other neighborhoods. Originally from uptown, Peter has expanded his chain of property knowledge beyond his antebellum townhouse to include the entire street he lives on. He generously shared his information on frequent visits to our excavation next to his house and photocopied a thick file of survey documents and photographs to assist us.

Genealogy as expressed through these house histories, at least in recent times, seems to be deployed as much for enhancing a sense of connectivity as for claiming privilege. It traces a rhizomic structure that runs underground, as significant in its horizontal as in its vertical extent. New residents are especially likely to take the time to research their properties through the Vieux Carré Survey or other records. They proudly share the evidentiary clues that connect their homes or businesses to well-known historical figures or events, or to archetypical ones such as smugglers and free women of color.

Many of the worries over the future of New Orleans voiced in the immediate aftermath of Hurricane Katina centered on the city's architecture and landscape. One preservationist worried: "The flavor and physical setting of the city's culture is locked up in the vernacular wooden houses of the nineteenth century and I fear for them now." An early pronouncement from filmmaker Ken Burns proclaimed that the "spectacular vernacular architecture is all but destroyed. . . . I'm worried the money will come pouring in and what we'll wind up with is a bigger, gaudier New Orleans, like Las Vegas." Fox Gotham notes that in the immediate aftermath of the storm, opinionated observers tended to have one of three future visions for New Orleans's post-Katrina landscape: as a Pompeii frozen in our memories in a moment of death, as a reconstructed Disneyland or Vegas-type faux imitation of its former self, or as a phoenix (the bird, not the town) with a renewed sense of its cultural value.[29] As time builds, so has confidence in this third possibility. However, a fourth future that melodramatic forecasts disallowed has recently emerged: that New Orleans might just return to a version of its same old self, with its stubborn social stratigraphy of economic and racial disparity.

In terms of the architecture of life, the population impacted the most may be those who formerly resided in one of the city's twelve public housing projects. Although demolition and rebuilding of these complexes began in the Clinton era, the process rapidly accelerated post-Katrina, with the federal and local government agencies claiming that storm damage made the structures unrecoverable, though in fact they were more flood-resistant than much of New Orleans's housing.[30] J.J.'s family had been in the projects near the French Quarter for three generations. Although he thought it was wasteful that such solid brick buildings were demolished, overall, he says it was a good thing to tear them down because they crowded too many people together. And too many bad things had hap-

pened there. He hopes to move into a brand new house someday. Nevertheless, historic preservationists and neighborhood activists united in an
effort to save some of the older units. These efforts failed to sway regu-
lators to save the complexes, although in each a token "Legacy Building"
will remain.[31]

Like J.J., Blue opined that it was a good thing that the projects had
been torn down. But he prefers old houses. In my interviews, one of my
standard prompts was to elicit opinions about the "Make It Right" building program in the Lower Ninth Ward founded by actor Brad Pitt, in
which architects from around the world (including Frank Gehry) contributed updated versions of the hall-less shotgun form. Some of the designs push aesthetically and speculatively into the future. Many use new
materials such as sheet metal. In our conversations, these houses provided
touchpoints about aesthetics, architecture, and local sensibilities. Blue at
first attempted to be diplomatic when I asked him what he thought about
them: "Yeah, real different, real different. To me, they don't fit . . . they're
just so modernized, it's just not New Orleans. Especially for that area. That
area never had no houses like that." I followed up by asking him whether
he thought people in that area (more than 90% African American before
the storm) liked old houses: "I think they do, I think they do. Well, I like
the way they look and if I had the money I would love to sweep up one
of those big houses. . . . It takes a lot of time to bring those houses back
and sad to say if we don't do something to get 'em and catch 'em, they're
all going to be torn down." He goes on to relate a story of his personal
outrage about a beautiful building in his neighborhood that was allowed
to fall down because the owner couldn't pay his taxes.

Isaiah is a self-made college student, the son of postal workers, who
traces his roots to Cuban Creoles on one side and English-speaking African
Americans on the other, going back four generations. He struggled to save
his grandmother's house in Holy Cross, the oldest portion of the sprawling Lower Ninth Ward, located on high ground next to the river. He also
seems to hesitate to express his feelings about the Make It Right houses.

> Isaiah: I think it has nothing to do with, I don't know, the architecture
> that existed there before. It's cool, I like it—sort of—but I just think that
> it doesn't sort of go with the area. I think that . . . it just brings this sort
> of modern or sort of semi- contemporary appearance to the area—it just
> doesn't—it's not what I remember. So it's sort of different.

Isaiah expresses appreciation for the help but clearly struggles with the
changes that the project has brought to his once-familiar landscape. His

experience is shaped by a heroic but failed effort to save his grandmother's house from demolition that involved petitions, forms, and several meetings with the city-appointed department that handles so-called blighted properties. In his eyes, the house was not a blight. I asked him to describe the house.

> Isaiah: It was a double shotgun that had been turned into one house . . . Of course it had the high ceilings that you find in New Orleans. . . . It had the original boards that you find on the Spanish ships that would be in the dock. Like most houses in that area would have. The house had been vandalized [after the storm]. Pieces had been stolen off of the house [doorknobs, brackets, millwork] . . . and they're usually handcrafted. And each one is different, you know. That's the thing, you know. Typically, you don't find the same one twice. I mean it's possible but normally every house has its own identity. And part of that identity is in those brackets. . . . I suppose you could argue that that particular area—a lot of the houses in that area before the storm were not really in a good condition. But they were also not in a condition where it was uninhabitable, where you couldn't live there.

> SD: How did you feel when you saw the house after the storm?

> Isaiah: It sort of made me seek culture in a different way because before when I would go visit my grandmother, I never really thought about those things, about what a house could mean or what artifacts could mean or just what being in that geographic location just looking at everything could mean. But after the storm it sort of made you sad, it made you want to cry, it made you think about everything you took for granted. You know, my grandmother for one, I hated going by her house. But now that she was gone. Now that her house was torn up. You know, it's just been something different. . . . It made me want to find out I guess what was near and dear to her heart.

For Isaiah, this modest little house had become a different kind of place through the experience of loss. His nostalgia is singular while also being critical. He has no kind words for city administrators and suspects that the forces of white gentrification were to blame for the bureaucratic roadblocks he encountered. The now-empty lot stands as a personal landmark unseen even by his neighbors who dump their garbage there, a convenient spot in an underserved neighborhood. He talks, half joking and half seriously, about doing archaeology as his only recourse left to connect with his grandmother.

HAUNTED HISTORY TOURS

The landscape of New Orleans presents a particularly dense palimpsest of landmarks, tall tales, omissions, iconic images, renovations, and "blight." But it is not an entirely unreadable one. Well-worn paths that natives and newcomers trek overlap at key points, though focused on different things, much like the coexisting but hardly mutual black and white landscapes that Dell Upton identified as coexisting on southern plantations.[32]

One can make an easy inventory of "must-see" sites in New Orleans for the visitor, and tours are readily available for a price on the streets of the French Quarter. Indeed, with the exception of a few Garden District and Cemetery tours, the vast majority of the city's tour guides grind a small, predictable circuit in the French Quarter. Following this route and the landmarks it highlights provides a useful exercise for gathering collective representations. While logistics of distance and access determine some parts of the route (particularly for the mule carriages), most of the choices seem to be made with one of two motivations: to stop at places where a good story can be told (usually about ghosts, pirates, or the War of 1812, straight out of the pages of George Washington Cable or Grace King) or to point out a hotel or bar of "special" interest. Entrepreneurial guides barely disguise the fact that this second motivation relates to a commission system for guest referrals. Tour guides in New Orleans must pass a test at City Hall and carry an ID and a license. However, they are not regulated by any agency with historical or cultural expertise. Rather, they operate under the management of the Taxicab Bureau. The role of the paid tour guide is understood to be akin to that of the bus drivers, cab drivers, and limousine drivers also regulated by this agency. They safely ferry visitors along a restricted route in the core tourist zones of the city. Monitoring the authenticity of the stories they tell is a low priority, much to the chagrin of long-term residents of the French Quarter who frequently complained to me about the shockingly shoddy facts provided on these tours. One resident I interviewed says he sometimes gets so irritated when he overhears yet another apocryphal story that he goes out on his balcony and shouts at the tour takers, "That's a bunch of b.s., nothing like that happened here! You people are wasting your money!"

The tours I sampled either started or ended at St. Anthony's Garden. At night when the "touchdown Jesus" statue casts a giant shadow over the rear of the church and the pirate-theme bar on the corner enjoys a loud business, the garden is an evocative spot (fig. 3.4). Other stops on the tours are chosen for their prominence in local history or for their aesthetic presentation: the Pontalba Buildings that flank Jackson Square trigger sto-

FIGURE 3.4. "Touchdown Jesus" behind St. Louis Cathedral. Photo taken for author by Christopher Grant.

ries related to a high-spirited Creole wife of a European baron. Ursuline Convent presents the most recognizably French-looking building in the Quarter, consistent with its prefire date of 1752 and its status as the oldest building in the Mississippi Valley. Certain hauntings figure prominently in the daytime mule tours as well as the nighttime walking "ghost tours." The Lalaurie Mansion is a celebrity building, said to be haunted by slaves who had been subjected to torture and vivisection by Madame Lalaurie and her physician husband in the 1830s. Jean Lafitte's Blacksmith Shop fronts a lively bar said to be where the pirate melted down smuggled goods. The documentary basis of this last story is weak, but the building sags sugges-

FIGURE 3.5. Lafitte's Blacksmith Shop. Photo taken for author by Christopher Grant.

tively and shows its age in its exposed cross-timbers and crumbling brick (fig. 3.5). Other stops on walking tours include the Old Absinthe House on Bourbon Street (where General Andrew Jackson and pirate Jean Lafitte supposedly met to strategize during the War of 1812); Preservation Hall, a performance space established in 1961 to "protect and honor New Orleans jazz"; and the Napoleon House, a restaurant established in a house built for Napoleon-in-exile (fig. 3.6). Like Lafitte's Blacksmith Shop, these buildings are among the most patinated in the Quarter. They show their age with layers of faded and peeling paint that glow with color. When the 1798-built Old Absinthe House, once featured on postcards as a near-ruin and "the oldest saloon in America," received a $3 million restoration in 2004, it disgruntled many old-timers, although the work may have saved the building from total collapse.

While we were excavating at St. Anthony's Garden, our project was incorporated into several creative mule drivers' tours. The guides mentioned archaeology as a curiosity and often stated that we were digging to find the earlier French colonial church (untrue). Although some guides proceeded cautiously, knowing we were within earshot, others unabashedly elaborated about gentleman duels in the garden, the apparition of a hanged pirate who could be seen from time to time, or the burial of Gypsy Rose Lee's baby beneath a crepe myrtle tree adjacent to our units. None of these events, or ones that could plausibly be an origin for exaggeration,

FIGURE 3.6. Napoleon House. Photo taken for author by Christopher Grant.

are documented in the written or archaeological records. However, many interesting stories could have been elaborated from our excavation, such as the discovery of an early-twentieth-century pet cemetery that included the burial of a cat topped with an inverted whole bottle, a known voodoo practice intended to trap bad spirits. But no one asked.

Conflicts between French Quarter residents and the "Haunted History" tour guides can be a bit fierce. As noisome as one might think that defecating mules might be in one's neighborhood, I found complaints about the carriage tours to be rare compared to those about the ghost tours. The lies and fabrications that these tours are seen as perpetuating consternate connoisseurs of the local landscape, many of whom can weave colorful enough stories on their own about the buildings around them (including the *real* ghost stories). On the ghost tour I went on, the guide emphasized to the group the importance of remaining discreet and respectful if we should encounter a local resident—crossing to the other side of the street, if possible.

These tours of New Orleans, with their projections of historic events, brushes with fame, and romantic or lurid hauntings, produce a storybook landscape quite different from that conjured up by a native New Orleanian returning home. Joe describes himself as a "Creole native" who was born the week of Hurricane Betsy (September 1965). As an adult, he has lived away from New Orleans for many years, working as a musician and crafts-man on the East Coast. He says, though, "I feel a great desire to return home and give back to my rich world that nurtured me." After Katrina, he was frustrated by the news coverage of New Orleans, finding few examples that were "historically considerate and truthful in my nostalgia from home, the only home I know." Joe does not oppose nostalgia to truth. He de-scribed for me a whirlwind trip he made back to the city in 2009.

> Joe: My experience was great. . . . My mom and one of my sisters walked up Jeannette Street and saw no one hanging on corners loitering and scary looking, to my surprise. We walked from Eagle Street deep in the hood and were greeted by so many who had returned and just gave us all hugs. We walked all the way to the River Bend to La Madeleine's for brunch. . . . [I] visited my favorite eye doc since I was a kid and asked if my favorite bar-tender still worked at Cooter Brown's and she did. We then got the street-car headed downtown. We proceeded through the French Quarter visiting places I worked and knew folks, from the Greeks at Mena's to Crescent City Books (where I worked), the jewelry store next door, the candy shop, and Lucullus antiquarian epicurean shop. We stopped at the Cathedral to pray and light candles, buy religious souvenirs and to the chapel of the first gen de colour saint, Delille, then to Faulkner House to see Joe DeSalvo, the owner who was already next door having a beverage [at a bar on Pirate Alley]. . . . [Then I went] touring the Bywater where all my stuff is stored. At Flora Cafe a Brazilian friend who worked there said "Hey Joe" from the bushes and I had not seen him—Bill—for years (since I was a kid) and then Ali the owner showed up and joined us. . . . And [then] a walk with Adé the owner of Cafe Brazil back to the St Louis Cathedral—you get the idea. Oh, my favorite part was the last visit with my youngest sister who is married to someone who is a Mardi Gras Indian. . . . [They] are keepers of the tradition, passing it on to their kids.

There are several remarkable things about the highly personalized map that Joe traced on his return trip home. First, Joe's nostalgic New Orleans stretches the full width of the city, from the Riverbend upriver edge down well past the French Quarter into the Bywater and the Lower Ninth Ward neighborhoods. His verbal cartography pauses in the little-known neigh-borhood of Hollygrove (Eagle Street in "the hood"), a majority black neighborhood located in the low-lying bowl of New Orleans, which suf-fered deep flooding and extensive damage in Katrina's floodwaters but has received no major assistance and little press (with the caveat that it is the home of one of latter-day New Orleans's major musical exports, rapper Lil Wayne). But Joe's tour also includes the heart of the French Quarter and diverse neighborhoods known only by locals.

Joe's New Orleans does overlap with the tourist landscape—it takes in the Cathedral, bookstores, antique shops, perfume shops, and restaurants. But Joe's Cathedral is different, he does not stand outside and look up at its fairy-tale architecture. He moves directly inside to participate in a ritual of visitation, knowledgeably attending to the image of Venerable Henriette Delille, the New Orleans Creole-of-color nun who in the antebellum period founded the educational order known as Sisters of the Holy Family. Sister Delille's canonization has not yet been confirmed by the Catholic Church, but this is of little significance to native hagiography.

The Faulkner House bookstore (where the author once lived) and the bar on the corner look out on the cathedral garden where our excavations took place, situated along Pirate Alley. In these secular spaces, Joe stresses a personal social connection to every locale, and his consumption of food, beverages, and collectibles is informed by the history of these venues and his relationship to the people who work there. It is *familiar* turf, in the kinship sense of the term. Further, in listing these sites off to me (whom he seemed to consider an informed neonative), Joe expects that I will be able to follow along on his whirlwind tour and participate in acts of recognition. Most of the shops, bars, and restaurants he mentions (indeed, even some of the individuals he runs into) are part of my own New Orleans, although Joe and I had never met before this exchange. With hundreds of cafés, bookstores, and watering holes to choose from, the tourist relies on guidebooks and Internet reviews to navigate New Orleans's consumer landscape, but to those "in the know," the selection is much smaller and more predictable. Preferred businesses have a long history of association with one's friends and family, as well as being subtly oriented to the tastes and sociability of New Orleanians, a kind of interior hospitality. Tourist-oriented simulacra of densely "local" establishments often sit side-by-side on the same street with the originals (such as antique stores along Royal or restaurants along Chartres Street) and have nearly indistinguishable facades and furnishings. Distinguishing them requires historical knowledge, social connections, and experiential density. Sharing this hidden landscape helps fuse social bonds and separate out true "locals." Locals are not necessarily natives, but those with an accumulation of this type of place knowledge and, among the insecure, an air of chauvinism regarding the authentic landscape. In fact, post-Katrina there has been such a population explosion

of new settlers eager to fit in, that some have cynically coined the phrase
"NOLA-ier than thou" (NOLA being the local abbreviated nickname for
New Orleans, Louisiana).

Joe's friends live all over the city and include many neonatives and international transplants. His New Orleans is neither white nor black. He identifies simply as "native Creole." Joe proudly recounts his family's involve-
ment in the living history of Mardi Gras Indian parading, a traditionally
black or Afro-Creole cultural practice.[33] While he could have used this
personal connection to one of the most prized of New Orleans's unique
performing traditions to stake a claim for his own authenticity, he did not
begin our conversation there. He felt no need to locate himself in that way.
Instead, he ended there, as if this connection through the generations was
taken for granted or already demonstrated by his mastery of the intimate
spaces of the city.

Knowledge of place is also a way that Jack, a nonnative long-term resident, establishes his belonging. I followed up to ask him what it takes to
appreciate the French Quarter.

Jack: I've been thinking about it. These buildings have a whole lot of numa
[numen],[34] is that the word?

SD: Oh, I don't know.

Jack: Numa or mana. It's like . . . basically the sense of history here is just
so palpable because this particular building, unlike the building on Chartres
Street [the so-called Beauregard-Keyes House featured on tours], which is
a very distinguished building, General PGT Beauregard actually lived here
for several years.

SD: In this building, where we are sitting right now?

Jack: Where we are sitting right now PGT Beauregard sat.

SD: Just for the record, can you just say who that is? [Jack assumed I would
know]

Jack: Pierre Gustave Toutant Beauregard, of the Beauregard-Keyes House,
Beauregard Circle, artillery instructor at West Point, who fired the first shots
at Fort Sumter in the Civil War, generally well admired New Orleanian.
And he—

SD: A military hero?

Jack: Military hero, yeah. I'm not a confederate partisan by any means. But there is a great deal of history. And it's like as you walk through here, history, it's palpable. Also, the buildings are just very aesthetically pleasing. And that's part of what I mean by numa, they show their age, and they show generations of association [he points to the multihued wall]. Maybe a better word would be mana.

SD: Spirit of some kind?

Jack: Yes, just some sort of a spirit. There's just layers of association that you can just [pause]—that one feels.

As in the exchange with Joe, we are connected because there are certain things that are understood: where a certain business is and who its proprietor is, the names of small local neighborhoods, who P. G. T. Beauregard was, and the fact that there's a National Historic Register site named after him nearby, where the truth-challenged mule tours stop. Jack displays his connoisseurship in being able to reveal the doubling of the landscape— that visitors and the poorly informed misidentify the locales of history and the haunts of the dead. P. G. T. Beauregard once sat on *Jack's* peeling, rusty balcony, not on the porch of the polished mansion down the street. His knowledge is intimate and tactile and occult—hidden until invoked. Jack calls forth the ghost of Beauregard, saying we—those who know the true history of these buildings and who live among them—are better spiritual mediums than those who parade for tourists. But it is not only dead soldiers who are summoned by the patina of New Orleans's buildings. Something larger and more diffuse dwells in old wood and brick. Jack calls it *numen* or *mana*, a spirit emanating from "layers of association."

Jack is not alone in feeling this spirit. One of the unexpected outcomes of my interviews was how many New Orleanians mentioned ghosts or the possibility of haunting once we got to the subject of old houses, although this topic had no place on my original list of questions. For example, J.J., who works at a bed and breakfast, said that another reason he was glad to be out of the housing projects where he grew up was that they were built over part of the old cemetery, cursing their inhabitants to a hard life. His mother, another employee, claimed she had seen a young girl in a nightgown several times in the B&B. Marie, from the Lower Ninth Ward, expressed a desire to move into a brand new house because a renovated old one could still be haunted by her neighbors who had died in the levee breaks. Patricia owns an antique shop on Magazine Street and says her neighbor bought an adjacent shop that had been closed up for decades, with all the furniture and goods left in place, collecting dust. In the upstairs apartment they found "satanic" symbols painted on the wall and had to call in a priest to conduct an exorcism. Then there's the sometime occupant of her own shop, cluttered with old glassware, toys, linens, and oak furniture.

> Patricia: Upstairs here, at one point, several people told me that they felt someone up there. It was an old man. . . . But when Katrina came, I think he moved. . . . No one's reported him since. . . . I have not met the man myself. But several people have reported him. They say he's friendly. He means no harm. He just wants to stay there. Maybe he moved to Iowa after the storm or something when Katrina came [laughs].

In response to a follow-up question, Patricia makes it clear that she believes these reports because "there are things we just don't know." A pattern of reporting *other* people's experiences of ghosts, although the speaker had no firsthand knowledge, was a common one in my interviews. However, with the exception of a Catholic priest, no one entirely denied the possibility. The priest did, though, elaborate on the criteria for miracles that would account for other visions that had occurred in the New Orleans area. Harry, who owns the bed and breakfast where J.J. works, is a devout adult Catholic convert, which may explain why his usually tropically lush storytelling faded to grey on this topic, though he did not shy away from it entirely.

> Harry: There are ghost stories, but I cannot give you first hand on any of those.
>
> SD: Who's seen a ghost?
>
> Harry: A lot of the guests. . . . [They] report it here or generally in this room [the dining room]. At the foot of the steps over here [pointing]. People are convinced, yeah. Or heard, it's more hearing. At the foot of the steps, a number of people have reported being tapped on the shoulder.

Harry's short, choppy sentences and lack of descriptive details suggest how uncomfortable he seemed with the topic. Other residents do report direct experiences. Brenda lives in the apartment above her perfume shop. Her narrative moves quickly from a ghost to her emotional attachment to New Orleans, to her experience right after Katrina.

> Brenda: Yeah, it's just a special place. And like we have right here in this corner behind this wall, we smell cigarette smoke all the time. This morning it was bad. Nobody here smokes. Nobody out there smokes [points to side-walk]. It's our little ghost, we've determined.
>
> SD: Oh really? A smoking ghost?
>
> Brenda: I guess. And it's like, you just sit here and go, "Oh, it's the ghost." He's back. [laughs]
>
> SD: He's trying to fight back the perfume smell? I mean with all the scents in here, I'm surprised you can smell it. [both laugh]
>
> Brenda: Oh, it's so strong some days, so strong—it's hilarious, I mean, we're just like, you know "could you lay off the cigarettes now, because we can't breathe." He comes and goes. . . . Yeah, I mean if you love this city, you can't breathe anywhere else, you know? . . . I just remember after Katrina. I was here. Nobody else was down here except this homeless guy, James, who's been down here for 20 years. So it was me and him hanging out. And he's cuckoo. And so I'd go get him MREs[35] or whatever every day. And one day he and I are just sitting out there [points to curb outside shop], having a conversation, and he's telling me how he talked to Walt Disney. And I'm just like, at that point, well, he probably did. And then when I'm going to bed that night, the city's totally dead, in the true sense of the word. And somebody is sitting out on a balcony, playing a clarinet. And it's like, where is that going to happen, but here? [chokes up and begins to cry]. You know, there's music, there's life, there's tragedy, there's emotion. There's everything in this little eight-block area.

For Brenda, evidence of the specialness of the French Quarter manifests in the form of a ghost, an unnamed and unseen one who makes himself known only through a waft of scent. As far as I could tell, despite her gentle laughter, Brenda sincerely believed in the smoking ghost, whom she brought up in a matter-of-fact way. This is not a ghost who will be featured on the haunted history tours for conventioneers. He is an intimate, local ghost who only makes his presence known to those who stick around.

In addition to the smoking ghost, Brenda cites two other figures emblematic of her attachment to the city—an equally disembodied jazz clarinetist whom she could hear but not see through the fog in the nearly vacated Quarter in the fall of 2005, immediately after the storm, and a homeless resident who claims to have met Walt Disney, the man most credited with vulgarizing the romance of the city. The clarinet of a traditional New Orleans jazz band, which typically sticks to a repertoire established before World War II, plays not just to the tourist crowd, but to the heartstrings of local residents while evoking a sense of pastness. Authenticating Walt Disney's encounter with a man of the streets of New Orleans may mean that the minstrel romance projected to entertain the tourists has yet some authentic ring for locals whose emotions are constantly being triggered by sensory cues. These vibrations are conditioned by a literary tradition ritually reenacted in multiple retellings, in the connoisseurship of architecture, and in the web of everyday associations that require a density of social experience to acquire.

The specific though quite anonymous hauntings reported by locals are undoubtedly enhanced by New Orleans's gothic reputation and touristic claims to be the most haunted city in America. Harry scoffs at the nonsense purveyed on ghost tours, and Father Kerry has more scurrilous things to say about them. Nevertheless, Jenny, who is a tour guide for the best-known haunted-tour outfit, is a treasure trove of information on the sociology of hauntings. A stout believer herself, as she affirms several times throughout our interview, she has no interest whatsoever in paranormal research or science's ability to prove or disprove the existence of ghosts. Of course, many of the tourists she encounters are among those predisposed to believe or to report experiences, particularly at their hotels. But she also gets her fair share of obnoxious (often drunk) skeptics who demand their money back at the end of the tour if they didn't see a ghost. Her tour focuses on ghosts and haunted sites in New Orleans that are at this point legendary, passed down from the same writers, including George Washington Cable, who originally popularized the city's decaying, decadent allure. She says many of her customers come on the tour already well informed by television shows such as *Ghost Hunters* and are expecting a retelling or a closer encounter with the space that for them is already supernatural. She relates all this, and some of the legends, with a matter-of-fact air: the sadist Madame Lalaurie, the hanged pirate of Jackson Square, the Creole mistress Julie who forever paces on the roof where she died waiting for her lover. Her manner becomes less rehearsed when I ask whether she's heard any post-Katrina stories. Naturally, she is a conduit for new local ghost stories. People are eager to share their personal accounts.

Jenny: I've heard it three times, from just random people. The first time I heard it was just after I had gotten back to New Orleans. . . . I had a guy come up to me . . . a federal officer and he showed me his badge. . . . He said, "I was called out post-Katrina to help out the local police force, you know, they needed assistance and I got called out, back when we had a curfew, but it was like two o'clock in the morning, was the curfew. I get this emergency 911 call at 3 o'clock in the morning: 'Get down here, there's a big fight going on behind St. Louis Cathedral. Rush! Right?' And I get out of bed and I rush down here and there is nothing at all. No one anywhere. Nada. Nothing."

This story of a night-time post-Katrina brawl behind the cathedral was independently reported to her by a customs agent and a resident. While it seems apt that post-Katrina ghosts reflect tension and conflict in a very public space (St. Anthony's Garden), Jenny observes that in general New Orleanians seem more sensitive to the paranormal. When I ask her why, she jokes that maybe it is all the drinking, but then follows soberly: "There's always a lot of death in New Orleans." Another reason she cites is the longevity of the architecture and the type of deep attachment that people form with the city. The specificity of the relationship between the people and the houses matters, as does its deep social stratigraphy.

Jenny: I think that a lot of people are attached to New Orleans so I guess it makes sense that after you die, you'd still be attached. Where I live now, I know was built as a rental for people working on the river, I live right on the river on Tchoupitoulas, in this double shotgun and I know somebody just slapped it up as some income property for longshoremen. And I don't think anybody ever felt like it was theirs and I don't have any inkling of ghosts now. I just don't think anybody feels like it's theirs. So it doesn't surprise me. But if I was in a place where somebody had built it and lived in it their whole life and had their children die in it. If they had really developed an attachment to it, then I would figure, they'd still be around.

Jenny's highly informed reflections on the hauntings of New Orleans suggest that in this field, as in the doubled tourist-local landscape, an important distinction exists between legendary ghosts attached to famous landmarks and the unnamed, often unseen spirits detected by residents. The local spirits index a more general sense of living-with-the-dead and a sense of pastness that is continually stimulated by contact with the aging materiality of the city. We can call this a historical unconscious, but it is diffused and scattered and not about a single narrative. It is also not a positive force for everyone. It depends upon which elements of history come to the fore, or how one's family fits within the city's social stratigraphy. In response to a question about whether he would prefer to live in an old New Orleans house or a brand new one, J.J. didn't hesitate.

> J.J.: I'll take the new one anytime. Like them old houses, you never know what done happened in those old houses or nothing. And me, I'm scary [aka, "prone to fright"]. Me, they talk about ghosts and what not, I'm scary. I'm scared of lizards and worms. [laughs] *Serious.*[36]

> SD: So you think old houses might have ghosts?

> J.J.: Yeah, I try not to think about it but yeah, I couldn't. I'd go with the new house. . . . Cause the slaves they probably was the ones that built those houses and that's way before my time. I just try to stay forward, not to go back.

While New Orleanians are highly attuned to the overlapping temporalities of their spaces, and of living *with* history, the associations they make with this past and with the possibilities of the future reflect their own genealogy and sometimes their own traumas, including, of course, Katrina and "the federal floods" that followed.

• • •

Digging through the literary debris of New Orleans, we can now see that it was around Latrobe's time in the 1810s that the city suddenly became old in its own imagination and exotic in the eyes of the newly arrived. This sudden aging and mystification occurred while New Orleans was experiencing an explosive demographic expansion and a threatened shift in political power, economic structure, language, and religion through the deluge of English-speaking entrepreneurs and frontiersmen following the Louisiana Purchase. Emphasizing difference in a positive, alluring light may have been as effective as emphasizing the deep roots of privilege held by the elite Creole oligarchy in keeping the flood under control to protect a familiar way of life. History repeated itself after the Civil War. The long and turbulent period of Reconstruction upended political and economic structures as freedmen and new waves of immigrants entered the city. Troops of native romance writers grew proportionately and engaged in a race-tinged nostalgia. On some level discomfited by a Jim Crow town increasingly defined by zones of black and white, they longed for the more tolerant Creole past they themselves had helped destroy.

As was well known by colonial descendants who had displaced local American Indians, autochthony does not automatically confer rights, nor does antiquity automatically invoke respect. However, the affective and aesthetic valuation of patina—the look of age—in the local urban context does have useful social effects. When residents attach sentiments to buildings and neighborhoods, it engenders community resistance to intentional demolition and structural change. To the extent that these threatened changes often displace established residents, saving buildings is a way to preserve structures of *habitus*, community networks, and some hard-won economic stability. Buildings and places do not simply shelter societies; they mortar them together. The historic preservation movement in New Orleans has at times buffered the center of the city not only from physical change but from some of the crasser promises of liberal capitalism. This potential for the landscape to assist in utopian resistance was fully recognized and mobilized by bohemian preservationists in the early twentieth century and is recognized today by many of the young artists and DIY hipsters now immigrating to the postdisaster city. They actively participate in a form of critical nostalgia that resonates at a national scale. Critical nostalgia may offer commentary on the present, but it would have to reach deep into practice to transform social stratigraphy. As seen in the cases of public housing and Isaiah's grandmother's house, the ability to mobilize historic preservation in New Orleans in order to resist social displacement remains unequal.

Still, in the case of "preservation by neglect," the endurance of old buildings has its effects on social life, providing a source of totemic power ranging from the almost unutterable aura of *mana* to the specificities of highly elaborate narratives about historic figures, catastrophic events, or the origins of quirky local habits. Houses are a medium through which locals bind themselves together, a means of incorporation and cohesion.

Valuing the look of architectural age acknowledges the depth of social stratigraphy. It is an aesthetic necessarily more multivalent than modernism. Like the palimpsest of its visual manifestations, the associated social levels are multiple and complex to those who want to find them. To embrace the aesthetic of patina means including the dead in social life, not simply as a form of ancestor veneration, but as a materialization of personal connection to place that one arrives at through local knowledge. This is why it is not necessary to be native-born to be a "real" New Orleanian. Knowing the history of the house in which one lives (whether you own it or not), or knowing the history of the neighborhood in which you walk, means being able to utter the names of those who went before you. If your neighbor has the same knowledge, the two of you are connected through these fictive dead kin. It is this recognition of the social forces at work in patinated buildings and oft-told stories that has helped me understand why so many of my interviews are peopled by ghosts. New Orleans is a "house society," or one in which inheritance of both material and immaterial wealth flows through the house rather than through blood descent, facilitating social bonds of totemic kinship, adoption, and flexible rules of endogamy. I do not mean to imply that this makes for one big, happy family. Some New Orleanians, like J.J. and Marie, have little access to this wealth except at the general level of the neighborhood. But I suspect they understand the terms of their own exclusion.

Although more articulate than most about the aesthetic of patina, Jack probably did not have Emile Durkheim in mind when he invoked *mana*. The anthropological resonance is therefore all the more powerful. In *The Elementary Forms of Religious Life*, Durkheim lays out his theory of *mana*, or the totemic principle, as an impersonal force detected by actors in many societies. It is an energy that fuels magic and in most religions becomes personified as a god. For Durkheim, this force represents the solidarity-building power of society itself, a projection of the principles that unite individuals into a workable collective. *Mana* is society abstracted. And it can be poured into palpable forms like sculptures, heirloom paraphernalia, boats, and human bodies. For Jack, the old buildings of New Orleans have *mana*. Their layers of paint embody mysterious social force. Old houses are totems that connect him to others, both to the dead who left their marks and to the living who can share his intimate knowledge of how to read the traces. Just as Jack sees Durkheim's mana, Durkheim would have seen Jack's patina. The French sociologist recognized that "time itself increases and reinforces the sacredness of things."[37] In our heavily secularized society, we seem to be returning to a form so elementary it verges on the profane—everyday objects and their ghosts.

CHAPTER 4

"French" Things

She is a lady with a past who is looking out for a future. —Storyville gossip column in the *New Orleans Mascot*, October 1896

As we screened and bagged artifacts from our excavation units at the site of Rising Sun Hotel in the winter of 2005, we began to notice that we were finding more than the usual number of ceramic sherds from a type locally called "faience rouge pot." These small, cylindrical pots made in France stand out among the bits of flat, white, British-made plates and teacups. The old-fashioned tin-enamel glaze is tinted *Clinique* green or powder blue on the outside and milk white on the inside. A heavy round base helps stabilize the pot so one can run two fingers through its contents without knocking it over (fig. 4.1). The pot's identification as a rouge container comes from word of mouth. In Diderot's *Encyclopédie*, identical pots appear under the simple heading "ointment jars." Some New Orleanians curate them as heirlooms from their grandmothers or great-grandmothers, and the local understanding of their original use has entered the informal training of Louisiana archaeologists, who regularly list "faience rouge pots" in their technical reports.[1]

For many outside observers, this high number of rouge pots offered sufficient proof to implicate the site as the original blues-song brothel, House of the Rising Sun—an excited forensics of New Orleans's renowned sexual license. The title of a front-page article in the *Los Angeles Times* about the excavation reads: "New Orleans Legend May Prove to Be Reputable: The Rising Sun Has Long Been a House of Musical Inspiration. It Could Soon Have a Real Address." The article goes on to say:

The simple folk song in a minor key always spoke to the sultry allure of this city from its first words, an opening line seared into one generation after another: "There is a house in New Orleans they call the Rising Sun."

FIGURE 4.1. Faience rouge pot recovered from an archaeological site in New Orleans.

No one has figured out—and many have tried—if the song depicts an actual bordello, and, if it does, where the real Rising Sun was. But a collection of pottery shards pulled from the ruddy soil of the French Quarter could prove to be the key that would unlock that beloved mystery.[2]

This desire to fix a historical mystery in space and make it tactile helps us understand the attraction of patina. The look of age is not unconnected to its sultry allure. New Orleans succeeds in making history sexy, not simply through recreating stories and stage sets of its legendary licentiousness, but by regularly insinuating that its "antiquity" equates with worldly experience and an intimate knowledge of the sensual that can be gained only through a long life. New Orleans is Old World, and an older woman.

The figuring of New Orleans as a woman dates back to the French period, with the abandoned and dying professional mistress and con artist Manon Lescaut, depicted in Abbé Prévost's popular early novel. Later, the same Victorian writers who antiqued New Orleans did their part to sexualize it. Hearn once described New Orleans from the point of view of the Devil, who had come to the southern city on a weekend break from a winter working in Chicago. The Devil was paying a visit to an old lover. Hearn's account mingles the good patina of faded beauty with the bad patina of mold and decay associated with unkempt morality:

> The Devil could not suppress a sigh of regret as he gazed with far-reaching eyes along the old-fashioned streets of the city, whose gables were bronzed by the first yellow glow of sunrise. "Ah!" he exclaimed, "is this, indeed, the great City of Pleasure . . . the fair capital which once seemed to slumber in enchanted sunlight, and to exhale a perfume of luxury even as the palaces of the old Caesars? Her streets are surely green with grass; her palaces are gray with mould; and her glory is departed from her. And perhaps her good old sins have also departed with her glory."[3]

Hearn's invocation of classical history underlines the orientalist principle behind the discursive and material package of New Orleans's patina aesthetic. The architecture and artifacts of the city express this tangle of the exotic, the erotic, and the antique. A generation later, the young William Faulkner echoed Hearn:

> Outside the window, New Orleans, the vieux carré, brooded in a faintly tarnished languor like an aging yet still beautiful courtesan in a smokefilled room, avid yet weary too of ardent ways. . . . This unevenly boarded floor, these rough stained walls broken by high small practically useless windows beautifully set, these crouching lintels cutting the immaculate ruined pitch of walls which had housed slaves long ago. . . . And outside, above rooftops becoming slowly violet, summer lay supine, unchaste with decay.[4]

A few pages later, he introduces Mrs. Maurier, the older, effusive hostess who clearly stands in for a major element of New Orleans society: "Her glance held a decayed coquetry."[5]

In these representations, the sketches are double-edged. The authors acknowledge an allure to the aging courtesan in her graciousness and "good old sins" but also offer a soft moral critique of her ruination. This negative patina resonates in the etymology of the word *brothel*; the Oxford English Dictionary reads: "Brothel. root: *to go to ruin*, from Old English brēothan, *to decay*."

In this chapter, I go deeper into how small objects evoke, seduce, and bind. They emanate a profane mana of their own, in which the emphasis is sometimes very much on the *profane*. An associative trilogy between

Frenchness, sexuality, and antiquity suffuses not just the representations of New Orleans, but sensual experiences of it and its souvenirs. We can take the word *souvenir* both in its French sense as memories of experience and in the English sense as objects that project both backward and forward in time. Tourist souvenirs materialize a temporally brief encounter with a different place while they promise the ability to recount that experience for as long as memory serves.

Doing a genealogy of "orientalism down south" requires paralleling the story of How New Orleans Became Old with a story about How New Orleans Became French. Frenchness packages an assemblage of representations and desires. This phenomenon is illustrated quite literally through *packaging*—select pieces of material culture, such as the faience rouge pots, that cite and reproduce New Orleans's shared fictive ancestry as well as its exoticism. In this chapter, I will offer the examples of cosmetic jars, wine bottles, and perfume. The port's hospitality economy has, since the early colonial period, helped create a sensorium that at first profited from a kind of nostalgia in its original meaning as homesickness. Over time, this sensorium began to do more complicated things as it attracted outsiders with a lust for the unusual, eventually encouraging the development of New Orleans's famous brothels. Interestingly, these houses were no less "antiqued" than uptown mansions. Here the focus zooms in on the role that small objects play in enhancing the imaginative mediation of experience—and of the past, present, and future.

In *Orientalism*, Edward Said describes a Western intellectual project from the eighteenth century to the present that focuses on the Middle East with an effort to describe, catalog, romanticize, and memorialize its difference. Writers, philologists, archaeologists, and colonial functionaries elaborated what they saw as the region's antiquity, backwardness, and sensuality. In doing so, they underwrote the imperial projects of Napoleon and Queen Victoria. Said's ideas have traveled. Many now recognize that the cultural phenomena and sociopolitical dynamics he observed have operated in other arenas (architecture and urban planning, music, and later cinema) and in other regions—in the Americas, in eastern Europe, in eastern Asia, and in Africa. Said's insights have exploded beyond their original scope because, "in an age of Western-dominated modernity, every nation creates its own Orient." The disposition of Anglo-America toward the South in general in the nineteenth and early twentieth centuries, and New Orleans in particular, provides a strong case of such a parallel.[6]

Consciously deploying the feminist terminology of "the Other," Said's comments on the gender politics of imperial culture were few but pointed in *Orientalism*. In later work, he recognized not only that "the Orient was routinely described as feminine," but that masculine competition and male-female relations reproduced the inequalities of colonialism in intimate settings. This dynamic reveals itself baldly in sexual fantasies on the literary plane and sexual economies on the structural plane.[7]

According to Said, Gustave Flaubert, who visited Egypt in 1849–50, represents a romantic type of orientalist who deliberately resisted the academic tendency to "get lost in archaeology," by which he meant a "regimented antiquarianism by which the exotic and the strange would get formulated into lexicons, codes, and finally clichés." Instead, Flaubert exemplified an approach that savored and reproduced the exotic, making it so sensually overdetermined that it resisted rational classification.[8]

In contrast to our contemporary world's association of sexuality with youth and the naked body, colonial sexuality and colonial economies were often infused with a patina aesthetic that evoked connotations of age and extrasomatic material signifiers. Orientalism, in fact, is inescapably about time. It amounts to a strategy for temporally "othering" regions and peoples that a political center is simultaneously attempting to bring under spatial control. Epistemologically, orientalism makes it possible to segregate diverse populations (by religion, ethnicity, language, race, etc.) as developmentally backward, denying them "co-evalness," to use Johann Fabian's term, so as to maintain difference as a basis for inequality. Otherwise, assimilation and spatial integration could undermine the very social hierarchy that imperialism was designed to benefit. *La différence* of the Other has at least as much to do with her place on a timescale as her place on a map.[9]

By "antiquing" colonial zones, metropolitan powers could incorporate them through acts of romance and preservation and thus stop or delay their participation in projects of modernity that might result in legitimate claims to social equality and political autonomy. This antiquarian approach to colonial acquisitions operated as much upon materials as upon discourse, not only in acts of archaeological exploration and classification that Flaubert dryly commented upon in Egypt, but also in efforts to describe and preserve the medinas or vieux carrés of colonial towns. The French Quarter has been romanticized and preserved in much the same way, and for many of the same reasons, as an Arab medina in one of France's North African possessions valued by orientalist travelers for the twists and turns of their streets, for their charming crumbling ruins, and for their colorful sights, sounds, and smells. Frozen antiquity promises a more sensual life than the "drab bourgeois world" of the commodified center. It excites the visual, olfactory, gustatory, and aural senses primarily through ethnicized, hand-crafted, or hand-me-down material culture. *Things* also accent the haptic experience of the exotic, through the accessories and space devoted to activities such as dancing, eating, drinking, grooming, greeting, and sex. We must scrape away at the patina aesthetic in order to understand the market magic that such places work upon the (masculine) visitor, resident, and consumer. In fact, without material culture, desire for more intangible things—belonging, achievement, love—would be impossible to construct.[10]

GOOD TIMES

There is a house in New Orleans
they call the Rising Sun.
It's been the ruin of many a poor girl,
and me, O God, for one. . . .
Going back to New Orleans,
my race is almost run.
Going back to spend the rest of my days
beneath that Rising Sun.

A recording of this old folk song appeared in the 1930s, performed by a Tennessee banjo player. Alan Lomax states that it probably descends from an English ballad and could be heard in the repertoire of white Kentuckians in the early twentieth century. In the eighteenth and nineteenth centuries, "Rising Sun" was a popular motif in English-speaking port towns, especially as a name for male meeting places such as taverns and coffee houses. The phrase may have had particular meaning for sailors or for those in the habit of entertaining themselves until sunrise. The popularity of the song has inspired many earlier searches for the "real" Rising Sun in New Orleans, although few have gone back as far as the early antebellum period. If they had, they would also have found that in 1808 a ship of the same name docked in the port and that in 1838 there was a Rising Sun coffeehouse operating on Decatur Street. The lyrics also seem to fit as a reference to the New Orleans Women's Prison, which is said to have featured a rising-sun motif over its main gate. In short, there have been many Rising Suns, even in New Orleans.[11]

But it is precisely in the character of the establishments that attracted this title that we find an important undercurrent to the sexualized aura of patina: the gender dynamics of the Atlantic world and its port cities. In New Orleans, as in its sister cities, large numbers of male travelers stopped in to refresh themselves and partake of food, drink, commodities, and general hospitality as respite from the hard work and brutal dynamics of their largely homosocial world on board ship, in military garrisons, and in the trading hinterlands. A major feature that distinguished the lifeworld in ports of call was the presence of women as residents, merchants, landladies, and hostesses. In the French colonial period, a majority of New Orleans women operated as heads of their own households and proprietors of their own businesses.[12] The feminine character of port cities did not escape the notice of male adventurers, whether or not local hospitality extended to sexual favors or prostitution. That this line could slip in the public imagination, or in the concrete realities of the local economy, is not a large surprise, but understanding how orientalist aesthetics and colonial economies intertwined remains a largely uncharted project. The eroticization of places like New Orleans did not simply produce a marketplace of floating representations. Such imaginative values were moored in the material transactions between men and women in colonial economies. Although the anthropology and history of tourism, particularly of sex tourism, does acknowledge the association of the aesthetics of "the exotic" with the crude realities of demand economies, they overwhelmingly point to the rise of advertising and mass consumption in the late nineteenth century as the period during which tourism as we know it was invented.[13] Examining the longer durée of colonial travel and hospitality—and the allure of antiquity—helps us see a deeper social stratigraphy to phenomena such as the baring of breasts on Bourbon Street during today's Mardi Gras.

Visitors have been coming to New Orleans to enjoy its pleasures since the early French period. The colonial capital served as a site of rest and recreation for deerskin trappers, soldiers, and sailors. While early reports focused on the familiar French delicacies available in the city's many inns and taverns, by the territorial period (1804–15), travelers' accounts emphasized the old-fashioned and exotic aesthetic of its markets and landscape. In the early nineteenth century, a large sector of the city lived off the hospitality trades, helping produce an economically vibrant small-business community that particularly benefited women and free people of color. The moral anxiety produced by this hospitality economy was also becoming well versed. In the early antebellum period, commentators frequently gave New Orleans names such as "the modern Sodom" or a "splendid Bedlam of a city."[14] The city thrived because of its strategic position at the gateway of the Caribbean and the Mississippi interior and attracted more travelers than its accommodations could handle prior to the Civil War. As mass transportation shifted to the rail system in the mid-nineteenth century, New Orleanians became anxious about their dependence upon the

travel economy. In the late Victorian period, hotel owners and restaura-
teurs began to adopt new advertising media and marketing techniques to
target potential investors and high-spending vacationers.

The Pitot House stands as a grand old dame of a West Indies plantation house overlooking breezy Bayou St. John, the peaceful waterway that
once connected the bay called Lake Pontchartrain to the Mississippi, and a
major transportation route from prehistoric times through the antebellum
period. Today the structure houses a museum that affords the visitor a
rare opportunity to see the inside of an archetypical elite Creole residence
maintained in the colonial style.

The large landscaped yard in which the house sits was the focus of archaeological explorations in 2005. In those shovel tests, we found evidence
of three major uses of the site: surface trash left by recent visitors and wedding guests at the Pitot House; extensive evidence of a late-nineteenth-
to-early-twentieth-century streetcar line; and the shadowy edge of a much
earlier structure and occupation in the form of a brick column support and
brick floor, scattered with the remains of two-hundred-year old stoneware
beer bottles. This earliest component corresponded to the Tivoli Gardens,
an "amusement park" dating to 1808 where men and women met for
weekly outdoor dancing and, apparently, beer drinking. We had found a
buried remnant of New Orleans's first "good time" district.[15]

The crossroads of Bayou St. John hosted a concentration of taverns,
restaurants, and beer gardens like Tivoli from the colonial period through
the early twentieth century. At the time of the Louisiana Purchase, Samuel
Kohn (later a part owner in the Tivoli Gardens) was running a well-known
"house of entertainment" just up the bayou where, his advertisement an-
nounced, "the best of liquors will be provided—separate rooms may be
had for private parties, and every care and attention will be observed to
render the house agreeable to those who may visit it." This language re-
sembles euphemisms used by known Storyville brothel operators in advertisements one hundred years later that included frequent references to
"attentive service" and the availability either of private rooms or of "ladies
rooms."[16]

These establishments appear to have been well known by word of
mouth, to the extent that their names or addresses were left out of newspaper advertisements. The ads simply informed customers of recent improvements, food specials, theatrical or musical presentations, or a scheduled ball, such as the one placed by Mr. Gautier in 1808, which directs
customers simply to "the usual Ball room." Another typical ad, taken out
by Monsieur Fourcade upon his reopening of the United States Hotel on
Bayou St. John, announces a special oyster and turtle soup dinner and em-

phasizes that his staff speak both French and English. Further, the house, "already so well known" had been updated with new furnishings. The appeal continued: "The billiard tables have been put in the best condition. The bar-room will be furnished with every kind of cordials, syrops, bitters, and wines of the best vintages. . . . Zeal and activity will reign throughout."[17]

These establishments developed out of roadhouses and country estate hospitality dating back to the French period and its itinerant population of colonial travelers. Smugglers especially preferred the bayou route into town. Travel writer Pierre Caillot mentions a brewery on the outskirts of town in 1730 that had "the air of the roadhouses [*guinguettes*] of Paris where a swarm of people come to divert themselves; there are also in the town many taverns and cabarets, where one is not only well served but can also be fleeced." As in Paris, the roadhouse on the outskirts of town served not only as a convenience for travelers but as a place away from family and neighbors for those wanting to carouse without judgment. These were not places where gentlemen generally spent the night, however. Caillot stayed in a New Orleans inn in the French Quarter for most of his time in the colony. French soldier Dumont de Montigny roomed at a guesthouse run by a wigmaker after coming downriver from the Yazoo Post in Indian country in the 1720s: "It was thus to this town that I came in search of my health," which by his own account consisted of prodigious amounts of alcohol.[18]

One reason that New Orleans attracted so many soldiers, traders, and woodsmen in the colonial period was that the *eau de vie* (brandy or any distilled liquor) cost half as much as it did at the outlying posts. The cheap local varieties consisted of corn liquor and a crude rum known as *tafia*, described as "made with the scum of sugar." Dumont punctuated his days with a "coup de l'eau de vie," and he clearly spent many hours carousing with friends in cabarets. In the eighteenth and early nineteenth centuries, coureurs de bois (Canadian or métis trappers) who dealt in salted buffalo meat and bear oil, lived in town a few months each year starting in the spring, occupying makeshift cabins in the backstreets and happily spending their earnings until the autumn hunt called them back to the woods. During the St. Anthony's Garden excavation, one of the earliest components (1730s-50s) we uncovered was a previously unknown outdoor market where these frequent visitors and their American Indian partners traded their goods to townies, leaving a scatter of fire rings, animal bones, lead shot, hide scrapers, and hundreds of colorful seed beads that had fallen off their deerskin clothing. The market's spatial centrality and early date underscores the force of the traveling trades in making the city.[19]

Caillot's account indicates that the larger homes in the Bayou St. John area on the edge of town formed a center of more upscale entertainment. With jovial detail, he provides our earliest account of a Mardi Gras celebration held in the city. He devotes several pages to describing how he passed two or three nights during carnival season in 1730 masking, singing, and reveling. He heralds the sensuous pleasures of the colony and the ways in which French drinks and delicacies were enjoyed on special occasions in New Orleans. He says, "In effect, I began that evening to taste the first pleasures in the colonies." The height of the celebrations occurred at the home of Madame Rivard on the bayou, where he fell in love with the young Mademoiselle Carrière. They ate, drank, and stayed up the entire night singing and dancing. His account elaborates the role that French imports and culinary connoisseurship played in urban colonial social life.[20]

His entire description pulses with sensual stimuli, of which food and drink comprise one part of the intense and pleasurable whole: "Assuredly, I thought that this day was made for love affairs, it being neither hot nor cold, the sun being covered by some clouds that only gave pleasure. A controversy of smells was stimulated by the woods with a confused murmur of diverse birds that seemed to be sharing their love with us. I am going to let you ponder just what a state we were in." He and his fellows teased the girls at the party, telling them the muscat wine they brought was Normandy cider, and "only the beautiful Languedoc girl" could not be fooled. The appearance at the party of the governor, who tried the muscat and danced two minuets, marks the elite colonial context for this tasting of France. After three hours of music and dancing, the hostess invited Caillot's party to join them for a late-night meal. The dinner party is impressive in its scale and lavishness, suggesting that by this time planter families such as the Carrières were well established in their wealth. He reports, "I began to taste new pleasures. . . . We were placed at a table where we were 46 in number. . . . We enjoyed a meal of 5 to 6 hours very agreeably but after we left the table our pleasure expanded infinitely because Bacchus had quit his empire to go find Venus." The guests finally left at 5 o'clock in the morning.[21]

Colonists and French travelers enjoyed New Orleans for the tastes of "home" that it offered. The city's market full of imports and a selection of cabarets, breweries, and inns distinguished it from the plantations and smaller posts of the colony. Sharing food and drink in these establishments offered not just simple sensual pleasures but fulfilled important social functions, bonding together a dispersed population of colonizers who were elsewhere isolated or outnumbered by American Indians and Africans. Caillot's text highlights the fact that the colonial capital brought together immigrants and passers-through from many different regions. Individuals who might have been separated by ethnic distinctions at home found common cause in redefining Frenchness in a foreign land, across the old divides of Parisians, Languedocs, and Bretons. The "home" they were nostalgic for was thus a blended construct of place and a moment frozen at the time they departed France, sometimes decades earlier. Hospitality intentionally designs a temporal bubble. Caillot's carousing also demonstrates that the tourist gaze was long anticipated by a colonial leer.[22]

Colonial soldiers and masculine travelers of the Atlantic World experienced a labor and consumption landscape that was dramatically gendered. The old stereotypes about sailors and their women in port towns undoubtedly resonated in the *old* Old World. However, prior to the development of the Portuguese caravel ship and the sprawling Atlantic system, their bouts of homosocial isolation were brief in comparison to the three to six months of sea travel or military deployment that become the norm for the foot soldiers of European empires. As a result, colonial towns such as New Orleans became more intensely loaded as ports of pleasure and sites of heterosexual adventure. These colonial desires and structural patterns form the stratigraphic foundation lying below the city's current tourist economy and circulation of sensual images. It is an old, patinated landscape of desire.

HOW NEW ORLEANS BECAME FRENCH

> Man sees the things of his clan as relatives and associates; he calls them friends and considers them to be made of the same flesh as he. Hence, there are elective affinities and quite special relations of compatibility between them and him. Things and men attract one another, in some sense understand one another, and are naturally attuned. —Emile Durkheim, *The Elementary Forms of Religious Life*

It could be said that the first step in the process of New Orleans's becoming French was not its colonial founding, which was due as much to African and American Indian labor as to Gallic, but the development of a hospitality economy that served homesick soldiers and sailors. What remains to be accounted for is how the city retained its Frenchness so long after the Francophone population had been swamped by Americans and other immigrants. Despite boosts from San Domingue refugees, Napoleonic exiles, and 1848ers, French-speakers had become a minority by the 1860s, losing out not only to Anglo-American entrepreneurs but to Irish and German immigrants as well as an influx of English-speaking freedmen after Emancipation. During the Civil War, French was abolished as a primary language in the public schools. By 1900, perhaps one-quarter of the population could still converse in French.[23] But in the same period, the Frenchness of New Orleans was reconstructed with a renewed focus on particular forms of materiality and consumption. The city's Frenchness became more pronounced in ever-expanding hospitality offerings and good times in the form of French food and consumables, in French gambling games, and ultimately in Storyville's purveying of "French" sex. As related in chapter 3, this materialized Frenchness can be seen in the insistence by historic preservationists and tour guides that the architecture of the Vieux Carré exhibits French qualities, despite the Spanish building code that dictated so much of its reconstruction after the fire of 1788. Today these physical references simultaneously enunciate New Orleans's eroticism and its antiquity by referencing the city's French colonial foundations.

In 1882 English travel writer George Augustus Sala expressed his delight in the persistence of French culture in New Orleans despite the "all-dominating influence of Anglo-Saxon language, institutions, and character" that reigned elsewhere in the nation.[24] In particular, he was charmed by the transplanted sights and sounds of France—*la bien aimée* (the beloved)—embodied in goods for sale, such as French newspapers, food, Catholic images, and even pharmaceuticals sold in the now-familiar faience pot. All these pleasant titillations that Sala lists suggest a commoditization of Frenchness.

Sala's citation of French pharmaceuticals returns us to the Rising Sun Hotel site and its many faience rouge pots. Archaeologists working in Louisiana have long identified these small cylindrical ointment pots as French-made based on their "faience" glaze (the French name for the tin enamel ceramic called delft in England and the Netherlands and majolica in Spain, Italy, and Mexico). They have also assumed that the pots contained the eponymous rouge, another borrowed French word and identifiably a French product.[25] These pretty little jars reflect the city's enduring French connection. Their ubiquity suggests that French rouge and ointment jars, as well as their contents, were more available and more desirable in the local economy than elsewhere in North America.

The fact that this particular faience ceramic type indexed France may have buoyed its popularity in nineteenth-century New Orleans. The manufacture of these tin-enamel wares had almost entirely died out in France by the early nineteenth century, yet the rouge pots retained a special niche for at least another century. One likely reason is that they reinforced the association of Frenchness with cosmetics. Since the eighteenth century, France dominated the cosmetics market, first as a site of innovation and then as a source of guarded tradition associated with a high-quality product. The antiquated retention of identifiably French packaging in the form of the faience ointment jar appears to have been a useful marketing device. Similar "antiqued" associations connecting national origin and quality of contents through packaging can be pointed to today with the impractical survival of "English" tea tins and the Cuban cigar box. The conservatism of the packaging communicates authenticity and historical value to the consumer. The heavy shipping weight of the small rouge pots, especially in proportion to the modest amount of product they could contain, further speaks to the communicative value of the packaging. We know by wear marks and their durability that New Orleanians reused and handed down rouge pots through the generations, but new pots were also marketed locally well past their peak production in France. In fact, their highest incidence on sites in Louisiana corresponds to the first third of the nineteenth century, when Anglo-Creole tensions following the Louisiana Purchase were at their hottest. Faience rouge pots represent a commodification of patina in a small everyday object. These old-fashioned things objectified an association with an older French regime, both exotic and venerable.[26]

Another example of commodity packaging that the local market clung to for its association with France and the past was French-made wine bottles, identifiable by their paler olive-green color, their rough flat-string rims, and their tendency to patinate quickly to a lustrous golden color (fig. 4.2). These bottles, particularly those of the straight-sided "Bordeaux" type, occur far more commonly on New Orleans sites in the nineteenth century than in comparable North American cities outside the Gulf Coast. The bottles are fragile and ship poorly, so importing in casks would have been more sensible, or purchasing the cheaper and more durable British-made black glass bottles that were widely available by the late eighteenth century. The production techniques for French wine bottles, as for the faience rouge pots, were conservative and intentionally anachronistic, with hand-blowing and hand-finishing techniques used since the Renaissance surviving well into the period when mold-blown bottles began to prevail elsewhere in the early nineteenth century. They evoked the Old World not just as a place but as a time.[27]

While the predominance of French-made bottles in the colonial period is not surprising, given the natural shipping connections to France and an official embargo against British imports, their persistence under the economic liberalization of the Spanish regime in the 1780s and their continued dominance in late antebellum deposits speaks to an extra effort to import this highly valued symbol of French culture. In New Orleans, old-fashioned handblown French wine bottles account for upwards of 50 per-

FIGURE 4.2. French wine bottles and seals from Maginnis Cotton Mill site.

cent of the liquor-bottle assemblage in nineteenth-century components, including those at the late Victorian Richardson Hotel, which replaced the Rising Sun. New Orleanians appear to have placed a special value on these bottles and curated them long past the period of their first distribution. In contemporary deposits from other port cities, such as New York or Boston, wine-bottle assemblages are instead dominated by the English- or American-made mold-blown bottles, often discarded after a single use. British and American wine importers had largely overtaken French merchant houses by the Civil War era. Although much of the wine still came from Bordeaux (the British vulgarly called it "claret" with a hard *t*), it arrived via casks. It was then carefully poured into the patinated French bottles—heirlooms from the colonial era—for presentation at the table.[28]

The symbolic capital of this antiquated, French commodity can be contrasted to the other imports available from the British and Anglo-American markets, which were readily adopted and widely available, often in violation of trading monopolies. Archaeological assemblages demonstrate that British-made ceramic tablewares such as creamware and pearlware were available in New Orleans as quickly as anywhere on the global market. In elite households, such as that of Captain Manuel de Lanzos, who rebuilt Madame John's Legacy to retain its French style, British creamware appears to have been a prized and fashionable tableware. It had almost thoroughly replaced French-made faience dinnerware by the 1780s. Likewise, single-event deposits associated with the 1788 fire dump at St. Anthony's Garden and with the 1794 fire at the Rising Sun Hotel site show that New Orleans's households were well stocked with the latest British ceramics, which constitute more than 80 percent of the assemblages. With the exception of special forms such as the faience rouge pot and American Indian collectibles (see chapter 5), everyday table ceramics do not appear to have been particularly symbolic of origin for colonial and nineteenth-century residents. This makes the selection and preservation of French wine bottles that much more significant. As with the rouge pots, the contents and the associated practices mattered. Wine-drinking was a distinctly French social practice, one that acquired greater significance in a colonial context where production was impossible and immigrants vied for cultural dominance. In fact, one salient architectural feature of West Indies and Creole Cottage floor plans are two flanking *caves*, or small, pantrylike rooms (later called *cabinets*) attached to the rear wall that were often devoted to wine storage.[29]

Further evidence of the special place these bottles held in the visual vernacular of New Orleans homes and hospitality establishments in the late-eighteenth through the nineteenth century comes from the incidence of imprinted, proprietary bottle seals (called blob seals, pressed into a hot circle or oval of glass applied to the bottle's shoulder). In New Orleans, not only do the more fragile French wine bottles predominate past the period of easy shipping connections to France, but local residents appear to have both preferred and curated those bearing identifiable French origin stamps in the form of these seals. Particularly prevalent are the ones with Bordeaux appellations such as "Haut-Médoc," "Saint-Julien," and "Saint-Estèphe," suggesting that Louisiana consumers preferred the fragile French bottles for their direct visual reference to France. Served at table, the bottles would have signaled not only the host's good taste but the person's totemic connection to the city's colonial past.

One particularly striking example comes from the house of Monsieur Poeyfarré, the builder of the indigo plantation buried under the Maginnis Cotton Mill (introduced in chapter 2). His cellar contained bottles marked "St. Julien/Medoc," an appellation that includes many well-known chateaus, including that of his own ancestral roots, the Leoville-Poeyfarré estate. While many French immigrants to colonial Louisiana came from Bordeaux, they were by no means a majority. However, Bordeaux wine merchants had easier access to the Atlantic ports and succeeded more than other French wine-growing regions in exporting their surplus. As a result, their wines became both a literal and a symbolic link to France for expatriots and their descendants. Perhaps no clearer proclamation of this regional commodity's special resonance could be had than the chant of the crowd on the streets of New Orleans during the 1768 rebellion against Spanish rule: "Hurray for the King! Hurray for Good King Louis! Hurray for Bordeaux wine! To hell with Catalonian rotgut!"[30] Although this political slogan evokes a kind of connoisseurship, it had more to do with ethnic than class distinction. The selection and utilization of "French things" in New Orleans's material culture entails complex class, race, and ethnic referents, depending on the context, but they are most emphatically, and ironically, used to emphasize *local* culture to mark off rooted locals from unenculturated newcomers and visitors. In the 1760s, this distinction ran along French-Spanish lines with high political stakes. Several French Creole rebels died before the firing squad for their resistance to the Spanish takeover of their colony. By the early nineteenth century, an even more fraught distinction arose between French Catholic Creoles and Anglo Protestant Americans. So shrill and real was this rift that the city literally broke apart in 1836, dividing into three distinct municipalities, and was not reunited until 1852.

THE SCENT OF HISTORY

Another example of the peculiar confusion of Frenchness follows a waft of scent—perfume. The case of French perfume in New Orleans presents a story more about reinvention than reuse. In the colonial and early antebellum periods, no evidence of a local market for perfume can be found, in either the archaeological or the archival records. Although it is likely that small, ornate perfume bottles were heirloomed and less breakable than other types of glass, there is little evidence to go on if one wants to make the argument that early New Orleans residents practiced the art of scent. However, today on Royal Street, two French-style parfumeries compete just doors apart. The first was established in 1843 by a French immigrant, the second in 1931. These small family-run establishments prepare proprietary batches by hand and purvey them in small bottles of early-twentieth-century form with labels reminiscent of parchment and script. Nineteenth-century lithograph portraits of women adorn many of the labels; others bear antique floral prints. Both establishments simultaneously emphasize their Frenchness and their long tradition. "Bourbon French Parfums" (originally Doussan Parfumerie) made a name change in the 1890s in order to emphasize its continental associations. The original proprietress of "Hové Parfumeur Ltd." changed the spelling of her married name from the English-looking "Hovey" to "Hové" with a French accent and also added the logo of a crown to invoke associations with the French monarchy of the eighteenth century. Today both shops sell small selections of antique gift items such as hand mirrors, soap dishes, and ornate perfume bottles, along with their perfumes. Also, "when the proprietors find antique reproductions that they feel are up to the standards of Hové's clientele, they will offer them in the shop."[31]

The websites, brochures, and interior signage of each shop provide a detailed history of the business, presented as a genealogical descent of proprietors, in one case emphasizing the careful apprenticeship and transfer of the traditions, recipes, and skills of the parfumeur and in the other case emphasizing the continuous family line in ownership. One shop is also decorated with the portraits of all the previous owners in a visual display of ancestry traced back to French immigrants. These shops were established during two particularly intense periods of commodity "Frenchification" of New Orleans. Three high points in this pattern correspond to the early territorial period (1800–1810s), the late antebellum period (1840s-50s), and the rise of historic preservation and cultural tourism in the 1920s-40s. In the first two cases, these developments took advantage of a local demand for French things, as well as the know-how and panache of new influxes of French-speaking immigrants. As one of the first perfume houses established in the United States, Bourbon French Parfums catered to visitors and filled orders from across the country in the nineteenth century. Nevertheless, according to the current proprietor, the majority of its business was local until World War II. Around this same time, Mrs. Hovey established the competing Hové Parfumeur to take advantage of the city's growing tourist trade. An extensive world traveler herself, she seems to have had a sense of what discerning visitors might like to take home. The scent lines for the two shops overlap somewhat in their themes, but Bourbon French emphasizes local florals and "traditional" recipes brought over from France 160 years ago and faithfully followed, while Hové carries several new fragrances with catchy, kitschy names evoking New Orleans's brand of romance—from pirate lore to love across the color line.

Perhaps no commodity wraps up the nostalgia and romance of New Orleans quite as blatantly as its perfumes. Looking at their names, marketing, and even their liquid recipes makes clear two important points—that these are products purchased to trigger memories, and that they do so for both locals and tourists, but in different registers. In other words, they can serve as either heirlooms or souvenirs. The difference is in the past they evoke—either sweetly familiar for the native, or exotic and tinged with oriental sexual fantasy for the visitor. Psychologists and neurologists in recent years have found that our common sense about the close link between olfaction and autobiographical memory is well founded. Olfactory nerves are located close to the centers in the brain that have to do with emotion and associative memory. However, studies also underscore that responses are filtered through cultural conditioning. So it is still important to look closely at the type of images or associations that scents call forth for different actors.[32]

While the marketing and labeling of this commodity visually evokes Frenchness, it performs more complex work in the realm of scent. Perfumes can be a trigger for the replay of autobiographical and shared local experiences, at the same time that they can supply a new sensory referent for nonlocal fantasies. These latter associations might be understood as false memories constructed out of a montage of movies, romance novels, and the yarns spun by tourism. The names and descriptions of the perfumes make clear these twin intents for local and visitor, a parallel of the doubled landscape described in chapter 3. Many perfumes cite local florals and the distinctive landscape, such as gardenia, magnolia, sweet olive, and even Spanish moss. Some are more vaguely French—Elan D'Orange, Louise Quatorze, Touché, Entre Nous, Sans Nom, or the aptly named Vous Souvenez-Vous? (do you remember?). Other names and descriptors attempt to create new associations with local history and landmarks, such as Carnaval, Pirate's Gold, Spring Fiesta, Rue Royale, Voodoo Love, and Bayou D'Amour. Others try to blend local associations and oriental sexuality, such as Kiss in the Dark, or Tonight, which, according to the shop's brochure, is "frequently worn by Latin women, who instinctively understand the full meaning of 'tonight.'" The scent of night-blooming jasmine bridges the Near East and the Near South. The flowering vine grows ubiquitously in New Orleans's gardens, and its scent is marketed in a "southern florals" line of the "vintage and exotic." Jasmine "since ancient times is described as feminine and seductive." Other product designs baldly attempt to resurrect a sense-scape of the past. George Washington Cable might be pleased to find that "Creole Days" is "a gentle blending of old-fashioned spices," while Purple Violet is "reminiscent of days a lot slower and life more gracious."

When I interviewed Brenda, one of the shop owners, she explained that their oldest scent is also their best seller. I asked her why this might be so.

Brenda: [It's] a very mild fresh, powdery fragrance that appeals to all ages. It's just a comfort fragrance, kinda, you know, like comfort food. . . . [In addition] we have a fragrance called Forever New Orleans which is kind of a compilation of those florals. . . . A lot of people after the storm were buying those single-note florals. Just, you know if you were here you know there was no nothing—it was all brown [referencing the landscape of dead lawns and gardens]. And it's just any little thing to make you better. You know it was just a $8 little roll-on cologne—you know it made you feel better today.

She added that since Katrina, the local customer base has grown significantly, suggesting that nostalgia for home and a desire to trigger memories of it peaks after episodes of catastrophic change.

A sentimental focus on the flora of New Orleans is not restricted to perfume purchasers. In my interviews with residents, another surprise pattern I noted was how many conversations drifted from architecture to gardens. Several interviewees lamented the loss of trees in the storm—not just trees in general, such as the loss of old oaks on St. Charles Avenue, but individual trees. Agatha lost a pecan tree, and Jane lost a cypress, both native trees. They also stressed that these trees predated their home purchase. There is something about the longevity of trees on the landscape as witnesses (and sometimes victims) to events over and beyond the human life span. Some of the most-cited stories about St. Anthony's Garden revolved around the date palm tree planted by Pere Antoine just outside his humble hut behind the cathedral. It stood for many generations after the priest had died and was colloquially spoken of as a kind of miraculous memorial. Although it finally died in the mid-twentieth century, the post-Katrina redesign of the garden brought it back to life with the planting of a new palm in the corner of an otherwise austerely symmetrical parterre French garden.

Agatha had a lot to say about New Orleans gardens, some of which are literally heirloom gardens.

> Agatha: When I moved here—I'm from the country and my idea was to plant everything that I had grown up with as a child [laughs]. Lots of nostalgic planting and two of everything [laughs] . . . [and] my father remembers roses that his mother planted. . . . He loved plants and older plants and remembered other plants from his mother's garden.

She elaborates that her own design aesthetic comes out of the 1940s and 1950s, when several historic-house museum gardens were established and quickly emulated.[33] These gardens used native and long-adapted plants and "had a romantic feeling about Louisiana." I asked her what might be typical of these gardens.

> Agatha: Certainly, the native magnolia, grandiflora is part of the mythology of our gardens . . . I think that Louisiana gardens smell very wonderful and sweet and there's always something wonderful to smell—ginger, all the beautiful jasmines and the nightblooming jasmine which is so wonderful

to smell on a summer night. And of course the sweet olive trees. And the sweet olive trees really don't grow very well in a slightly colder place so they are very much a part of New Orleans. And of course they change. They smell wonderful—the flowers. The trees burst into bloom when the weather changes from warm to cold or from cold to warm. So you've got that wonderful smell off of them in the spring and in the autumn. And that to me is the smell of New Orleans because you really don't smell it so intensely anywhere else that I know of.

Agatha's description of old-fashioned gardens stresses the olfactory over the visual elements, as well as nostalgia and the sense of time cycling. Peter had a more sanguine comment on the ubiquity of sweet olive trees, while not denying their dominance on the scentscape: "Prior to 1900 you didn't have a sewer system in the French Quarter, you didn't want to live down here in the summer. You know where did the Sweet Olive trees come from? To cover the smell in front of your property . . . of the open sewer." Unprompted, he went on to describe the smells of today's French Quarter, which at night smells like beer and piss, but "since the hurricane, they have a new company . . . almost every morning he [the company man] comes through and powerwashes and sprays a nice scent, a little stronger than Sweet Olive, but that's OK." I had noted myself that the spray smells a bit like bubble gum, and is the same color. This strange new cleansing operation has reinforced some complaints about the "Disneyfication" of the Quarter, a bright morning cover-up of its nightly reality.

Clearly, there is a shared scentscape that resident New Orleanians, especially those who stay around for all seasons, can cite that evokes strongly shared memories. After Katrina, local customers sought the floral scents above all others (including the best-selling mythical magnolia and sweet olive). Bought online by displaced residents, or by residents surrounded by a deadened landscape, these purchases were nostalgic acts in the original sense of the term—a yearning for a lost home. Other scents are purchased as a bottle of more personal associations. I asked Brenda for her thoughts on the connection between smells and memory.

Brenda: It's the biggest déjà vu generator there is. You know, because there are things we smell and it makes you think of your grandmother or where you were at a certain moment in time.

SD: So do we want to smell like our grandmother because we miss her or—?

Brenda: No. [both laugh]

SD: Why don't we want to smell like our grandmother?

Brenda: Because it *smells like* [emphatic] your grandmother [laughs]. Sometimes people will get it and spray it on their pillows or something—for that comfort issue. But you know, the changes, if you look through the fragrance industry, back in the 60s, it was the heavy heavy opium fragrance, you know the orientals, the patchouli and all. So right now we are in a period of light, clean, fresh. So it'll make the circle. And we'll come back to those heavy fragrances. But, you know right now they don't want *that* smell.

According to Brenda, scents can be associated biographically with a particular person, such as a family member, but they can also bring up entire lifeworlds, such as the India-inflected era of hippies, opiates, and free love. These lifeworlds can be delineated by time or by space. Contradicting the shops' own efforts to market perfume to the consumer's self-conception (perfumes are variously described as suitable "especially for the conservative," "for those who are outgoing and who like bright colors," or for "those who love the outdoors," etc.), Brenda reveals that perfumes may be used as much to keep alive the memory of family members, or a lost way of life, as to spin the identity of the living. As commodities, the desires they package are not always, or simply, narcissistic. In fact, the association of smells with the dead was quite vividly enunciated when our conversation took a surprising turn toward the "smoking ghost" who haunts Brenda's shop (chapter 3).

In the marketplace of New Orleans, many other commodities accent and reproduce the Frenchness of New Orleans, especially types of comestibles such as French Market coffee, beignets, and Creole cuisine generally. The three "French" commodities I have discussed here—rouge pots, Bordeaux wine bottles, and perfume—are connected not only by their antique-style packaging, but by the social practices they enable. The wearing of French cosmetics and perfume marked the family body as French, regardless of the actual origin of one's near ancestors. Of course, makeup, perfume, and getting a little tipsy also help make things sexy.

FRENCH SEX AND ANTIQUE FANTASY

During its heyday, the legalized red-light district of Storyville (1897–1917) concentrated some of the most elegant brothels in the United States, as well as backstreets full of dilapidated houses cut up for 50-cent cribs. It was a dense, specialized development. The largest, most elegant brothels

=MUMM'S=
EXTRA DRY
What?
Yes!
over one third of total import-
ations of 36 brands of Champagne for year 1902, amount-
ting to 125,719 cases. :: ::

THINK OF IT

Can't beat it!
Why?
Because it is always
the same---The Best

One of the gorgeous "dens" in Miss Arlington's, 225 Basin St.
If seeing is believeing, then you can judge for yourself
the cost Miss Arlington laid out on her Mansion

FIGURE 4.3. Blue Book Storyville advertisement. Courtesy of Historic New Orleans Collection.

(or "houses," as they were called) fronted Basin Street, overlooking the French Quarter, in plain view of train passengers arriving at the adjacent depot. The architecture of the street has been called "Robber Baron Victorian." Legalization followed an already established practice and geography, however. In 1866 a writer with the *Southern Daily Star*, while complaining about the "low classes of immodest and impure women" moving into the neighborhood, also grudgingly admired the "spacious and elegant house, costing from thirty to fifty thousand dollars," that belonged to prominent madam Hattie Hamilton. A fascination with the opulent interiors and collecting tastes of the successful madams became a recurrent theme in Storyville journalism. Photographs taken of the interiors of the brothels indicate different thematic rooms, such as the "Conquistador" room (fig. 4.3), complete with a suit of armor, where patrons could act out fantasies that had as much to do with being somewhere else, in some other time, holding some other social status, as they had to do with sexual pleasure.[34]

Popular nineteenth-century notions of Frenchness and sexuality became entwined in this sector of the city's business, a bald-faced marketing of erotic orientalism. Partly because of France's precocious home industry of pornographic literature, lithographs, and photographs, American and

English consumers in the eighteenth and nineteenth centuries often associated promiscuous sexuality with Frenchness. Photographs of female nudes were known as "French pictures." The work of the Storyville photographer E. J. Bellocq further entangled these strands with the history of New Orleans, as did the popularization of his work in Louis Malle's 1978 film *Pretty Baby*.[35]

The branding of "French sex" took place on an international stage, but the insinuated parallels between New Orleans and Paris worked market magic for local entrepreneurs. Timothy Gilfoyle, in his study of nineteenth-century prostitution in New York, shows that Frenchness was often a central theme of the discourse on sexual disorder. During the 1840s and 1850s, madams advertised "French love," and the "French association" used Tammany Hall as a venue for suggestive masked balls. The latter may have been inspired by New Orleans's own tradition of masked balls, dating to the territorial period. Storyville merchants and "sporting men" continued this tradition, giving it a heightened sexual charge. They organized several carnival organizations (for example, the CCC Club and the Red Light Social Club) to put on public balls. The unofficial mayor of Storyville, Tom Anderson, sponsored the best known of these. By 1883, he and his partner were hosting a "Grand Fancy Dress and Masquerade Ball" that became an annual tradition. After legalization in 1897, they renamed it "The French Balls" (1898–1905). The transparent advertising made possible by legalization unveiled the commercial character and social underworld behind the event. According to Gilfoyle, a French Ball was the "most erotically charged Victorian institution" and "probably the most significant public forum for testing the boundaries of urban sexual behavior." By the turn of the century, "French box" became an English euphemism for a brothel and "French love" an exotic catch-phrase. Sexual props were "French imports." In 1907, reformer Francis Kellor lamented, "There has grown up a great trade in what is known as French Houses. . . . These women will stoop to practices that the ordinary American girl could not be induced to do."[36] Kellor nods to the greater specificity "Frenchness" had acquired in the American market by this time, where "French Love" referred to fellatio and a "French Studio" was one that specialized in oral sex. The New Orleans sex industry capitalized on this association to attract out-of-town visitors and became renowned, even within the business, for catering to the most outré Edwardian tastes, offering "circus shows" of kink allegedly ranging from lesbian live acts to bestiality, as well as "Olivia the Oyster Dancer." Local proprietress Emma Johnson advertised herself as the "Parisian Queen of America" and actively sought out convention business. New Orleans's Frenchness enhanced its reputation for sexual indulgence, and vice versa. More surprising, perhaps, is the large role that antiques and fancy things played in the commodification of sexual fantasy.[37]

Perhaps nowhere is the transferability of the patina—and thus its unstable relation to social distinction—as trackable as in Storyville. The high-end brothels sported elaborate interiors, decorated with pieces that were both "French" and antique. In 1869 an investigative reporter described the interior of Kate Townsend's "house," emphasizing how the furnishings sent disturbingly mixed messages: "The decorations of the rooms, in the pictures that hung on the walls, the plated mirrors, the delicately tinted furniture . . . evidently [were] intended to embody a sybarite's dream—luxury and repose. The grotesque and bizarre aspect of everything—splendor without comfort, glitter and sparkle suggestive of death and decay—gave rise to singular reflections."[38] For the viewer, malignant patina glinted in the premature sheen of purchased gilt and the anticipation of decay. "Splendor without comfort" indexed the dangerous appropriation of the domestic accoutrements of elite uptown wives by proprietresses who were anything but respectable in the eyes of the newspaper's readership. The danger that the visitor, if not the occupants themselves, could misread this spellbinding material world as a sign of respectability and social esteem is signaled in the reporter's eagerness to see the elegant and glittering furnishings as "already decaying." He may not have been aware of the Old English root of *brothel*, "to decay," but his verbal excess enunciates the moral and material entanglement that houses of assignation excited in the Victorian imaginary.

An updated description of Townsend's boudoir appeared in an 1883 edition of the *New Orleans Daily Picayune* with details such as, "Next to the armoire was a rep and damask sofa and over the mantel was a French mirror with a gilt frame." This reporter admired the fact that not only had Townsend acquired the goods, but she had acquired the taste to distinguish them, an acquired skill elites thought they had reserved for themselves: "In the left-hand corner was a magnificent étagère [a French bric-a-brac shelf], upon which were statuettes, the work of renowned artists, and small articles of *verdu* [curios], betraying great taste both in selection and arrangement. . . . Around the walls were suspended chaste and costly oil paintings. The bloodstained carpet was of the finest velvet." The only taint in this well-read tableau that disturbs what might otherwise be a clear case of Bourdieu's bourgeois distinction, was the blood from Townsend's murder at the hands of her lover.[39]

Newspaper accounts also grant some respect to Madame Gertrude Dix for her collection of art and rare books. Lulu White and Willie Piazza competed in their reputations for cutting stylish figures and hosting memorable parlors. Josie Arlington's four-story brothel was renowned as the fanciest one in the District. In an advertisement she placed in one of the Blue Books (surprisingly transparent consumer guides to the district), not a single mention is made of her female employees or the services her business provides. Rather, the advertisement presents a drawing of the four-story house with its skyline-piercing cupola and a long list of furniture and renovations; she does not shy away from mentioning dollar figures for her improvements. In another promotional piece, Arlington enunciated the oriental sophistication of her accommodations, including a Turkish Parlor and a Japanese Parlor, as well as a Hall of Mirrors. A visit to her Storyville house offered theatrical tableaux of other times. She knew that if you suspend guests in a bubble of time, they are more likely to linger. And she well understood another precept that the New Orleans tourism industry has long capitalized on: there is something erotic about pastness.

Arlington's business plan aimed to attract "only refined gentlemen with a taste for 'amiable, foreign girls.'" But these interiors made an impression on everyone. Pianist Clarence Williams, one of many black musicians legally allowed only to work, not frequent, the brothels, reported that they "were really something to see—those sporting houses. They had the most beautiful parlors, with cut glass and draperies, and rugs, and expensive furniture. They were just like millionaires' houses." The heavy investment of high-end brothels, sometimes called fairy palaces, is documented in the large credit accounts of the city's prominent furniture dealers. Some stores allegedly went bankrupt when Storyville closed in 1917.[40]

Arlington's focus on architecture and furnishings was not unique. Remarkably, almost all of the surviving advertisements from Storyville spend at least two-thirds of the copy space and images (including the *only* photographs) detailing the "splendor" of the material setting rather than the beauty of the employees (figs. 4.3, 4.4). Typical entries from the 1906 edition of the Blue Book include those of Miss Lillian Irwin, whose "home has been pronounced extremely gorgeous by people who are in a position to know costly finery, cut glass and oil paintings, foreign draperies, etc.," and for Miss Flo Meeker: "Bon vivants and connoisseurs pronounce her mansion the Acme of Perfection. Her furniture and fittings were all made to order from her own designs; many of the articles in her domicile, such as paintings and cut-glasses, came from Paris and Germany and the late St. Louis Exposition. Her new Mirror dance hall, recently put in at great expense, is the talk of the town. See it."[41] Miss Meeker's style may have run a bit more to the contemporary, but her focus on material connoisseurship of European art and the latest collectibles from the arcades of the world expositions echoes other aspects of the cult of the antique and curio.

FIGURE 4.4. Storyville dining room. Courtesy of Historic New Orleans Collection.

Clearly, brothels were as cluttered and as "distinguished" as any elite or aspirant interiors of the Gilded Age—loudly and insistently so.

Fancy houses offered taste in fine things as part of their general package of hospitality. As many have noted, their major revenue came from the sale of drink, food, and entertainment (music, dance, and occasionally theater) rather than sexual services. High-end French champagne (Veuve Cliquot and Mumm's Extra Dry) and oysters appear to have been favorites, as corroborated by Storyville pianist Jelly Roll Morton and by archaeological assemblages from known brothels in other American cities. According to reports, mastery of the rules of etiquette complemented the material appointments of the downstairs parlor. A dress code required patrons to arrive in formal wear and "hostesses" to maintain a large wardrobe of silk dresses and lacy dressing gowns. Anonymous editorials claimed that working-class children were sometimes voluntarily recruited into the business because they "envy the sinful elegance displayed before them and hanker after the pleasure enjoyed by their possession." The objects, not the women, lured them into the underworld.[42]

Perhaps it was the same with the johns. Why were the furnishings, architecture, and food and drink of brothels so important, perhaps even more important than the physical attributes of the women, to judge by advertising decisions? We can speculate on the possible fantasies that drove individual men, depending on their background and class position. For the sporting men of the well-heeled crowd, the surroundings would have been generally familiar, not unlike their mother's house on St. Charles Avenue. For them, perhaps there *was* some comfort in the splendor, with the idea that they were enjoying just another privilege of their class. Familiar surroundings naturalized their activities. In fact, one factor that may have contributed to the rapid expansion of fancy brothels after the Civil War was the displacement of sexual practices elite men had become accustomed to within slave society. In other words, prostitution provided a new home for the "privileged" practice to which planter-class men had become accustomed: having ready sexual access to enslaved women. This social stratigraphy below Storyville prostitution had a significant material dimension. In the vernacular of Louisiana architecture, wing extensions off the back of plantation great houses are called "garconnières"—or "boy's rooms." Most Louisiana tour guides will tell you that teenage boys moved into these wings separated from the main house in order to have discreet but easy sexual access.[43]

In the story of Storyville, we observe a dense accumulation of entwined sensuality, power, and colonialism. In its sinister aspect, plantation slavery and its practices of sexual predation lay just below the surface, even echoed in the architecture of the district through its barrack-like cribs. Deeper still lay the ruins of colonial nostalgia for the French girls that soldiers left behind when they embarked on their male-dominated missions. And built *over* Storyville's stratum, we find Bourbon Street's good-time excess and the foggy erotics of historic preservation.

Al Rose, the author of the quirky but still best-documented historical account of Storyville, recalls that when he grew up in New Orleans in the 1920s and 1930, adults around him were already recalling the District "with a certain nostalgia." Such sentiments countervailed concerted efforts by others to demolish the physical remnants of Storyville and its archive. In his decades of exhaustive research and collecting of Storyville memorabilia, Rose discovered that newspaper files in the public library, the *Times-Picayune*'s photo files, and even real estate plat books had been vandalized, with insalubrious details of Storyville excised. Other attempts at public erasure occurred in the renaming of streets. Within a few years after the district's demise, anonymous censors renamed almost every one of the shorter streets (those that did not extend far into "respectable" neighborhoods) of Storyville as well as the older antebellum sex districts known as Gallatin and Perdido.[44]

Whether they were seen as the good old times or the bad old times, not everyone wanted to erase the patina of Storyville's heyday. Within a generation of the district's closing down, concerned citizens were mobilizing nostalgia in an effort to save its remains of saloons, brothels, and even cribs from the federal wrecking ball. The importance of the area to the history of jazz, but also as a revived site for tourism, motivated boosters in the 1940s. Although the National Jazz Foundation succeeded in restoring Basin Street's name (having been cloaked as "North Saratoga" for a while), it did not win against the slum-clearance project that transformed the space into the Iberville public housing project. Not even the sponsorship of *Esquire* magazine, which briefly got behind this historic preservation effort, could save Storyville.[45]

Bourbon Street, which came to inhabit the same imaginative space as Storyville's Basin Street, makes residents nostalgic for Storyville. Although they rarely frequent upper Bourbon Street, leaving it to college students, midlifers-gone-wild, and conventioneers, most residents agree with Al Rose's assessment in the 1970s, when it already seemed aged and tawdry. For him, the "junk" of Bourbon Street manifests in its negative patina and the ultimate after-object of the aged bawd: "[It] is a welter of unattractive and usually dirty saloons . . . [with] harridans in varying stages of physical decomposition (some are in their fifties)."[46]

Walter Benjamin was enchanted with the prostitute as a metaphor for the commodity and the Freudian complexity of our attachment to things: "Love for the prostitute is the apotheosis of empathy with the commodity."[47] One of the paradoxes of the prostitute that parallels the biography of commodities is how time waits in the wings to erode promised value. Prostitutes age, decline, even "decay" if afflicted with the symptoms of untreated venereal disease. The value they tease with their catcalls or come-hither looks in fancy parlors lasts, according to disappointed johns in the moment, less than three minutes. As recycled commodities circulating in the market in new clothes and jewels, most know that their clock is ticking. The majority of prostitutes legally registered in Storyville were between sixteen and twenty-four years old. Although a few went on to become madams, others descended into the cribs when their beauty or health faded. A few escaped and married out. Most died young. But some hung on, cultivating their own knowledge and experience as a marketable asset. In the society column of the *Mascot* of October 1896, we read: "Kittie Archer, the Ancient Hibernian . . . was very mad last Friday when she read what Bas Bleu said about her youthful attributes. Kittie declares that she is no 'Old Curiosity Shop' but that she is a walking encyclopedia. . . . Kittie is proud of posing as a blue stocking in New Orleans. In New York and other large cities, she is a mere footprint on the sands of time; she is a lady with a past who is looking out for a future."[48]

Hearn or Faulkner couldn't have said it better. The city-courtesan is acutely aware of the passage of time while she defiantly flaunts it. She uses the erotics of heterogeneous time to command brief moments of power. She knows that her value contradictorily depends upon her accumulated experience *and* that this value is headed toward certain decay. She is a patinated object, having a sheen of experience acquired through repetitive human strokes, powerful with tabu, hot with bad mana.

• • •

Looking back over the long history of nostalgia in New Orleans, we can identify three different types associated with its Frenchness. The first equals the longing for home felt by colonial travelers and settlers who had left France behind. The second consists of a critical nostalgia that took root as an embattled minority lost its former dominance over the political and cultural landscape. In this form, "things were better when we were more French." And finally, there is the exotic and erotic Frenchness of orientalism. Although each of these forms may have predominated in certain periods, from the early French colonial period to the present day, they are not exclusive to any one era. They can, and do, coexist in the complex landscape of New Orleans's material signs and practices of hospitality.

When I asked Eliza, an eighty-one-year-old native of uptown to describe the aesthetic preferences of New Orleanians, she replied with the linked trio of "French-antique-garden": "They like gardens . . . [and] I think they like old things more than new because the French antiques are old." I later asked Peter why New Orleanians like to collect antiques. His reply went straight to local hospitality.

> Peter: You live in another period when you entertain. You're using fine silver, fine china, fine crystal. And that's how you entertain at a formal dinner party. You don't have a BBQ pit on your balcony.
>
> SD: And people expect this?
>
> Peter: People live it. You don't do business with people until you've had a meal with them. You get to know them. People prefer not to discuss business at a meal. Part of that is a European lifestyle. And as you know, there's a huge French influence here.

By the early nineteenth century, New Orleans had become a marketplace for tasteful French things where knowing locals were connoisseurs and visitors could acquire some sought-after souvenirs and sensual experience. Presenting and scenting the body as French was one way to mark oneself as a local. For the tourist, a bottle of perfume or a jar of rouge would also make a nice souvenir of the city's eroticism. The hospitality exchanges of New Orleans's very active social life provided important occasions for the presentation of self and the display of connoisseurship from the eighteenth century forward that included (and includes) dinner parties, garden picnics, balls, Mardi Gras parades, teas, and theater events. In the colonial period even French visitors remarked upon the exhausting pace of the entertainment calendar. To understand and participate in the events where Bordeaux wine flowed from antique French bottles was to belong to a special social world. One could marry into this world. Or, with time, one could acquire the cultural facility to insert oneself into the chain of title through intimate knowledge of townhouses, rouge pots, and shared scents. Consumption of old "French" things binds this world together.

The early colonial city was a place nostalgic for an imagined France left behind by forced immigrants and soldiers. By the American period, it had become a doubled space of the familiar and the strange. Today, the city is nostalgic for itself. Mourning every loss—a tree in Katrina, a grandmother dying, the sale of a house—offers an opportunity to savor and reassert the spirit of place. In contrast, the visitor pursues nostalgia for a time and a place that is so exotic it has never existed, except perhaps in the parlor of a brothel. The Orient down south.

Through their interiors, the prominent Storyville franchises sold much more than sex, which in its stripped-down form could be bought in the abject cribs on the backstreets. Their collections of French antiques and fancy things emanated profane mana—a seductive force associated with both pleasure and death. It fascinated neighborhood children as well as the journalist viewing its incarnation as blood on an oriental carpet. The profane mana flowing through Storyville's brothels confirms the old anthropological observation that such a force could be both dangerous and contagious—moving between people, and between things. Like mana, the material sign of patina could quickly oscillate from "good" (respectable, quaint) to "bad" (decaying, morally decrepit).

The product brothels offered was often packaged as an experience of uncertain vintage. They sold a fantasy of masculine achievement on many planes. In the Japanese and Turkish boudoirs, with the attentions of "amiable foreign girls" (most of them, in fact, Irish) and fabled octoroons, johns could travel through time and space and become colonial adventurers. Fancy brothels represented dazzling heterotopias. Or perhaps better said, chronotopias. They actively, sensuously created bubbles of time.

Although prostitutes have been called "frail goddesses in glass houses,"[49] the patina aesthetic provided some salvation from obsolescence. Senior madams were among the most admired and sought-after figures in Gilded Age New Orleans. In their many appearances in court and the newspapers, they espoused a way of life that embraced good times over hard labor. As such, they served as loudly dressed mouthpieces for New Orleans's deep history of hospitality. The French colonial euphemism for a madam was "hostess." Upon closer inspection, the trope of New Orleans as an aging courtesan seems to be right on the money. Well beyond Storyville, the city is an arcade that promotes "the good *old* times" as an alternative to the despiriting forces of less playful markets.

CHAPTER 5

The Antique Fetish

A real true collector likes patina. —Tom, dealer in antique clocks

A fetish is a story masquerading as an object. —Robert J. Stoller, *Observing the Erotic Imagination*

Ursuline Convent, another prominent landmark in the French Quarter, makes a reasonable claim to be the oldest surviving building in the Lower Mississippi Valley (fig. 5.1). It is a regional antique. The building, the second one built for the nuns on the site, was completed between 1751 and 1753. Situated on the far downriver end of the French Quarter, it survived the city's disastrous late-eighteenth-century fires unscathed. Our archaeological investigations in 2011 in the rear garden aimed to understand the daily labor of the convent, particularly as it related to gardening and food preparation. Since its earliest occupation (1734), the site has been a center of Catholic service, from operating a pharmacy and hospital, to the administration of the archbishopric, to providing a parish for Italian speakers in the late nineteenth and early twentieth centuries. However, the convent's longest-lived mission centered on education, first for girls and young women of the French colony and later as a coed school for neighborhood children.[1]

The artifacts we found supported our original research interests. However, we were surprised to find that the gardening component of the institution's life continued well into the mid-twentieth-century period of what otherwise appeared to be a rough-and-tumble schoolyard with makeshift basketball hoops. Around the edges of the playground, we encountered numerous strange sherds of what could only be described as novelty flowerpots. One had bark texture on the outside to make it resemble a stump; others were painted with bright enamels. But the ones that stood out most were those that were clearly attempts to replicate ancient Greek or Roman designs. They possessed molded laurel wreaths, an "antico rosso" body, or

FIGURE 5.1. Ursuline Convent. Photo taken for author by Christopher Grant.

a roughed-up bronze glaze to further cite their antiquity, not just by mimicry of form and design, but through a fake patina. Of course, we were a bit amused to find such "archaeological" sherds mixed in with bottle caps and toy marbles.

These fragments of a citational garden call to mind a more common type of artifact found in New Orleans's yards and courtyards: fragments of thick Provence olive jars. Like the faience rouge pots discussed in chapter 4, these ceramics can date back to the colonial period and are strongly associated with French origins and habits. Originally used to deliver the precious cargo of olive oil to the colonies, these massive pots (some over four feet tall) came to be reused as cisterns and planters in outdoor spaces. Their distinctive thick sherds are a common find on nineteenth-century sites in the Creole neighborhoods. Whole, the pots can still be encountered in the verdant spaces of the French Quarter and the Garden District, along with the occasionally repurposed plantation sugar kettle. French Quarter antique stores offer them to the discerning gardener or designer wanting a historic Louisiana touch. A single jar can cost thousands of dollars in today's market. In contrast, those mid-twentieth-century Pompeian flower pots that once held geraniums at St. Mary's School on the convent grounds were probably cheap to begin with and destined never to accrue much monetary value.

This chapter explores how artifacts like pots, pipes, strands of Mardi Gras beads, and pieces of furniture acquire value through two processes, circulation and narration. Whether faked or real, patina singles out some objects from other commodities. What is the significance of the "antique" and other temporally marked artifacts like souvenirs, heirlooms, and retro-style commodities? The process of answering this question will cover some varied ethnographic ground and wind up at a discussion of what I call the *antique fetish*. In the final section of the chapter, I gather the strands of my argument about patina laid out in the previous chapters and set a course for some broader reflections on ontology, value, and the politics of nostalgia.

Like humans, objects have distinct biographies, even personalities. They sometimes reference a deep past linked to totemic ancestors: colonial settlers, American Indian hunters, or enslaved craftsmen. The connection need not be authenticated, and the artifact need not be old, although objects with the look of age are much more likely to be elevated to special status. While negotiating the storefronts, private interiors, and littered streets of New Orleans, one is reminded over and over again that the past *matters*. As we will see, heirlooms may be valued antiques, but just as often they are quirky curios, containers for family narratives with trajectories that may not articulate strongly with the local landscape. In both the shared and the idiosyncratic cases, select patinated objects can become "signs of what was," and thus a force in the social present. Archaeology shows that such objects have functioned this way since the colonial period. People in New Orleans have been collecting and displaying antiques and souvenirs since the late eighteenth century. It is not a particularly modern phenomenon. Nor is it unique to "the West"; the Aztecs collected Toltec antiques. But heirlooms, antiques, and souvenirs mediate the past and the present in a manner resonant with the dominant preoccupations of the local social context. Framing these practices simply as "memory" cannot capture the active work they do. For the Aztecs, looting and collecting related to an effort to legitimate a legacy for their insecure empire while operating as a mode of fictive ancestor worship.[2] In the context of contemporary capitalism, antiques and heirlooms present themselves as ambiguous objects that trouble the supposed dominance of impersonal commodities in object-human relations. Old things offer one means of ameliorating alienation, a way to re-enchant the world. When held apart from commodity flows, antiques and heirlooms can become like objects in the Kula ring, or what Annette Weiner called "inalienable possessions." They change the terms of value through their movement and through their unique biographies.[3]

REAL FAKES

St. Anthony's Garden (fig. 5.2) can be viewed but not entered by any pedestrian walking the streets of the French Quarter. A tall, Victorian-era wrought iron fence surrounds it, with a gate opening onto Royal Street, the French Quarter's main artery of well-preserved Creole townhouses and antique stores. Passersby can peer through the fence to see a modest obelisk monument and, further back, a marble statue of Jesus in the sacred heart pose. At night, lights in the garden illuminate the statue to project a huge, imposing shadow of Christ over the back of the cathedral, perhaps meant as a silent reminder of daytime devotions for the noisy, inebriated nocturnal crowd. A bold and simple clock face overlooks the ensemble space.

Some parishioners and history buffs know the story of the strange temporal artifact of the obelisk. It was erected in 1914 to memorialize French sailors who had died of yellow fever en route from Mexico to New Orleans nearly sixty years earlier. Before Katrina, the obelisk and its contemporary Sacred Heart monument could barely be seen through the leafy shadows and branches of two massive oak trees and companion magnolias and sycamores. Although Katrina's floodwaters spared the French Quarter, the

FIGURE 5.2. St. Anthony's Garden. Photo taken for author by Adela Amaral.

trees did not fare so well in the winds. Remarkably, the trunks and major branches fell to either side of the sacred heart statue, clipping a thumb and a finger but otherwise sparing the church, the obelisk, the statue, and the surrounding townhouses. The trees, now remembered as "ancient and magnificent," according to a popular tourist's guide to post-Katrina New Orleans, fell in the only way they could in this tight space without doing any major structural damage. Locals, devout and irreverent, soon quipped that Jesus had sacrificed his fingers while flicking the worst of the storm toward Mississippi. Nevertheless, Archbishop Hughes, in his first post-Katrina homily held within the cathedral, vowed that the statue would not be repaired until New Orleans was healed. He stopped short of proclaiming this close call a miracle but he acknowledged that the French Quarter had been spared while much of the rest of the city had been devastated.

In June 2008, Monsignor Crosby Kern, the rector of St. Louis Cathedral, said to me: "I want those fingers." He half-jokingly anticipated that our excavation in St. Anthony's Garden would recover the amputated fingers of the statue, making possible a future restoration of the statue and, symbolically, of the city. One week into our work, while sifting through the dark loam and architectural rubble of an upper level, one of the students picked up an odd-shaped cylindrical object. It appeared to be made of smooth white marble: "I found it!" Members of the crew circled around the sorting screen and took turns fondling the artifact and making pronouncements. Few thought it was a finger, since the archaeological instinct is to doubt folklore. Only with washing at the garden faucet did the object assert itself more clearly as, indeed, a marble finger. However, when I walked up to the statue of Jesus and held the finger up to the sunlight, comparing it to those still attached to his outstretched hands, something just didn't fit. Or rather, the finger didn't fit. It was too big. Further, our fragment lacked the detailed fingernails and skin creases evident on the statue's remaining fingers. Despite these doubts, I shared our find with Msgr. Kern, who was initially excited. But later in an interview he confessed, "I have to tell you this, those fingers were broken before and were re-glued on a couple of years before Katrina. So I'm not sure whether maybe a branch might have touched it and those weak little fingers are gone. But we found some of them. And you know, so, just leave them be as it is, it's a good sign of what was."

At first I wasn't sure what to make of this qualification to the miracle of preservation. Our finger is a fake. But the broken hand of the statue is "a good sign of what was." Now I take the misfit finger to be as apt an allegory as there could be for the strange layers of truth and invention, literary and material, that encrust New Orleans's landscape and gloss over the ruptures of its history. New Orleans overflows with small objects that reference the past, some merely with a vague aura of another time, some with a quite specific historical narrative spun around and through them. When viewed as dialectical objects—those that bring the past and the present into a charged proximity that changes both—such things proactively function as "good signs of what was." To do so, they need not be "real"; they only need reference a relevant narrative or evoke an experience of pastness.

That fake patina works just as well in some cases highlights the fact that it is the qualia of the material appearance of age that is the relevant signifier in the present.[4] Such objects crop up in private homes as heirlooms and collectibles, in antique and junk shops, and in the damp clayey soils of the city. Affectively charged qualia or a peculiarity in their biography can cause certain objects to get selected out for special attention. They can become a personal talisman for individual owners. Others serve as shared conversation pieces that spin threads of connectivity. With a little storytelling, artifacts become indexes of missing pieces and larger wholes. They can stand in for the dead, for past traumas, for social stratigraphy, and for fictive ancestry. That misfit finger stood in for generations of rupture and re-making.

SOUVENIRS

The objects archaeologists uncover are usually called artifacts. They may once have been souvenirs. Excavations at numerous sites in the city have produced a small but consistent percentage of hand-built pottery, much of it with recognizable American Indian forms and decoration (fig. 5.3). Some of the sherds are small and nondescript, of a plain local shell-tempered type that colonists may have acquired as substitute utilitarian ware. However, sherds from the best-preserved deposits bear ornate incising associated with groups further away, such as the Natchez Indian chiefdom located almost two hundred miles to the north. Others have a delicate red-slip paint, pointing to a Creek or Appalachee source to the east. The vast majority of the forms are indistinguishable from prehistoric types, with fewer than five vessels suggesting colonial-period accommodation to European vessel types or tastes (commonly called "colonoware" in North America). Chemical analysis indicates that most of the pots were imported from outside the New Orleans area. Given their diverse geographic origins, their stylistic variety, their similarity to precontact types, and their wear patterns, the explanation that best fits is that residents of these households collected the pots from archaeological sites or from American Indian pot-

FIGURE 5.3. Aboriginal pottery from Madam John's Legacy site.

ters early in the colonial period.[5] They occur most frequently in relatively elite household assemblages of the late colonial period (primarily Spanish, 1763–1803) and do not appear to have been used as substitutes for utilitarian kitchenwares, which are plentiful.

American Indian pottery in colonial New Orleans households seems to have fulfilled a symbolic role in what has been described as rather spartan though tasteful Creole interiors. Displayed on shelves, mantel pieces, or the dinner table, they would have referred to the prehistoric past as well as to the exotic other. As conversation pieces, they could evoke stories of the owner's service at one of the colonial outposts, or a past trading expedition. The households where the largest concentrations have been found archaeologically belonged to high-level military or administrative officials (the commanding officer of the town regiment, the colony's head engineer, a top official of the Company of the Indies, and a member of the governing Superior Council).[6] But these pieces appear also to have been curated for many years.

There are several points to make about this discovery of collecting by colonial Louisianans. As others have argued about ethnographic collecting, these objects may have helped inscribe a story of conquest and othering. Second, given their contexts within households dominated by military men whose duties involved long-term assignments at outlying posts in Indian country (when not fighting in the Natchez and Chickasaw wars), they likely began as souvenirs—objects that commemorated specific events, exotic experiences, and masculine activities in which their collectors had participated. Third, as these artifacts traveled through the generations against the background of a shifting political landscape, they became heirlooms of an originary act of settlement, casting a vaguely sacral air over Creole autochthony.[7]

While I am highlighting antiques valued for their narrative condensation and aura, they can also, of course, be artifacts of luxury and taste. The familiar argument that antiques function to create social distinction does have some merit in New Orleans contexts, both historically and contemporarily. I did have one interviewee, unquestionably the wealthiest and most highly educated of the group (she has three master's degrees), rather self-ironically explain her own antique collecting as "a class thing." However, this social distinction is not necessarily inherited. In fact, it can be earned, learned, bought, sold, and counterfeited. Or perhaps, in the case of prehistoric pots, looted and stolen. One of my present-day informants mourned the damage Katrina had done to an extensive, but very private, collection of pre-Columbian figurines from Mexico and South America, the provenance of which would not stand up to legal or ethical scrutiny. As cultural capital, antiquities and antiques are mobile and fungible but not necessarily available for public display. Their illicit route disqualifies them from becoming what Malinowski called "objects of parade."[8] Their stories cannot be told, at least not too loudly. They represent a highly rarefied form of inconspicuous consumption.

Admittedly, old Indian pots stand out as somewhat unusual types of souvenirs. But by the early nineteenth century, commodities intended for the tourist trade began to appear in local markets. As recounted in chapter 4, some of these objects evoked New Orleans's Frenchness, whether they had been manufactured at home or abroad. Both locals and visitors consumed them, though with distinct associations. And, "as early as 1887, the French Market was already peppered with 'fake' souvenirs made in New York rather than New Orleans, enough to confound the visitor on the hunt for something 'typically southern.'"[9]

Some souvenirs commemorated specific events. New Orleanians had been celebrating Mardi Gras with feasts and balls since the early French period, but it became a more public event in 1837 with the first recorded city parade. By the 1870s, parading was well established, and the Twelfth Night Revelers formalized a tradition of giving keepsake "throws"—small gifts thrown to the crowd by krewe members on the floats. Early in the nineteenth century, carnival riders primarily threw sweets, such as sugared almonds and bonbons, although some hazy historical sources refer to flowers and bead necklaces gifted as early as the 1840s. By the 1920s, the practice of throwing souvenirs was widespread enough that businesses cropped up in town specializing in the importation of cheap Czech and Japanese glass beads. In 1884 Rex (the king of parades) introduced small medallions or doubloons, and other krewes quickly emulated the practice. In the mid-twentieth century, goblets (later plastic "go-cups") appeared and became especially prized throws. Both doubloons and cups are usually embossed or printed with the year and the name of the krewe or parade, marking them as single-event souvenirs. The frenzied exchanges between parade riders and parade goers came to distinguish New Orleans's carnival from other pre-Lenten celebrations. Significantly, most of the throws represent forms of fake wealth—precious jewels, coins, and goblets.[10]

At St. Anthony's Garden, after cigarette butts and bottle glass, the next most common artifact type we collected from the ground surface was Mardi Gras–type souvenirs—plastic beads, go cups, and other cheap souvenirs.[11] An archaeologist working centuries in the future might be challenged to understand a society that left an extraordinarily dense deposit of cheap jewelry and feasting objects across the city, with concentrations in the French Quarter and in linear scatters along broad, tree-lined boulevards. More puzzling, the seasonality of zones would be distinct, with evidence in the French Quarter of year-round ritual celebrations and in the outlying areas of a massive early springtime event.

A visit to Leah's house in a neighborhood far off the tourist beat helps explain the peculiar pattern of Mardi Gras accumulation. Her well-maintained arts and crafts bungalow in Uptown is brimming with books and kitchenwares in the expected places, but small piles of clothing and clusters of toys are also scattered about in corners, or piled up on un-repaired, funky furniture. She admits to being a compulsive "dumpster diver" who salvages "junk" to give to her friends, family, church members, or the homeless people she serves in a soup kitchen. A few of the quirky vintage pieces she cleans up and keeps. With some embarrassment, she acknowledges that some of the best finds came from sidewalk piles of personal effects resulting from forcible eviction, but she does wait several hours to see if the owners come by first. She just hates to see things "go to waste." More peculiar to the local story (although Leah herself is a West Coast transplant), this house assemblage includes bags and bags of Mardi Gras throws that fill a large corner of one bedroom. Thinking of my son, Leah rummaged through the bags and retrieved a fistful of beads with medallions and plush toys that she thought a boy his age might particularly like—featuring alligators, fishing, and football. The means of collecting these items, however, is quite different from that of the other piles. Family members have acquired these trinkets from years of attending Mardi Gras parades that flow through their neighborhood during Carnival season. When the parade season ends (sometime in February or March, depending on the Lenten calendar), most New Orleans residents have amassed a couple of shopping bags full of such disposable treasure. What to do with it after the excitement of attainment wanes is a common problem. Most residents will save the largest, gaudiest, and most unique throws, which they usually receive from float riders via verbal charms, dancing, masking (i.e., wearing a creative costume), or holding up adorable children or pets. But those special items account for a small percentage of the total haul, which consists mostly of simple strands of single-color cheap plastic beads. Acceptable ways to thin the pile include regifting items to children and out-of-town guests, draping them over tree branches and iron fences, and melting them down to make Christmas ornaments. More rarely, they are sorted and repackaged to be thrown again next year. Mostly, they are a form of conspicuous waste.

Anyone who has participated in even one season of parading (there are dozens of parades in the New Orleans area each year) faces the quandary of such plastic wealth and how to get rid of it, store it, or recycle it. In the face of such a surfeit, it would be quite absurd to ever go about buying the equivalent in the souvenir shops of the French Quarter. And to do so is considered nearly as crass and nonsensical as baring your breasts to strangers. In fact, you can't buy equivalents, which is the whole point of the singular value of the Mardi Gras throw. What gets offered in tourist shops are oversized, extra-gaudy simulacra of some of the most coveted throws (those with oversized and figurative beads such as chili peppers, animals, or Mardi Gras theme objects such as masks or crowns). They lack the medallions or annual theme icons that identify the specific parade, the krewe, or the year. They are timeless and thus even more worthless than the usual throws. Tourists mark themselves off as embarrassingly gauche in local eyes first by *purchasing* these beads rather than receiving them as a gift, and then by wearing them out of season, or anywhere besides a large public celebration where bead-wearing is consensually accepted (St. Patrick's Day and Saints football games, for example). To locals, purchased throws are *fake* souvenirs because they are unconnected to the commemorating event of a specific carnival season and named parade or the exhilarating act of catching the little treasure from one of the masked float riders. Of course, to the tourist, they seem authentic enough—they commemorate a visit to the French Quarter, virtually the only place where fake beads are sold, and sold all year round.

FIGURE 5.4. Fake or toy pipe (Ce n'est pas une pipe!) from St. Anthony's Garden.

The point is not that we should evaluate souvenirs along a scale from the authentic to the fake, but that their value inheres in their relationship to temporality and circulation. Some souvenirs capture this relation in a complicated, even playful, fashion. While we were excavating at St. Anthony's Garden, about a foot below the surface, but not nearly deep enough to be in the colonial-era deposits, we encountered a nearly whole white clay pipe of the shape and type that fur trappers would have clenched between their teeth in the eighteenth century (fig. 5.4). It took us some cleaning and puzzling to figure out that this copycat of a common colonial artifact was really a toy souvenir from the early twentieth century that evoked the French past at the same time that it (probably more enjoyably) blew bubbles. According to a ninety-two-year-old informant who ran the shop across the street that her father had established in the 1920s, these faux historic bubble pipes were usually sold to children and tourists. The pipe and many other examples that one finds for sale in the Quarter (including the embarrassingly still-available "Mammy" saltshakers) make it clear that a tourist souvenir from New Orleans and many other "old" places is a temporally complex object. It references the event of visiting a place, but a place that is also understood to be *of another time.* The American Indian pots in the colonial households similarly compounded the event of conquest with the misty place-time of prelapsarian America. The orientalist confusion of time and place can be located as much in a hand-held souvenir as in the business names along Pirate Alley or the furnishings of a Storyville boudoir.

"Fakeness" in a manufactured souvenir tenders no scandal. It may even grant part of its appeal as a piece with little utilitarian value, a poor person's luxury. What risks more of a scandal is fake wealth. In all the excited writing on the politics of Mardi Gras, the prevailing symbolism of the throw has been overlooked. Capitalism operates through mimicry and mechanical reproduction.[12] In a sardonic twist, applying these same operations through the fake wealth of Mardi Gras (in the form of plastic coins and jewels) mocks the very foundations of the commodity form—labor-time and money. It does this first by producing throwaway plastic copies of wealth and then by making them so abundant that the poorest child can walk away with an armful, having committed neither crime nor real labor. In the act of catching a coveted Mardi Gras throw, the relationship of labor-time and the arbitrary sign of money are revealed as absurd fictions. Like other objects considered here, the value of the souvenir Mardi Gras throw derives from its peculiar temporality. It is the product of a relation in which abundance is produced not by long toil but by short bouts of play. And it is the product of an exchange that takes place on a specific day in a specific year, often stamped on the throw itself. Carnival celebrations around the world perhaps have been overly romanticized as "the world turned upside down."[13] However, most of them do retain an element of social and political satire, a defining feature of the annual themes of New Orleans's parade floats. The fact that faux riches constitute New Orleans's special spin on carnival can be understood as a form of satire that carries over from year to year. Laughing at the absurdity of wealth and its questionable relationship to labor fits with the slowly stratified, wary critique of capitalism that has built up in a city with a legacy of slavery and wild cycles of booms and busts. The dirty mass of jewels strewn across the surface of New Orleans glimmers as an allegory of the city's partial rejection of market modernity. But with time, even fake lucre can acquire a new kind of value. Old glass beads and vintage trinkets buried deeply enough can resurface as antiques.

HEIRLOOMS AND GRANNY-HAD-ONES

One would think that after the Gilded Age indulgences in the antique, local elites would have turned away from old things and toward an aesthetic for the new, as happened in cities like New York and Paris. But modernism never acquired a strong following in New Orleans, nor really in many parts of the American South. The antique remained. One might explain this via the phenomenon Grant McCracken argues occurred in the Renaissance, with a turn toward the authentic family heirloom among white elites to stress old class over new money as their footing in the social hierarchy slipped. In fact, I expected to find in my interviews a strong distinction drawn between antiques and heirlooms. A distinction did emerge, but not one that my informants expected to be readable by anyone except their own family members. The object biographies of heirlooms gave them an idiosyncratic, highly affective value, but interviewees often downplayed the value of the pieces for anyone but themselves, saying that inherited furniture was "large and clunky," "ugly," or "not worth anything," although they mourned its loss in Katrina or were grateful for its rescue. Often, what was an antique to one generation, acquired through shopping, became an heirloom to the next generation as pieces got handed down through inheritance and became attached to family narratives. Asking people about their habits of collecting and caring for antiques and heirlooms helps clarify the strongly social character of these objects and the sometimes quite intimate relationships they form with individuals. Locally, the dynamics of an alternative system of object value were already well developed before architectural and artistic modernism began to spread in the 1920s.[14]

Ann is a sixty-something resident of the mostly affluent and mostly white suburb of Metairie, although she grew up in a New Orleans lower-middle-class neighborhood and attended the city's Catholic schools. Our interview focused on the experience of losing her house of thirty-six years and most of its contents.

> Ann: I think the main emotional part is the loss. I know it's people's quote "stuff," but it's *your* stuff and the reason you have it is cause you like it and you want it and then to have it just sort of taken away by the water like that, it's tough.

> SD: What do you miss the most? what do you wish you had saved or salvaged?

> Ann: Well, a couple of pieces of furniture that I really miss—one was a grandmother's armoire . . . they're usually very pretty, pretty old wood because in the early days there were no closets in houses so they were built to store your clothing either folded and/or hanging. . . . From the other grandparents' house, I had a bedroom set and that was salvaged . . . a dresser and a wash stand.

My question to Ann had been of a general sort about what she had lost or salvaged, and her response immediately focused on heirlooms. Similarly, Peggy (introduced in chapter 2) saved about ten pieces of furniture, all antiques, from her ranch-style house in New Orleans near the lakefront. She said the modern pieces "were not worth saving" and immediately followed with a digression on what *was* worth saving:

Peggy: Mother had a dresser that she had bought when she and my father married and it was in my daughter's room and it had been blown against the door to the room—in pushing the door open—the dresser just fell to pieces. Which, you know, was sad—it was my mother's.

As with most interviewees, the items most mourned by Ann and Peggy were photographs and heirlooms that connected them to family members, some of whom had died before they were born. The first thing Jane did upon returning to the city was to go to her grandmother's house and retrieve quilts and a bisque doll her grandmother herself had inherited. The older the items, the more they were valued.

My discussion with Ann moved on to how she was going about furnishing her new townhouse, and I asked her if there was a particular style she had in mind.

Ann: What are you going to do? I think New Orleans is an old city and I think people like old furniture and antiques. . . . I think we have a special way of looking at all that, I really do.

SD: Do have any ideas about why that might be?

Ann: When it's a family piece, it's naturally memories. We have a funny old Chinese chair. I don't think they're very valuable at all. But they came from my husband's grandmother's house. You saw it as soon as you walked in the front door. You know those old carved Chinese chairs, very carved and kinda black looking and all. And it's loose. It needs attention, I think. But anyway, it went through pretty good in all that water. And we have that with us and of course we love it.

I have a friend who's very good—a decorator type person—and she said, "Oh the chair needs to be moved." . . . and I thought, "No, that chair ain't gonna get moved. That chair's had a life." We laughed—the children like it—everybody likes the chair because it's just sort of a fun chair, you know [laughs]. The chair's *not* gonna get moved.

In reply to a question about the general New Orleans obsession with antiques, Ann answered with an account of a chair that's "had a life" and for which her family has a humorous affection, quirks and all. She stresses that it's not "very valuable" and that other people, such as her decorator friend, may not appreciate its style. Her response stresses that patina value adheres to the biographical heirloom with storytelling properties and idio-syncratic referents as much as it does to distinguished antiques. It is not the valued design of the object that matters (her armoire was a simple country Creole type, while her bedroom furniture is ornate Victorian) so much as the stories and feelings it evokes. She downplays the possibility that there is anything elegant or upper-class about her furniture. I then ask whether she has acquired any new antiques since the storm.

> Ann: Well, you know, we're so fortunate here. We have several auction houses. . . . We have shops on Magazine Street. We have shops on Royal Street. Everybody caters to antiques, and the almost-antiques, granny-had-ones—there's a lot of that on Magazine Street. So everybody likes granny-had-ones.
>
> SD: What's a granny-had-one?
>
> Ann: You know, your grandmother had one like that, so it's familiar, so it's like "Oh yeah, it looks just like my grandmother's. Good memory—I'll take that." Right now everybody loves French furniture, but the granny-had-ones are kinda Victorian so they're more ornate. My bedroom furniture is Victorian—the two saved pieces—but Fred [a collector friend] says the Victorians will one day have their day, it's just a question of time. Because they're beautiful—the workmanship, you know, they're just [pause]—now *modernists* wouldn't go for it [laughs].
>
> SD: So you think they're not appreciated much right now?
>
> Ann: I think they're not that much appreciated. You know I think most people that have them have them because they're family pieces. That's what I really believe.

In Ann's fast-moving explanation, she recounts how many people are refurnishing their houses with "granny-had-ones"—familiar pieces, often Victorian, that do not catch a high price on the antique market but are more likely to provoke an experience of pastness from their intimate, homey associations. She calls these associations "memories" but describes how they bring about an affective ambience rather than trigger the recollection of specific events. In local logic, a "granny-had-one" in a Magazine Street antique shop is a family piece as much as it is an alienable commodity. It is an heirloom inherited from a local collectivity to which you belong by right of residence, rather than by right of blood or marriage.

Sociologist Fox Gotham, in his work on tourism in New Orleans, interviewed one resident who described antique collecting as a local social activity and mode of integration for the newcomer: "I had never really been into an antique store until I moved to the French Quarter and began visiting them. And that got me interested in collecting antiques, which I have been doing now for over thirty years."[15] This transplant then grows nostalgic for the type of cluttered antique shops operated by friends that one could once find in the neighborhood, saying that antique collecting helped "create and project a magical and enchanted world" in the French Quarter. Many local collectors would say that the enchanted landscape of antique shops did not disappear; it just moved to lower rents on Magazine Street, away from the throngs of tourists.

My informants also pointed to antique collecting—or antique watching—as an important activity in their family's lives. It is a practice that accentuates heterotemporality. The habit of object collecting itself gets passed on within generations and marks important points in the life cycle, such as the death of a parent or a wedding. The antiques Peggy owned before the storm dated from when she and her husband first married and made purchases to establish their household, or they were inherited from her mother.

Peggy: Mother collected antiques, well, antique glass. She had antique furniture, but she especially collected antique glass. And as a child [in the 1920s-1930s], I hated to go antiquing. She and her two sisters would go antiquing and sometimes I would have to tag along. But she had collected a nice collection of antique glass and as I say, most of that was alright. It was saved [from Katrina]. So that, you know, was good.

Eighty-one-year-old Eliza notes that her grandmother's generation also cherished old things and old houses. Unlike Peggy, who inherited her mother's antiques but not her mother's penchant for antiquing, Eliza characterizes herself as a collector, having amassed an assortment of English pieces over "years and years," most of which she lost in the storm.

Eliza: I never bought anything impulsively in the French Quarter. I would always go down for a whole day *looking* at antiques. I love antiques. And I love wood. My children used to say: "What would you want in the whole wide world if you had a million dollars?" and I said "Old wood. A lot of old wood." [laughs]

For Ann, antiquing was a year-round activity that tied her into a larger social network outside her family.

Ann: When I was younger two things I loved to do if my children were in school, I loved to go to jazz funerals as a young person. . . . And the auctions. I'm glad that the auction houses still exist. And you'd be surprised. Some of the pieces that you never see anymore—some of the historic houses had some pieces of furniture that you used to see come in all the time and you don't see them anymore. I think they're staying in families. You see I think if it's a charming, fun, smallish piece that somebody takes it—a daughter, a son, a grandchild—someone takes that piece of furniture.

SD: So it's not in the market anymore?

Ann: It's not in the market. Doesn't get into the market anymore. I can tell you that pretty authentically. . . . I have a dealer here who used to tell me he was going to charge me an entertainment fee. [laughs] I never bought anything. I didn't have any money. . . . We would just go sit and listen and watch all the people buy all the wonderful things and listen to the descriptions. I just liked it.

For Ann and other New Orleanians, participating in the antique market is akin to attending a jazz funeral—it is a local pastime that creates a sense of community and requires local knowledge to fully appreciate. Both activities connect one to rehearsed traditions and, quite literally, to the dead. Ann perceived certain heirlooms from the historic houses as personages. She had no intention of possessing them, but she wanted to have some brush with their life cycle and with the people who passed them around. And she *knew* them, had a familiarity with particular items. Her assertion that many old object friends have "disappeared" (an assertion she went on to elaborate with accounts of pieces that had been reclaimed from museum collections by family members) offers a contemporary American example of Annette Weiner's "keeping while giving": the idea that even after an exchange, an inalienable claim persists between the original owner and the object. Ann's gossip about what happens behind the scenes of the auction echoes the mystique that surrounds Kula ring items, as recounted in the thick anthropological literature descending from Bronislaw Malinowski. Weiner revised the original thesis of the Kula ring as a complex but reciprocal gift exchange of personified objects, to show that many Kula traders actually resisted reciprocity by keeping the best items out of circulation for as long as they could, while maintaining their connection to the renown of the piece. Ann's account suggests a parallel in New Orleans, that of an exchange system of "old things" that operates with a different value system and circulatory pattern from those in the dominant market in alienable commodities. Given local skepticism about the good that capitalism has to offer, this interpretation seems especially apt. While nowhere nearly as formalized as the Kula system, the constant motion of junk and antiques within the city articulates a system of value that, like the plastic coins of Mardi Gras, exists in critical tension with conventional capitalist logic.[16]

Agatha is a native Louisianan, an artist who lives in a historic center-hall house in a downtown Creole neighborhood. In contrast to Ann and Eliza, she downplays collecting as an activity, although her answers suggest the importance of heirlooms and a highly attuned connoisseurship that assesses the "fit" of small things within the household. This connoisseurship has guided key acquisitions. In fact, she participates in a highly selective (thus infrequent) collecting activity that punctuates her own life cycle with connections to the local space-time continuum.

SD: You have a really beautiful old house that looks like it has some antiques. Do you collect antiques?

Agatha: No. [laughs]

SD: These are just things that people have given you?

Agatha: They are things that people have given me, that have come down—some things we have bought. . . . The proportions of the furniture to the rooms is rather tricky and the old Louisiana furniture just obviously fits into the rooms so beautifully. My brother and I inherited a very nice, 1950s sofa from his Aunt Mabel. It's upstairs now covered with things because I can't find anywhere in the house where it looks nice. It's not the right shape, it's not the right size.

Agatha then goes on to discuss her coming-of-age as a connoisseur, with the deliberate acquisition of one of the most identifiably "Louisiana" furniture pieces, a cypress armoire.

Agatha: I actually purchased an armoire when I was sixteen. My parents—We lived in a house in Thibodeaux and my room had no closet, we had just moved into the house. And so, the landlord . . . [said] come on up to the attic space, I've got about 10 or 12 old armoires up there. [laughs] And so I went and all of the armoires were very Victorian, with you know mirrors and fancy things and then there was this one armoire that was perfectly plain and I thought it was just beautiful and I said, "Oh, I just had to have it." And so I said, "how much?" and he said, "$15, would that be a lot?" [laughs] And $15 was a lot for me you know, I was 16 and it was, you know, many years ago. I still have that armoire and it is a Louisiana piece. It's not something you know that a probably a collector would want . . . but it's just very, very simple and so nicely proportioned.

With this coming-of-age story Agatha exhibits her knowledge of what locals identify as the true Creole aesthetic of unadorned but beautifully worked and proportioned wood. But she denies that she collects. Agatha briefly mentions a few other pieces that she and her husband inherited, but then elaborates on another purchased piece that stands as another exception to her noncollection.

Agatha: So I felt very fortunate in that I've had some nice pieces to put in the house and I didn't have to go out and look for things. Although we did purchase some things—a very pretty chest and beautiful bed from Orange Grove Plantation, a really nice old bed. I always wanted a four-poster bed. It's a bed that probably was used by children or a servant because it's not particularly fine in the details but the proportions are just so nice. And it was falling to bits and it was in an antique shop on Bourbon Street. And the owner of the shop had, on commission, all this furniture from Orange Grove Plantation.[17]

So that's a piece that was fun to restore and we had to—it was missing its headboard so we designed a headboard from a picture of an old bed, an old Louisiana bed. But basically we were not collectors, and we just were lucky to inherit things and to like the things that we inherited. And I feel, I love to have pieces that belonged to someone else or that have a history, a family history, [that] tell a story.

As with the armoire, the modesty and simple proportions of the bed are what Agatha highlights, as well as the object's biography and the social context of her acquisition. In both cases, she rescued the objects from ruin and oblivion. Despite her emphasis on liking old things with a story to tell, the main story she shares is about the way her relationship with the objects began and how they connect her to local space-time regardless of blood ties. I interpret her refusal to label this as collecting as her desire to distance this sort of object relationship from the usual market acquisition. Through her narration, she transforms these purchases into heirlooms. They tell a story about connectivity and care. And over the course of our conversation, she reveals that she knows a great deal about the social stratigraphy that the pieces have participated in—slavery, the deforestation of native cypress stands, the migration of the rural population into the city. The acquisition of such hand-worn furniture helps place her within that stratigraphy, for all its traumatic complexity that she openly acknowledges.

A personal relationship with old objects can also be emphasized by those who self-identify not only as collectors but as agents in the antiques market. Tom, the seventy-one-year-old dealer and clock collector introduced in chapter 1, comments that while antiques are definitely a market commodity and investment for him, at auctions certain ones leap across this category. "These clocks even find me," he says, pointing to favorites in his jam-packed store that he has marked with handwritten signs, "not for sale." Tom lived in a middle-class suburb near the lake. His house and its contents were almost a total loss after the storm.

SD: So you really like clocks? I mean, is this like a passion of yours?

Tom: Yeah, I have about 300 of them.

SD: 300? wow. Was it hard?

Tom: I was very angry after the storm—very, very angry. One clock in particular I lost about 9 foot long or tall, and it had a porcelain dial, and a colored jeweler's regulator and a mercury pin. . . . That thing just flipped over—I salvaged the movement. . . . It was quarter-sawn oak that had such a nice patina, almost a bright walnut. It wasn't real dark, it wasn't really light like some oak. So that was my favorite clock.

In the interview, Tom actually goes on for nearly ten minutes about this particular clock: how he acquired it, how he was inexplicably drawn to it, how he meticulously restored it, what it looked like, how he fought with his wife over it when it seemed too tall for their ranch-style house, how they resolved this conflict and she grew to love it too when he had a carpenter cut a three-foot hole from their ceiling into the attic to accommodate the clock's ornate pediment.

We then talked about local collectors. In Tom's view, many of them don't know enough to appreciate clocks. They mostly want Louisiana-themed artwork and Louisiana furniture, which he says is an identifiable style because "It's copied after some of the country French type furniture with you know nimbly kind of legs—but country pieces, they're not city pieces. They're not really frilly kind of things." He despairs a little that "now all the young people want of course, it's black ebony—they want the brand new black type furniture . . . [but] it'll flip over. Maybe not in my lifetime. But once they get older, they'll start to appreciate antiques a bit."

Our conversation then moves around the store while he shows me his antique clocks, with their doubled reference to the passing of time. We discuss restoration and repair. He again despairs that some customers want a piece that looks "brand new" and can't discriminate between an antique and a reproduction. The connoisseurship and care involved in appreciating object life without erasing signs of age are matters of skill and aesthetic sense.

Tom: So, this particular one, I'm pretty good—I don't like to refinish, but this one I bought at an auction and it was crummy. Yeah, well, it needed spiffing up. This is a little more spiffy than I like to see 'em but I kind of gave it to a guy and he uh . . .

SD: What do you mean, it was more spiffy than you like to see them?

Tom: It's too clean.

SD: It's too clean—you like them a little dirty?

Tom: Not dirty—but just, let's see, kind of like this [points to another clock]. I cleaned this up. It was dirty but you can see some wear here and that didn't bother me. But this is a clock probably from the 1830s. . . . It had over a century of dust on it—crap—'cause they had fireplaces and so on and so forth. So, this has a good patina. I like something with a little patina.

SD: Why do you like the patina?

Tom: I guess I've just been in the antique business. A real true collector likes patina.

SD: Why do you think that is?

Tom: It just reminds you of the past and what the piece has been through. Now I don't like it real dirty or anything. I'll wax it up. But I don't like it [that] this one had to be stripped. I'll go to great pains to keep original finishes.

Without missing a beat, Tom goes on to describe how he uses wax and steel wool to give a piece the right patina after the dirt is removed. A "real true collector" likes patina—and knows how to fake it.

I am struck by the ways in which many of my interviewees switched back and forth between the aesthetics of the objects we were discussing and their history—either within the era of their original production and circulation, or within the biography of the current owner. As Tom says, patina "reminds you of the past and what the piece has been through." As with his anger at the loss of the grandfather clock, old things are also a reminder of what we ourselves have been through. It is a "sign of what was," a trigger for storytelling that negotiates the relationship between personal experience and collective solidarity. Narratives accrue to old things like patina.

Harry has a special talent for finding the stories in things and adding to them. He runs a rambling bed and breakfast just outside the French Quarter that is stuffed to the eaves with antiques, odd artifacts, and things guests have left behind. This material has accumulated not only by his own collecting activity, but by generations of family collectors. Each object he points to launches a long and often humorous story. A taxidermied peacock contains the story of Harry's alcoholic and dearly beloved brother who led an eccentric life as a caterer to the stars in Hollywood. The particular story of the peacock related to a failed starlet marriage perhaps doomed by such an inappropriate wedding gift (the dead peacock). Although the bird had no connection to New Orleans before Harry inherited from his late brother, he says of it, "so that's a New Orleans type thing, you know," presumably because it embodies such a tragicomic romance.

A wardrobe trunk in the room I was staying in also seemed to hold an element of his brother's spirit. The long story of how this item from the set for *Gone with the Wind* traveled by train to New Orleans seemed to be as much about how Harry's southern bachelor brother ended up living in Hollywood. A hand-painted tapestry evokes the story of another relative, "who invented and hybridized the Alberta peach—all those big peaches out of California were named after his first wife. This was painted by his second wife, Ms. Pearly. And so he also was the first person in Georgia to ship fruit by refrigerated cars—think *East of Eden*." And so on. Much of the interview wound in and out of the clutter of the house and the clutter of Harry's family history, with its collection of politicians, bootleggers, and agronomists who ventured out from the South only to come home in one form or another.

After discussing the house, which is a historic Creole side-hall cottage that Harry claims in the past served as both a funeral parlor and a brothel (though not presumably at the same time), I asked Harry why he likes old houses and old things.

> Harry: It's very important. It's a part of the continuum. It a part of what makes community. And this of course is one of the great tragedies of putting all of the old people in nursing homes and everyone in the neighborhood makes the same amount of money, is the same age, you're losing this whole—that's an aside—not specifically related to New Orleans. But it is a horrible thing that has happened. Because you lose that pass-on information that basically tribal information, in a sense, and it's all gone and of course everybody's now getting their information from T.V. And don't get me started on that.

On the activity of collecting, he points to family habits, particularly of his wife, her grandmother, and his late brother (although he himself is not immune—he talks about china he acquired *before* he was married, making fun of himself: "Can you *imagine?*"). Harry characterizes himself and his wife not as connoisseurs but as rather indiscriminate magpie collectors.

> Harry: We're really just packrats. Margaret's grandmother was a big collector.

> SD: So Margaret's grandmother, she collected furniture or other things?

> Harry: Anything that she could afford to buy or could wheedle out of somebody.

> SD: Was there a theme to it or a particular thing she liked?

> Harry: No, if she liked it. If she liked things that she described as odd, meaning unusual . . . That's from Margaret's grandmother [pointing], that pie safe and china cabinet, various things—beds. . . .
>
> I mean Margaret rides her bike up to the lakefront . . . and she would call me on the phone and said come to X and Y corner and there'll be something—some wannabe treasure—put on the street. Scavenging—that's

why we don't have a pick up truck cause then it would get ahead of us. It's already pushing us. It could be deadly . . . and all the pictures and this [pointing to objects in the hallway] come from various places. . . . And so there's just various ways [of collecting]—we've been around a while. I mean I'm 71 years old, been married 42 years so we've had a lot of time to collect.

While the pleasure of collecting unabashedly relates to the pleasure of sharing connected stories (some, one suspects, with a bit of faked patina in the form of Mark Twainish elaboration), Harry and Margaret also collect objects as a form of archiving for the future. This activity seems unrelated to any calculation of future market value. These objects are far removed from systems of commodity value; they are discards, and Harry and Margaret have no interest in selling anything. If they slough off objects (which he says is rare), they end up back on the curb for another scavenger, not in a consignment shop or on eBay.

> Harry: We just don't throw anything away—Margaret said to me once, she said, "These boxes in the attic, now we've moved house three times since they've been unpacked, do you think it's time to throw them out?" "Certainly not," I said, "Who knows what treasures might be in there?" But Mary has a real problem. We had to kind of clear her grandmother's house—and her grandmother had Margaret's report cards going back to the first grade—and worse. I mean *unbelievable* stuff. . . . And we still left probably about as much stuff there as we took out. I don't mean furniture but I just mean dresses on long pipes in the attic going back generations—you get the picture.

Harry and Margaret's boxes in the attic will one day haunt their own children during the life transition of death and inheritance, though not with the same ghostly presence of human-shaped, threadbare dresses strung out on a pipe, reaching back into ancestral time.

My pursuit of interviewees who could speak to the obsession of collecting old things in New Orleans relies heavily upon a subset of the demographic: primarily white and older than fifty, although they otherwise ranged over class and between native and adoptee. African American interviewees were less likely to bring up heirlooms and old things when we talked about Katrina losses. As voiced by J.J. when we talked about historic houses, "old things" may have too much of an association with negative heritage, but collecting (even free curbside "junk") requires stability of housing that many poorer residents have never known. One partial exception was Isaiah, who grew up in various predominantly black downtown neighborhoods. While talking about the house his grandmother lost in the historic district of Holy Cross within the Lower Ninth Ward, I asked:

> Does your mom have anything from that house? Or passed down from her parents that she holds on to?

> Isaiah: Yeah, she has some things. They sit up in a closet. She doesn't mention them. I find stuff all the time in the closets that I know belonged to my grandparents, you know whether it's a Chinese case full of Chinese money because my granddad served in China or whether it's anything. There's all kind of stuff that we have no explanation for at all.

> SD: Like what else?

> Isaiah: Sometimes you find, you know, weird ceramics or you find just things that look real old like stools or benches or anything that's just put up where nobody can find it. And it just has, like, this really really old look to it that I think—I want to hear the story about it. I want to know where it's from. I know it's not my mom's. And she'll even say that, "Oh, you know, I got that from your grandmother. I got that from your great granddad." But that's it, that's as far as the story goes. . . . My family isn't one for like, talking about history.

As with Harry and Margaret, boxes of artifacts sit up in the attic, full of narrative potential and an unknown future value. Quite unlike Harry and Margaret, Isaiah's family "isn't one for talking about history." History in the form of objects is silent but not discarded. They survived Katrina, and Isaiah promises to keep pestering his mother and grandmother for their stories. As mute as the objects are, and as painful as their stories might be—about slavery, about war, about a father who abandoned his children to lead a good-time life—they are still safeguarded as the stuff of connectivity across generational time. Of course, not all objects become heirlooms or collectible antiques. Only a tiny fraction of the things that flow through our lives get elevated to such a pedestal, to become a fixation for emotional associations and storytelling. But once they do, they can become quite powerful pieces in our social flows. How and why does this happen?

THE FETISH

Fetishism is the cult of baubles. —Max Muller

Within anthropology, perhaps we have always been ontological. At least, we have always been fascinated by other worlds and willing to believe in them, by phenomena that exceed our classificatory schemes, and by objects that seem to have agency, if not a type of spirit, like the old houses and things of New Orleans. Thing theory at present does not account very well for why some objects play a much larger role in our social lives than others. Not all objects are equally agentive. In their special properties, old things set aside for curation seem to have much in common with what we used to call totems and fetishes. So perhaps fetish theory can help thing theory appreciate some nuances of the more intimate and affective relations between things and people.[18]

Over time, fetishism has earned a bad name and scholars have been quick to point out its "sinister pedigree."[19] Talking about fetishism usually involves the idea of a kind of misidentification, or mistake. Taken naively, this judgment risks dismissing the role that material things play in our intangible lives via memory, affect, and association. Some degree of misidentification, projection, or displacement may be not only a quite common means to handle emotional and social complexity, but an effective one. A more nuanced approach to fetishism can help us understand these strategies. An additional attraction of the fetish is that it invites us to escape the old divided dualities of subject-object and abstract-concrete. Fetishes make a mishmash of these categories.

Fetish theory has three main, though intertwined, branches: the fetish as a magico-religious object as described by history and anthropology; commodity fetishism via and beyond Marx; and sexual fetishism via Alfred Binet and Sigmund Freud. In contemporary literature, commodity fetishism is by and large the version most commonly invoked in anthropology and critical theory. It traces back to references in the first volume of *Das Kapital*. Marx's comparison of religious fetishism with the masquerade of the commodity—in which a relation between person and thing cloaks a relation among persons—has been taken by most interpreters to represent a condensation of his argument about the mystification and false consciousness both necessary to and produced by capitalism. Specifically, the commodity appears to have some intrinsic value, an exchange value or price, a natural worth in an objective marketplace of human desires. But in fact, according to Marx, its value can only be reliably measured by the labor-time that went into its manufacture. Like the practitioners of magic, consumers misidentify the significance of an object. Marx's use of fetishism was the allegation of a nonbeliever.[20]

As a metaphor for *im*personal social forces, commodity fetishism stands in contrast to fetish theory grounded in psychoanalytic ideas of sexual displacement. The most useful ideas from Freud's brief treatment of the topic are (1) that the object of focus is a substitute for something unseeable; (2) that the object represents something lost or whose potential loss is feared; (3) that the meaning of the object became fixed during a brief, sometimes traumatic, event in the past; and (4) that the fetish often compresses contradictory ideas and feelings.[21] Dr. Robert Stoller, a later psychoanalyst critical of many of Freud's theories, offered a positive revision of fetishism (now called paraphilia), saying that "an object (inanimate thing, animal, or body part) becomes a fetish when it stands for—condenses in itself—meanings that are, wholly or in crucial parts of the text, unconscious: a fetish is a story masquerading as an object."[22]

According to William Pietz, author of several important articles on the intellectual genealogy of fetishism, the idea of the fetish in both its Marxist and its psychoanalytic variants can be traced back to early modern Lusophone Africa, where colonialists were confronted with a belief system focused on eccentric objects. Travelers inevitably perceived African practices through the lens of the Inquisition and Europe's campaign against witchcraft. So while Europeans and Christians may have found these types of objects threatening, they were not entirely unfamiliar. Colonial writers bestowed the fetish label on objects or assemblages having an accretion of debris, biological matter, or evidence of repetitive action that were believed to have magical or personally efficacious powers. Through colonial writing and collecting, these objects entered the consciousness of Enlightenment Europe, becoming things that Europe liked to think with—most famously Kant and Hegel. They used the fetish as an example of an error of logic called hypostatization, or the fallacy of misplaced concreteness for abstract ideas. Not unrelatedly, the "irrationality" of African systems of value was explained away due to a propensity—identified as fetishism—to personalize and personify artifacts rather than see them as having a natural, neutral, price or use-value rationally calculated by the world market.[23]

Bridging this intellectual history with later ethnographic explorations of these types of objects, Pietz identified some common properties of fetishes. With some glosses of my own added, I find his points helpful in thinking through the place of patinated objects in contemporary life. The first is *historicity*. A fetish results from historical acts of accretion or the trauma of a specific event. Next, the fetish has an *irreducible materiality*. The power of a fetish, unlike that of an idol, comes not from its semiotic references or visual conventions, but from its aura of pastness. The materiality of the fetish is untranscended and untranslatable. It bears a heavy load of qualia but weak symbolic content. Third, a fetish acts by being *socially recursive*. From the analyst's point of view, a social process develops the meaning and value of the fetish. Or, as Deleuze says, "The fetish is the natural object of social consciousness as common sense or recognition of value."[24] Pietz argues that the fetish depends upon a particular order of social relations to produce its meaning and value, which it in turn reproduces. Put another way, we can understand the fetish as constitutive of social relations. Finally, I would add to Pietz's list of traits the fact that, from a distance, the fetish is perceived as *dissimulating*. In all three fetish theories of the Western intellectual tradition, there is a persistent qualification of the fetish as an object that perpetuates a con or a fraud, duping the human agents who have faith in its value and efficacy. Per Marx, it mystifies in a superstitious way; he was quite clearly disparaging of the parlor trick the commodity performs. In psychoanalytic terms, it substitutes or displaces normal sexual arousal. And according to early ethnographies, the fetish claims to contain spiritual entities that do not exist according to the Western observer's ontology.[25]

Many antiques and heirlooms would fit Pietz's description of a fetish. They have experienced repetitive handling and use, if not traumatic events, evidenced through scratches, fading, and the patina of dirt and skin oil. Of course, they are irreducibly material, an aspect not unrelated to their untranslatable affective qualities and the capacity to evoke an aura of pastness. An unusually well preserved object that looks "good as new" does not have the qualia to be a true antique. Many antiques and heirlooms are so historical that they tell stories. Or, per Stoller, they *are* stories. As meaningful objects that circulate in an alternate circuit of value, they have effects on their human handlers and help constitute a field of social relations. Finally, they cannot be entirely trusted. They might be fakes or reproductions, with the patina added not by history but by intentional surface treatments. However, since lack of authenticity does not necessarily alter their evocative efficacy, I would like to take a step back from the skepticism we have inherited about fetishes to appreciate what they actually *do* for their human interlocutors.

The process of fetishization entails the creation and perpetuation of a social use value. In the case of the antique, fetishization becomes ever more likely as an object endures beyond the era of its production and initial exchange, and still more likely if it survives whole human generations. It becomes an allegory of shared social stratigraphy and it is more likely to have a personality—or to house a spirit. Durkheim himself verged on naming the antique fetish: "It is feelings inspired by the ancestor and projected onto the material object that make it into a kind of fetish."[26]

I am not entirely abandoning the Marxist notion of the fetish, but pulling at a tension between commodity fetishism and antique fetishism. Another frame to put around antiques and heirlooms (unless handmade) is to consider them commodities that have entered a stage of the afterlife. As such, they are more likely to take on an uncanny quality. Souvenirs, too, buck standard commodity logic. They can never be replaced because the event that they embody can never be repeated. They are temporally "singular," as Igor Kopytoff first termed the quality opposite to that of the mechanically identical commodity. The biography of the commodity, as soon as it enters the hands of a purchaser and travels home, becomes entangled with the biographies of individual humans, with their life passages of birth, marriage, and death. Adopted into a household, the object begins a process of singularization by means of a relationship with particular human handlers and a unique series of events resulting in the marks of wear and tear. The mold seams that indexed it as a mechanically reproduced clone identical to an uncountable number of siblings can be rubbed away. From a romantic view, patina returns things to a more natural order. It de-standardizes them, remanufactures them by the touch of a human hand. The singularization process reverses Marx's alienation. It also reveals that different circuits of value coexist, sometimes cantankerously, with the marketplace and its fixation on new things.[27]

Old things possess their unusual value because they bear the marks of human touch. In the case of heirlooms, they were removed from, or have never been in, the commodity circuit. They pass from hand to hand through time, and in the case of long-rooted New Orleans families, they may not move through physical or social space at all. The conservatism of their movement against the landscape informs their value. When we focus on circulation through time rather than circulation through space, we can see that heirlooms and antiques are used as citations of social stratigraphy: the past events and structures that produced the shared conditions under which residents live. These strata are littered with the dead, some named and some only vaguely sensed as the original makers, purchasers, and users of old things.

Seen against the map of their movements, antique fetishes become objects that, "circulating as a possession possessed by no one, prompt people to think of one another."[28] At auctions, antiques with long provenances seem to exchange themselves, coming in and out of view periodically, as in the case of Ann's voyeuristic account of "old friends" circulating through the auctions. Tom's clocks "find him." With old houses, the pattern flips. It is the people who pass through the objects. And most old buildings have the sign—the patina—of having circulated through time. Ultimately, the antique fetish expresses a desire to re-enchant the object world.

• • •

When former commodities become elevated to the status of an emotionally charged fetish, Freud's theory takes over from Marx's. Objects stand in for something the actor needs, which is often immaterial and incorporeal. The actor may fear losing the object's referent or it may already be missing. The connection to nostalgia as loss crystallizes. The antique fetish can be a displacement for a lost world or a dead loved one, but it can also be a kind of preservation of something you *fear* losing in the future. Collectively, in "antique cities" like New Orleans, old objects stand in for something larger and unseen. It is both something to which you belong and something that is a part of you. *It* possesses *you.*

While talking about things people chose to salvage from their homes, I asked Jane:

SD: Do you think our attachments to things all trace back to childhood?

Jane: Yes, but I also think traumatic experiences, things that happened with Katrina, that make us bond with elements of our environment here. It's an amazing thing. . . . People have bonded with some strange things, like when they moved one of the boats that was stuck on Hwy 90, when they finally got it out of the way, people were upset. They had bonded with that boat.

That boat had been through some history. For some, it was a good sign of what was—of the pre-Katina community, now damaged by death and exile.

Illuminating the antique fetish has been one of the final steps in understanding the social processes and nostalgic practices related to patina. The antique fetish is a conglomerated object. It is a story, but at the same time its aesthetic and affective allure exceeds narration. Fetishism names a charged relation that can simultaneously be an economic, psychological, and spiritual one. Even under the conditions of modernity and industrial capital (or perhaps especially under them), people need to understand some things as animate, as infected with an old spirit, or what Jack called mana. This is not a misidentification. It is concrete social experience made thinkable. For some actors, constitutive events may be too painful to dwell on, or they may have experienced too many repetitive ruptures to find anything restorative about the past. Others grasp at the flotsam, trying to stay connected as time carries them along. The fake finger is *real* as a fetish—as "a sign of what was" and as an agent of the present. This concreteness is not misplaced.

CHAPTER 6

Conclusion: Patina, Chronotopia, Mana

> Nowhere can a collective feeling become conscious of itself without fixing
> upon a tangible object. —Emile Durkheim, *The Elementary Forms of Reli-*
> *gious Life*

The central argument of this book has built up like patina itself, with lay-
ering, contact with different materials, and a steady chipping away. The
result is not seamless, but cumulative. I have sought to show what patina
is, in both its social and material senses, and how those connect. To return
to the question *What does patina do?*, I argue that it does two powerful
things. It critiques and it bonds.

Patina is an aesthetic modality that protests commodity capitalism and
modernity's fixation on linear progress. It questions the creed that everything new is necessarily better. Patina enables a critical nostalgia. This is its
outward aspect, a subtle protest against global conformity.

On the interior walls—touching individuals, families, and neighbors—
patina does something different. It serves as a qualisign of heightened singularization that makes evident the intimacy of human-object relations. By
doing so, it materializes the totemic dead who gather together the living.
It cites social stratigraphy. It emanates mana.

Out of my investigation of a particularly local fixation on old things
has come a broader engagement with aesthetics and temporality. This bit
of profane archaeology has aimed to understand the ways in which the
world we experience consists of a dense matrix of people, actions, ideas,
and things that have built up over time. The effects of this stratigraphic
matrix are not always expressible by those caught within it. But redeeming
nostalgia and the category of the fetish have, I hope, helped illuminate
important formation processes.

Nostalgia in New Orleans as produced through its historic preservation
programs, storytelling, and a penchant for object collecting presents the
past not as a refuge, nor as a foreign country, but as a heterotopic sphere

that feeds diverse future imaginaries. Nostalgic practices can serve conservative retrogression, bohemian languor, or a revolutionary rejection of mass consumer culture. Historic preservation efforts in some ways *are* a Disneyfication, a term often thrown around the anxious city as a pathologizing label. The overdone effects of historic preservation in New Orleans stimulate a spectrum of fantasies by not getting too specific on the details. To choose a particular set of facts or even the style of a certain era would deny the palimpsest quality of the landscape. Much of the aesthetic effect of the French Quarter could not be said to be historically edifying or informative. It is, through its vague prettiness, a kind of antihistorical coquette. Past traumas are not replayed too intently for the visitor, although their signs may be easily read by residents. Patina and the narratives that attach to New Orleans's ruins operate much more at the level of the mythic and the totemic than that of a linear historicism or memorialization. Patina does a lot of work to create a sense of social belonging for residents and fleeting communitas for visitors. Locally, patina is curated to provoke an involuntary memory of ancestors, and for that social purpose, it is more effective if the referents are fictive, vague, and shifting. The French Quarter presents what Susan Stewart calls "the infinite time of reverie," the temporality of a dollhouse, with its idealized domestic routine you know never really existed. Yet nostalgia in New Orleans is not particularly melancholy. It is, rather, celebratory. Like Mardi Gras, it can even be satiric. Its purpose is not to roll back time but to goad the future.[1]

The patina that accents the critical nostalgia of New Orleans is messy, the effect of preserving "dirt." In contrast, sites of *restorative* nostalgia, such as Colonial Williamsburg, are kept meticulously clean and renovated. Why is dirt not "out of place" in the patina aesthetic? If, as Mary Douglas observed in her classic work on purity and danger, an obsession with controlling and removing dirt, and signs of wear and tear, is an important index of social meaning, then surely the opposite—the aestheticization of dirt—also has social meaning. Eastop, in observing the treatment of dirt in museum conservation efforts, notes that "soiling and creasing are retained when they are considered to be part of the 'true nature' of the artefact, e.g. the blood staining on the clothes of heroes or martyrs."[2] Thus, we might understand the dirty patina or valued grit of places like New Orleans not simply as an aesthetic effect but as part of its "true nature" that has resulted from multiple layers of historical processes. In this view, patina invites a forensics of events both dramatic and quotidian—of trauma, work, and play. In recognizing the passage of time but not erasing it, the curation of patina contributes to a heightened temporal consciousness. Such a disposition is not antimodern. It has movement, but it is not a linear one. Places characterized by critical nostalgia assert the immanence of a present that reassembles fragments of the past. Many have described a similar everyday aesthetic in places such as Istanbul, St. Petersburg, Barcelona, Amsterdam, London, and Buenos Aires (and once-upon-a-time New York and San Francisco). These cities are characterized by a playful give-and-take between the old and the new and a delicate balance between good and bad patina.

The critical nostalgia of New Orleans is made possible, one might say even enacted, by an accumulation of old objects. The proclivities of romanticism and the picturesque, as exemplified in the city's literary productions, entwined themselves in the relationship between the physical and the social worlds. The extent to which that relationship had an old and colorful history fascinated visitors and local observers alike. As much as New Orleans thrived as market port for new commodities, prior to Katrina, it had also become a place where old objects got caught in a gentle eddy, a collection of historical detritus that shaped each new generation of inhabitants. Many of those old objects were swept away or eaten by mold after the levee breaks, but newish ones are slowly taking their place.

As an orientalized place, New Orleans has been recursively shaped by the people flowing through it and the erotics of the host-guest relationship. It caters to the fantasies of a national market of consumers who may view themselves as living in a world that is too fast, too serious, too disconnected, too impersonal. A dip into New Orleans's sensuality and slow time offers a tonic for threatened anomie. The city's nostalgic practices also define local groupness against an outside other, a good-time culture that pities the impoverished rationalism of Protestant capitalism. If one could say there is a dominant ideology unique to New Orleans, that would be it.

This is not to deny that nostalgia sets up an ethical mechanism for the evaluation of authenticity that can be politically conservative. Residents often utter the phrase: "Now that's *real* New Orleans." They recite it with a touch of humor and in an adopted Yat accent that only those who have been in the city a long while will attempt (it still surprises many visitors from other parts of the United States that the most identifiable local accent is almost indistinguishable from Brooklynese). Authenticity here functions not so much to check the pedigree of the object or the performer, but to appreciate the density of narrative that can be attached to one or the other. As Stewart says, authenticity can be achieved "only through narrative." Authenticity does not sacralize history-as-text in a biblical fashion, asking, "Does it tell the one and only truth?" Rather, the test of authenticity for nostalgia is "Does it tell a New Orleans story?" (as in Harry's interview). Of course, a good story means mixing familiar plot lines and comforting tropes with some well-placed variation and invented detail. Still, when the

time-valued objects that anchor nostalgia begin to move through space, it can create anxiety about origin, narration, and valuation. Can we be sure of their stories? The larger the geographical circuit, the more likely a policing discourse of authentication will appear. Objects of uncertain provenance are the Martin Guerres of the object world. Heirlooms are much more trustworthy than antiques, even if their recognized value is much lower.

Speaking of storytellers, anthropologists and archaeologists are notorious romantics. As Michael Taussig says, "precapitalist societies acquire the burden of having to satisfy our alienated longings for a lost Golden Age." New Orleans takes this burden upon itself through its auto-orientalism. While some aspects of the resulting sensorium affirm fleshly indulgence, a slow life, and the kindness of strangers, others evoke "tropical gothic"—a macabre sense of humor and a romantic fascination with death, violence, and tragedy. This is a cultural disposition nourished by a landscape of patinated objects and a palimpsest of narratives. Taussig, channeling Walter Benjamin, says that nostalgia has revolutionary potential: "Melancholy is the gaze that penetrates the images of the past, transforming them from dead objects into images vibrant with meaning for the revolutionary encounter with the present. . . . Nothing could be further from the conservative nostalgia for the past."[4] But as we learn from Storyville interiors, nostalgia also casts an erotic gaze on the past and on places far away in the imagination. Some forms of nostalgia are powered by the little motor of orientalism, rooted in the masculine fixations of colonialism. Nostalgia may be characterized more by dissatisfaction than revolutionary ardor. The past is fetishized in New Orleans to satisfy a desire for the intangible, an erotic and consumable substitution for an elusive completion of the present.

Although known for its laissez-faire (some say just lazy) attitude, New Orleans keeps busy in its work against alienation. A conviviality flows from shared knowledge and fictive ancestors. Residents of the city seem to enjoy, rather than suffer from, what Simmel famously called hyperaesthesia, or "the fear of coming into too close a contact with objects," an overstimulation of the senses. Filtering objects via collection, narration, and fetishization provides a way for locals to manage this overstimulation. On the other hand, tourism has long banked on the fact that temporary overstimulation is exactly what many visitors seek. One elegant definition of the New Orleans style of tourism could be a "romantic effort to derange the senses."[5]

Walter Benjamin would have loved New Orleans. Not simply because it represents a wilder, more messianic version of Paris, but because he would see it as a place that takes on the hubris of capitalism with a sense of ironic play. Whereas his romantic Paris (via Baudelaire and Simmel) played up the tragedy of modernity's contradictions, New Orleans plays up its dark comedy—and makes a good buck doing so. The city has narrowly, and repeatedly, avoided catastrophe by not taking progress too seriously. Time is already understood as a bit twisted and folded, and disaster and trauma as inevitable. Society presents itself simultaneously as a ruin and as a kind of playland.

Another aspect of New Orleans that Benjamin might have liked is that residents tend to value things for the way they transcend their own commodification. For the way they become humanlike through a process of singularization and patination. If the machine-reproduced commodity is fetishized elsewhere for its ability to deliver an imagined future for aspiring consumers, in New Orleans the hand-produced heirloom or recycled object is fetishized for its ability to call up the spirits of an imagined past. The new commodity and the used object provide foils for each other. The clutter of New Orleans, even after the forced purge of Katrina, defies some of the more obvious mechanics of the market commodity. It offers a rich ground upon which to explore the social significance of artifacts that resist, or have fallen away from, the commodity system. New Orleans could be viewed, without too much exaggeration, as a sprawling, ramshackle arcade of ragpickers, salvagers, and collectors of idiosyncratic junk.

Contra Pierre Bourdieu's thesis about art and distinction, the living-with-old-things habitus in New Orleans does not naturalize the national social order so much as it satirically comments upon it. At the same time, it allows the local social order to reassemble itself in response to ruptures and influxes of newcomers. One thing that seems true about all forms of nostalgia is that social cohesion is almost always imagined to have been stronger in the past than in the present. Although Blue still thinks New Orleans is special, he worries that in some neighborhoods "there's no love in the streets." He describes an earlier time, when both people and things were a little more appreciated across the lines of color and class: "And even though you might have been on the other side of tracks, or whatever, but you *know* people. You may have gotten hand-me-down clothes but they were good things to get and you learned to appreciate what you had at the time. You know what I'm saying? So, people are good. . . . They built up a love for each other, you know?" Being able to imagine a time of greater connectedness in the past may be a necessary condition for making some small enactment of it possible in the present. Durkheim recognized this need for utopian images: "A society can neither create nor recreate itself without creating some kind of ideal by the same stroke."[6]

An older anthropology would see occasions like All Saints Day and Mardi Gras, when traditions are dusted off and old objects are brought out to become reacquainted with the living, as a ritually induced liminal state between the past and the present. Such rituals allow society to pause and reflect upon itself and create a communitas of effervescent connection. By taking on the material mantle of past social relations, actors are able to temporarily transcend present-day conflicts through the enactment of a *chronotopia,* a utopia that exists in another time dimension. Chronotopia plays off of Foucault's *heterotopia.* In his brief development of this idea, Foucault focused more on space than time and used cemeteries, museums, gardens, and vacation villages as examples of heterotopia. For him, these are places marked off from the quotidian landscape by their unique materiality in order to concretize abstract ideals of social life. For me, they are also places that create a peculiar experience of time. Another way to think about them is that they are intentional anomalies in space-time. The French Quarter presents such a wrinkle, or from some perspectives, perhaps the whole city of New Orleans. The city's playful manipulation of time is certainly one cause for the oft-repeated worry that New Orleans will become a Disneyland.[7]

In New Orleans, museums, gardens, cemeteries, and brothels are not unrelated chronotopias. And these chronotopias have real effects. They are moneymakers. Museums have been accused of being a form of entombment for objects—killing them by stopping their biographical journey through time. If a museum is a tomb for objects, is a historic district a tomb for houses? The city promotes the romantic sex-death complex and commodifies it as carriage rides, ghost tours, souvenirs, and exotic tourist experiences. In a landscape of vampires, to hurl an accusation of entombment toward its preserved structures is simply to recognize the fetish appeal of objects taken out of their normal life cycle, particularly those that cheated the death of their human makers. They live on as a kind of soulful undead.

The city's self-love demands an alternative temporality to quick linear time. As Blue said, "it's always been a slow go" in New Orleans. A deliberate effort to slow things down may help explain why gardens come up in the same breath as old houses and grandmother's perfume. In addition to confusing the artificial divide between production and consumption (they are both), gardens represent a quasi-magical space set aside from the banality of the market. When tended by owners, they transform acts of productive labor into performances of leisure. Gardens exist in a temporal reality separate from capitalism's compulsive newness. New Orleanians especially appreciate gardens full of heirlooms and well-established features such as trees, shrubbery, and perennial vines. Some trees, such as the renowned palm of Père Antoine, may predate any living memory and thus humble the surrounding bustle. A garden proclaims itself a slower, older place than the swirl of urbanity around it. Strolling through a space like the antebellum pleasure garden at St. Anthony's, the pedestrian traces a sliver of romantic resistance to clock time.

From the time of Baudelaire, writers began to complain that the world was changing too quickly, so quickly that actors were losing touch with the world to which they supposedly belonged. Early social scientists equated the modern condition with an anxious alienation from the face-to-face, reliable social networks of kin, village, and parish. However, examining the writing of the romantics reveals that what they spent more time explicitly worrying about was alienation from the *physical* world. They expressed anxiety about losing a connection to objects and forgetting the stories of houses, furniture, and baubles that tie people together. Thus, nostalgia as a longing for what is lost can quite literally be taken as a longing for *things*. As Peter Stallybrass tells us, even Karl Marx was not immune to the antique fetish, or what Benjamin called "the aura of the habitual" (chapter 1) that his family's things possessed.[8]

I do not want to be read as overstating the case about the edifying effect of critical nostalgia and the antique fetish. For some individuals, patina does little to create cohesion and instead brings up melancholy and fear. J.J. links his dislike of old houses with slavery and his desire to keep moving beyond that history. Similarly, Marie has too many traumatic memories associated with the Lower Ninth Ward to want to remain in one of its old houses. These responses suggest that if there is *too much* trauma associated with the past, then no longing for return develops and thus no corresponding veneration of the antique. In that case, people see a negative patina, not of moral decay but of scarification. But the point remains: whether positively or negatively valued, patinated objects are alive with associations.

It is also the case that many of the same working-class people who have moved around the city without acquiring the collecting habit tend to focus on intangible heritage—on jazz, Creole cooking, and the second line parading tradition in which the Mardi Gras Indians participate. While it would have stretched the canvas of this study too thin to include the intangible traditions of New Orleans, these practices clearly play a huge role both in constituting a self-aware community and in attracting tourists in search of "authentic" expression. Like their tangible counterparts, these performances and ephemeral forms of consumption have heterotemporal effects. Actors knowingly repeat performances scripted in a much earlier time, in a much different context. As Peter said, "You live in another period when you entertain." Performances have a repetitive tempo that glosses over unique events and emphasizes reproduction and continuity. Anyone who has experienced the transition from pre-K to post-K New Orleans can attest to the fact that there are now parades for just about *everything*, in an almost compulsive effort to rehearse the city back to a predisaster state. In contrast, tangible heritage in the form of scarred objects can emphasize social change. This "wounding" capacity is due to the biographical nature of ruins and aging objects, with qualia that signal unique life events, sometimes catastrophic ones. While both forms of heritage reference the past, they do so according to distinct temporalities.

The one performance I *have* touched on is Mardi Gras, an annual chronotopia enacted on a mass scale. At carnival time, the gift-commodity duality (if ever real) not only breaks down but gets deliberately parodied through "throws" of fake wealth. Local customs of hospitality, even when played out in the context of commercial hotel and restaurant service, also blur this line and nostalgically invoke a time when life "wasn't all about money." Of course, Mardi Gras is also the biggest moneymaker for the city.

It would be easy to be cynical about the alternatives to fast capitalism that the chronotopia of New Orleans holds out. In a city riven by tremendous economic disparity that has only grown since Katrina, a claim that residents resist the commodity's elusive allure in preference to the antique's enduring charm, or the souvenir's ephemeral one, risks claiming that imagined historical connections trump present-day inequalities. I am not claiming that. But I *am* suggesting that what we find on the underbelly of the romance is a fantasy rejection of exchange value in favor of a system that highlights singularity and the aging object. The implication of such an alternative system of value would be that human beings themselves cannot be reduced to an economic index, or a youth index. This is why Walter Benjamin wanted to redeem outmoded and discarded commodities—the umbrellas, hats, crystal lamps, toys, dusty knickknacks, and velvety chairs of *The Arcades*. It was an allegorical practice in the revolutionary redemption of people.

Igor Kopytoff's contribution to *The Social Life of Things*, in which he turned the commodification of the slave upside down to view an object as a slave—one with a humanlike biography—has been highly influential in material studies. But I think his bold thesis could be pushed further. Not only do objects have biographies of birth, peak activity (perhaps reproduction), old age, and death, but they can appear to their human interlocutors as animated by spirit. The more objects seem to have a humanlike history, the more likely they are to be fetishized as agentive. What Kopytoff calls the singularization of objects closely parallels Western psychology's ideas about personality development. Freud himself referred to the process of consciousness emerging as a form of scarification.[9]

To extend the comparison between the slave and the fetishized object as perceived by others, both have an extremely limited range of agency, largely determined by their possessors. The slave is attributed with spirit, but her biographical history and thus her disposition may only be guessed at by the appearance of scars and aging. As Walter Johnson reminds us, New Orleans was *the* most important domestic slave market in the antebellum South. Slaves were sold at prominent auctions, when not inherited or sold among friends and family or lost to debtors. But Johnson's most important insight regards the emotional aspirations that owners projected onto their slaves—they could never be sure that their gaze was returned in the same way.[10] Like the fetish, this produced anxieties about dissimulation and misrepresentation. Buyers could be sure of ownership but not of (spiritual) possession. The greatest internal contradiction of the slave system was that ontologically slaves were both persons and things. By the nineteenth century, the subject-object divide was more unstable in daily life than it was in philosophy.

Today New Orleans serves as a hub for the antique trade in the United States. I propose that these markets are not unrelated. The point is not to reduce enslaved people once again to the status of objects through comparison, but to explore the modes of value, temporality, and agency that their ontologies share that may account for the peculiar local trade in personified, aging objects. In fact, the implicit connection between the market in slaves and the market in old things may be another reason that many descendants of the enslaved have little interest in collecting and historic preservation. Both enslaved people and antiques are animated by histories and are highly singular, although commodification may attempt to mask their living qualities. Both slaves and antiques defy the commodity logic that is the very condition for their appearance in a market.

Arjun Appadurai claims that "auctions accentuate the commodity dimension" by creating a tournament of value. Slave auctions and antique auctions indeed do this as a form of obfuscation, to hide the biographical life force of the person/object that is not entirely under the control of either buyer or seller. Something even more vital than the social relations of production is being masked. We might understand auctions as an attempt to dim the aura (in Benjamin's sense) of persons and things by making a spectacle of reduction and equivalency. However, auctions of unique beings produce more contradiction than Appadurai suggests, as their singular histories must be visible enough for an evaluation of authenticity and provenance. Aura needs to be dimmed enough to suggest the possibility of possession, but not so much as to suggest the presence of counterfeit.

Does the "tournament of value" succeed? The history of slavery is rich with accounts of the many ways, petit and grand, that slaves resisted their commodification, exchange, and use. Although lacking the undeniable agency of a human being, antiques communicate their singularization at the point of sale and in this way resist commodification. They were not made for the market; they were made through some unreplicable, often unpredictable, process. New Orleans's antique market presents a sentimental paradox. At the point of their appearance in auctions and collector markets, antiques are priced at the same time that they are inalienable from the possession of a larger social body that knows their stories. Their attributed "family histories" reduce the strangerness between seller and buyer. This animating effect occurs particularly with highly narrated objects. Thus objects with the longest family histories and object biographies in an auction catalog will often catch the highest prices.[12] It is hard to say whether these antiques are persons masquerading as commodities or commodities masquerading as persons.

Equally, it is hard to escape the suspicion that the antique fetish in its New Orleans variant arose in part as a response to the contradictions of slavery's commoditized humans who were spiritually unpossessable. The slave who became too old to work was a figure that stretched the system's logic to the breaking point. Such slaves either had to be discarded, with any traces of their humanity ignored, or treated as fully human and deserving of care. To mock the "rational" economy that created such an unstable condition (through Mardi Gras and the city's other alternative circuits of value) was easier than resolving it. Such markets purport not to deal in commodities, but in personlike possessions. In both cases, buyers can indulge in denial of their role in putting a price on life. The results are equivocal. The antique fetish often fails to realize its utopian potential to transform relations. But it does resist compulsive obsolescence and thus slows down consumption and discard. Instead of the commodity's alienated abstraction of congealed labor, the antique represents the barely captive accumulation of subjective experience and affective inheritances of thoughts and habit.

Antiques are not the only objects to trouble commodity value. Souvenirs and heirlooms rarely enter tournaments of value, because they are "often attached to locations and experiences that are not for sale."[13] Not unrelated to the yearning of nostalgia, "there is clearly a yearning for singularization in complex societies . . . that governs the fate of heirlooms and old slippers alike."[14] Two desires coexist: for the youthful, replaceable commodity and for the old, well-worn object in the process of becoming a human story. Most new commodities lose resale value as soon as they are purchased, but eventually, with preservation and the acquisition of a unique biography, they can become antiques or collectibles. Via a multistage process, an object that begins as a generic and replaceable commodity transforms into an idiosyncratic possession with little shared worth and later into a collectively valued treasure. It then moves between human interlocutors who act more like hosts and caretakers than like owners and collectors. The antique and the old house are recognized as objects whose experience transcends human memory. An object that has not only acquired a sort of worn appearance but has done so over several human generations is among the most singular of all. The heirloom that is never allowed to reenter the commodity market, that is exempted from the debasement of circulation and exchange value, belongs to another realm altogether.[15]

The power of the antique fetish derives in part from the dimension of time. Like the magico-religious fetish, it "is never positioned in a stable here-and-now and thereby confounds essentializing strategies that aim for neat resolutions and clear-cut boundaries among things and between persons and objects."[16] As such, it cannot be entirely accounted for by constructivist arguments that focus on instrumentality in the present. Analyses such as the invention-of-tradition approach to heritage require a flattening of time and a denial of social stratigraphy.

While I acknowledge the operation of the commodity fetish, I refuse to generalize fetishism as pathology and deceit. I believe it is a common and understandable mode through which people try to understand the historicity of their social worlds. As in the case of haunted houses and personified chairs, the fetish "is both discursive creation and material reality. . . . It points to an aesthetic sensibility in which the direction of mutual influence of human subjects and thinglike object can be reversed."[17] Or put another way, in the fetish the forced division between subject and object breaks down. In the case of the antique fetish, it is a way in which the dead constitute the living and the living keep the dead present. It is where we locate much-needed ghost stories.

While strong versions of the object-agency argument can be taken too far, objects do possess a kind of autonomy, and they respond to human touch. They can persist beyond human lifeworlds, and they can migrate between them. As Jack described the old buildings of the French Quarter, they have *mana* or "layers of association." An old neighborhood is perhaps the best illustration of the uncanny fact that "artefacts often have longer lives as collectivities than people do."[18] This distinction between people-time and thing-time parallels the difference between historical and archaeological interpretation.

One of my priorities has been to emphasize the temporal aspects of object circulation and value. Archaeology, generously conceived and broadly received, can be a major help in this effort. It operates along intergener-

Truth of patina
in. material? (> modern torm

ational time scales that allow us to see at least three different long-term processes: the unspoken dialectics between the human and object world, the buildup of social stratigraphy, and the development of cultural habits of preservation. Deepening the time dimension helps us better see how communities are constituted by old objects: "Not only are humans as material as the material they mold, but humans themselves are molded, through their sensuousness, by the 'dead' matter with which they are surrounded."[19] And it *is* a matter of the dead. As we witness in New Orleans, houses and other objects that are allowed to rest in a condition of benign neglect eventually become haunted by ghosts. Like the unique art object, old things emit an *aura*. They are individual and solidly authentic, if indexing something not entirely knowable. They almost return our gaze.

Heirlooms and antiques produce social relations between the dead and the living that generate totemic, rhizomic connections. In New Orleans, old things are particularly prone to collective fetishization. This fact relates directly to their accumulation of patina. It is the process by which objects become social things, accumulating signs of their traumas and biographies parallel to, or mimetic of, human lives: "That chair's had a life" (Ann's interview).

Acknowledging the role of ghosts in social life made manifest in old, singularized objects does not negate certain readings of Marx. Derrida, for example, characterizes the relationship between objects and subjects, or matter and thought, as a "specter" that moves in and out of both. Bill Maurer elaborates: "A shadow from another time, whose time has gone, but yet manifests itself in *this* time . . . is *out of sync* with the rest of today's time-space . . . not quite fully in or out of it."[20] I want to emphasize the temporal aspect—the "out of sync" quality of this relation between prior things and present thoughts (and vice versa). I also want to read the "specter of Marx" quite literally, as related to New Orleans's ghost stories. A suitable ending for this story.

Marx's specter ~ Benjamin's aura ~ Durkheim's mana? These ideas address different but related concerns about invisible forces, social relations, and materiality. As seen in the examples illuminating this book, patina captures these forces, these abstractions, and makes them temporarily concrete. Marx's specter represents the history of human relationships that haunt every object. Benjamin's aura corresponds to the singular qualities of certain objects that cannot be reproduced in the commodity form. And Durkheim's mana refers to an evocative force that runs through some objects that makes people feel like they belong to a collectivity.

Valuing patina acknowledges that the surrounding object world preexisted the viewer's consciousness and that it was largely created by other, now unknowable conscious beings. The past is, of course, populated by the dead. By specters. They have a reality that secular society attempts to deny. In addition to setting the scene for chronotopia, patina value demands an awareness of the continuing effect of past generations on the materials and habits of the living, a recognition (not a misrecognition) of social stratigraphy.

Susan Stewart claims a psychoanalytic significance for the patina of sepia-toned photographs and distressed antiques: "The acute sensation of the objects—its perception by hand taking precedence over its perception by eye—promises, and yet does not keep the promise of, *reunion*." Implicitly, patina promises a frustrated reunion with the dead.[21]

> SD: Why do you think people like to hear ghost stories so much?
>
> Jenny: As much as people might want to deny it, they do need to know that there's something beyond them. I mean it's a lonely world. If there's any endemic problem I think in modern Western society, it's loneliness—it's a huge problem.

This huge problem concerned Émile Durkheim too, as did its cause, what he called *anomie*, the loss of social connectivity. *Elementary Forms of Religious Life* can be understood as a nostalgic work. Although he did not advocate a return to animism, Durkheim longs to preserve something that seemed threatened with extinction by the conditions of modernity. He believed that so-called primitive societies were rich in mana, or the totemic principle, "an anonymous and impersonal force . . . an impersonal god . . . immanent in the world, diffused in a numberless multitude of things."[22] I'm not sure what he would have made of New Orleans. It is not a particularly anomic place—quite the opposite. Durkheim's was a melancholy gaze, but New Orleans shows us that it may have been a preemptive one. Space-times that offer alternatives to the lonely, fast aesthetic of modernity and its dominant political economy have not gone away. Over time, they may have even become stronger, thriving off the dialectical tension that makes them exotic and desirable. Perhaps Durkheim's contemporary R. R. Marett could have helped with his more profane definition of mana as "the common element in ghosts and gods . . . the supernal and the infernal, the unknown within and the unknown without."[23] New Orleans often gets characterized as an ungodly place, but one cannot say that it is an unghostly one.

NOTES

1. All direct quotes of New Orleans residents are from recorded interviews conducted between 2008 and 2011 under University of Chicago Institutional Review Board protocol #H08055. Recordings and transcripts are archived by the author. Aliases for the interviewees were chosen or assigned to protect their identities. In some cases, I have slightly modified biographical information when an individual and/or the person's professional affiliation might be easily deduced. In the transcriptions, I omitted false starts and repetitive fillers such as "um" and "you know" and used standard American English spelling, although phonetically some local accents are quite strong. I did not, however, correct for grammar or oddities in local lexicon (these are explained when necessary). Ellipses represent sentences or phrases I omitted from in-text quotes for the sake of brevity.

2. David Dillon, "Big Easy Faces Big Questions," *Dallas Morning News*, November 19, 2005.

3. On Disneyfication, see Jonathan Mark Souther, "The Disneyfication of New Orleans: The French Quarter as Facade in a Divided City," *Journal of American History* 94 (2007): 804–11.

4. Daniel Sieberg and Soledad O'Brien, "Preserving New Orleans' Military History," *CNN American Morning*, November 11, 2005.

5. Lori K. Gordon, *The Katrina Collection*, 2008.

6. To name just a few works on other "antique" cities: Alaa El-Habashi and Ihab Elzeyadi, "Consuming Built Patrimony: Social Perspectives and Preservation Strategies in Modern Cairo," *Traditional Dwellings and Settlements Review* 10, no. 1 (October 1, 1998): 18; Christoph Brumann, "Outside the Glass Case: The Social Life of Urban Heritage in Kyoto," *American Ethnologist* 36, no. 2 (May 1, 2009): 276–99; Teresa Stoppani, "Venice, Time, and the Meander," *Log* 12 (April 1, 2008): 131–43; Susan Kepecs, "Saving Old Havana," *Archaeology* 55, no. 2 (March 1, 2002): 42–47; Morna Livingston, "Houses That Dream in Cuban: The Crumbling of Old Havana," *Traditional Dwellings and Settlements Review* 6, no. 1 (October 1, 1994): 69–70. Of course, "imagined community" comes from Benedict R. Anderson, *Imagined Communities: Reflections on the Origin and Spread of Nationalism*, rev. ed. (London: Verso, 2006).

7. For example: Eric Arnesen, *Waterfront Workers of New Orleans: Race, Class, and Poli-*

tics, 1863–1923 (New York: Oxford University Press, 1991); Richard Campanella, *Geographies of New Orleans: Urban Fabrics before the Storm* (Lafayette: Center for Louisiana Studies, 2006); Leonard N. Moore, *Black Rage in New Orleans: Police Brutality and African American Activism from World War II to Hurricane Katrina* (Baton Rouge: Louisiana State University Press, 2010); Peirce F. Lewis, *New Orleans: The Making of an Urban Landscape,* 2nd ed. (Charlottesville: University of Virginia Press, 2003); Lawrence N. Powell, *The Accidental City: Improvising New Orleans* (Cambridge, MA: Harvard University Press, 2012); Michael Eric Dyson, *Come Hell or High Water: Hurricane Katrina and the Color of Disaster* (New York: Basic Civitas, 2006); David L. Brunsma, David Overfelt, and J. Steven Picou, eds., *The Sociology of Katrina: Perspectives on a Modern Catastrophe* (Lanham, MD: Rowman & Littlefield, 2007).

8. In 2012 New Orleans hosted 9 million visitors, or twenty-four times the number of its residents. In 2005, 77 percent of resident New Orleanians were born in Louisiana, according to www.datacenterresearch.org/.

9. Although they recognized that something beyond Marx's alienation was taking place, thinkers such as Georg Simmel, Walter Benjamin, and Theodor Adorno did not agree on whether the commodity and the city were ultimately dangerous in their enchantment. For excellent overviews of these conversations, see Wolfgang Fritz Haug, *Critique of Commodity Aesthetics: Appearance, Sexuality, and Advertising in Capitalist Society* (Minneapolis: University of Minnesota Press, 1986); and part 1 of Neil Leach, ed., *Rethinking Architecture: A Reader in Cultural Theory* (New York: Routledge, 1997).

10. I follow convention in here using *modernity* to describe a general ideology of progress and its attendant institutions in development since the late Enlightenment, and *modernism* to describe the aesthetic principles of art and architecture that dominated the twentieth century. Both should be considered global phenomena, even if the loudest mouthpieces came out of Europe.

11. Svetlana Boym, *The Future of Nostalgia* (New York: Basic Books, 2001).

12. "American Indian" is the preferred term, according to the *Chicago Manual of Style,* 16th edition, and a plurality of U.S. Indian activists and scholars. It is used here as equivalent to "Native American" and "First Nations," terms for which there are also appealing rationales.

13. On the IRB, see note 1.

14. This is not to say that I do not produce work from these same excavations within the more accepted archaeological paradigm. I have and I will continue to do so, but that is not the aim and mode of this book.

15. For recent volumes that set an agenda for the archaeology of the contemporary, see Alfredo González Ruibal, ed., *Reclaiming Archaeology: Beyond the Tropes of Modernity,* Archaeological Orientations (Milton Park, Abingdon, UK: Routledge, 2013); Paul Graves-Brown, ed., *The Oxford Handbook of the Archaeology of the Contemporary World,* Oxford Handbooks (Oxford: Oxford University Press, 2013); Paul Graves-Brown, *Matter, Materiality, and Modern Culture* (London: Routledge, 2000); Rodney Harrison and A. J. Schofield, *After Modernity: Archaeological Approaches to the Contemporary Past* (Oxford: Oxford University Press, 2010).

16. Graeme Gilloch, *Walter Benjamin: Critical Constellations* (Cambridge, UK: Polity Press; Malden, MA: Blackwell, 2002), quote on 114; see Walter Benjamin, "Excavation and

Memory," in *Selected Writings, 1931–1934,* ed. Michael W. Jennings, Howard Eiland, and Gary Smith (Cambridge, MA: Belknap Press, 1999), 576. As noted by others, archaeological tropes emerge throughout Benjamin's work in several contexts and uses. I am not alone in attempting to bring Benjamin to bear on archaeology proper. See, for example, Laurent Olivier, *The Dark Abyss of Time: Archaeology and Memory,* trans. Arthur Greenspan, Archaeology in Society Series (Lanham, MD: AltaMira Press, 2011); Jeffrey Schnapp, Michael Shanks, and Matthew Tiews, "Editor's Introduction," *Modernism/Modernity* 11 (2004): 1–16. For my own position on temporality and the anthropological subdisciplines, see Shannon Lee Dawdy, "Clockpunk Anthropology and the Ruins of Modernity," *Current Anthropology* 51, no. 6 (December 1, 2010): 761–93.

17. Walter Benjamin, *The Arcades Project,* ed. Rolf Tiedemann, trans. Howard Eiland (Cambridge, MA: Belknap Press, 1999); Walter Benjamin, "Surrealism: The Last Snapshot of the European Intelligentsia," in *Walter Benjamin: Selected Writings,* 2:207–21 (Cambridge, MA: Belknap, 2004).

18. Susan Buck-Morss, *The Dialectics of Seeing: Walter Benjamin and the Arcades Project* (Cambridge, MA: MIT Press, 1989); Max Pensky, "Method and Time: Benjamin's Dialectical Images," in *The Cambridge Companion to Walter Benjamin,* ed. David S. Ferris, Cambridge Companions to Literature (Cambridge: Cambridge University Press, 2004), 177–98.

19. Miriam Hansen, *Cinema and Experience: Siegfried Kracauer, Walter Benjamin, and Theodor W. Adorno* (Berkeley: University of California Press, 2012), 106.

20. Cited in ibid., 107 and 108.

21. Emile Durkheim, *The Elementary Forms of Religious Life,* trans. Karen Fields (New York: Free Press, 1995), quotes on 191, 327.

22. Mary Douglas, *Purity and Danger: An Analysis of Concepts of Pollution and Taboo,* Routledge Classics (London: Routledge, 2002); Edmund Ronald Leach, *Political Systems of Highland Burma: A Study of Kachin Social Structure* (Boston: Beacon Press, 1967), 12.

23. *Merriam-Webster Collegiate Dictionary,* 11th ed.

24. Randolph Starn, "Three Ages of 'Patina' in Painting," *Representations* 78 (2002): 86–115; Filippo Baldinucci, *Vocabolario Toscano dell'arte del disegno* (Firenze: Santi Franchi, 1681).

25. E. H. Gombrich, *The Heritage of Apelles* (Ithaca, NY: Cornell University Press, 1976).

26. Eileen Cleere, "Dirty Pictures: John Ruskin, 'Modern Painters,' and the Victorian Sanitation of Fine Art," *Representations* 78 (2002): 116–39; Darcy Grimaldo Grigsby, "Patina, Painting, and Portentous Somethings," *Representations* 78 (2002): 140–44; Starn, "Three Ages of 'Patina'"; Boym, *Future of Nostalgia,* 12.

27. Grant David McCracken, *Culture and Consumption: New Approaches to the Symbolic Character of Consumer Goods and Activities* (Bloomington: Indiana University Press, 1988).

28. Grigsby, "Patina, Painting, and Portentous Somethings"; Starn, "Three Ages of 'Patina.'"

29. John Ruskin, *The Seven Lamps of Architecture* (London,: Smith Elder, 1849), aphorism 30, pp. 86–87.

30. Ibid., 178, 194–95.

31. Leach, *Political Systems of Highland Burma,* 12.

32. Alois Riegl, "The Modern Cult of Monuments: Its Character and Its Origin," in *The Nineteenth-Century Visual Culture Reader,* ed. J. M. Przyblyski and V. R. Schwartz (New

York: Routledge, 2004), 56–59; Mike Gubser, *Time's Visible Surface: Alois Riegl and the Discourse on History and Temporality in Fin-de-Siècle Vienna*, Kritik: German Literary Theory and Cultural Studies (Detroit: Wayne State University Press, 2006).

33. Madalina Diaconu, "Patina—Atmosphere—Aroma: Towards an Aesthetics of Fine Differences," in *Logos of Phenomenology and Phenomenology of the Logos: The Creative Logos: Aesthetic Ciphering in Fine Arts, Literature and Aesthetics*, ed. A. T. Tyminiecka (Dordrecht, Netherlands: Kluwer, 2006), 131–48, quote on 133.

34. Henry W. Nichols, *Restoration of Ancient Bronzes and Cure of Malignant Patina* (Chicago: Field Museum of Natural History, 1930), 130.

35. The cultivation of patina, whether faked or preserved, plays a prominent part in Boym's reflective nostalgia that "lingers on ruins, the patina of time and history, in the dreams of another place and another time." Boym, *Future of Nostalgia*, 41.

36. Yuriko Saito, *Everyday Aesthetics* (London: Oxford University Press, 2008), 184. On environmental aesthetics, see Allen Carlson, *Nature and Landscape: An Introduction to Environmental Aesthetics* (New York: Columbia University Press, 2009); Martinus Antonius Maria Drenthen and Jozef Keulartz, eds., *Environmental Aesthetics: Crossing Divides and Breaking Ground*, Groundworks: Ecological Issues in Philosophy and Theology (New York: Fordham University Press, 2014); Jack L. Nasar, ed., *Environmental Aesthetics: Theory, Research, and Applications* (Cambridge: Cambridge University Press, 1988).

37. Walter Benjamin, "The Work of Art in the Age of Mechanical Reproduction," in *Illuminations*, ed. Hannah Arendt, trans. Harry Zohn (New York: Schocken Books, 1986), 217–51, quote on 239. See also letter no. 47 in Theodor W. Adorno, Henri Lonitz, and Walter Benjamin, *The Complete Correspondence, 1928–1940* (Cambridge, MA: Harvard University Press, 1999). I am grateful to William Mazzarella for pointing toward Benjamin's *distraction*. I otherwise would been too distracted to notice!

38. Technically, however, qualisigns are a kind of icon in Peirce's overlapping trichotomies for classifying the sign-referent relationship. Being faithful to his complex taxonomy is not as helpful as fleshing out examples of his different types to understand how they work. Munn's application and elaboration of Peirce's qualisign have been quite influential in anthropology. See, for example, Nicolas Harkness and Lily Hope Chumley, eds., "Qualia," special issue, *Anthropological Theory* 13 (March–June 2013).

39. Terry Eagleton, *The Ideology of the Aesthetic* (Cambridge, MA: Basil Blackwell, 1990), 13.

40. For a similar view from another angle, see Ben Highmore, *Everyday Life and Cultural Theory: An Introduction* (New York: Routledge, 2002).

CHAPTER TWO

1. For details on the site's history and the archaeological project, see Shannon Lee Dawdy and Juana L. C. Ibáñez, *Beneath the Surface of New Orleans's Warehouse District: Archaeological Investigations at the Maginnis Cotton Mill Site* (New Orleans: University of New Orleans, College of Urban and Public Affairs, 1997). All of the author's cited archaeological reports are available online. Current address: http://home.uchicago.edu/~sdawdy/home.html.

2. Jack D. L. Holmes, "Indigo in Colonial Louisiana and the Floridas," *Louisiana History* 8, no. 4 (1967): 329–49.

3. *History*, when defined separately from *the past* (what happened), is usually understood to mean a linear narration of events selected as being important for explaining something (a major event like a revolution, a collapse of a civilization, conditions of the present). What is meant by *collective memory* is more troubling, and I have not been able to resolve my frustration with the literature sufficiently to become comfortable using it, although I do at times refer to individual memories. While I resist heavy-handed versions of the invention-of-tradition thesis, I feel that most collective memories can *only* be inventions, particularly when projected back into past generations and given that the intangible record of experience is subjected to the same taphonomic processes that affect physical evidence. For some popular definitions, see R. G. Collingwood, *The Idea of History,* rev. ed., with lectures 1926–28 (Oxford: Oxford University Press, 1994); Maurice Halbwachs, *On Collective Memory,* Heritage of Sociology (Chicago: University of Chicago Press, 1992); Paul Connerton, *How Societies Remember,* Themes in the Social Sciences (Cambridge: Cambridge University Press, 1989); Brigittine M. French, "The Semiotics of Collective Memories," *Annual Review of Anthropology* 41 (2012): 337–53; David Lowenthal, *The Past Is a Foreign Country* (Cambridge: Cambridge University Press, 1985).

4. Charles S. Peirce, *Writings of Charles S. Peirce: A Chronological Edition* (Bloomington: Indiana University Press, 1982).

5. Pierre Nora, "Between Memory and History: Les Lieux de Mémoire," *Representations* 26 (1989): 7–24. See also Marie Louise Stig Sørensen, *Heritage Studies: Methods and Approaches* (New York: Routledge, 2009); Lynn Meskell, *The Nature of Heritage: The New South Africa* (Hoboken, NJ: Wiley, 2011); Beverley Butler, "Heritage and Present Past," in *Handbook of Material Culture,* ed. Chris Tilley et al. (Thousand Oaks, CA: SAGE, 2006), 463–79; Rodney Harrison, *Heritage: Critical Approaches* (Milton Park, Abingdon, UK: Routledge, 2013).

6. Eric J. Hobsbawm and Terence O. Ranger, *The Invention of Tradition* (Cambridge; New York: Cambridge University Press, 1983), 1–2.

7. Lowenthal, *Past Is a Foreign Country,* xvi. Cf. Reinhart Koselleck, *Futures Past: On the Semantics of Historical Time* (Cambridge, MA: MIT Press, 1985).

8. Martin Heidegger, *Poetry, Language, Thought,* His Works (New York: Harper & Row, 1971); Hannah Arendt, *The Human Condition,* 2nd ed. (Chicago: University of Chicago Press, 1998), 96.

9. Edmund Husserl, *On the Phenomenology of the Consciousness of Internal Time (1893–1917),* in *Collected Works,* vol. 4 (Dordrecht, Netherlands: Kluwer Academic, 1991). For helpful explanations of Husserl's ideas, see Gavin Lucas, *The Archaeology of Time* (London: Routledge, 2005); Robin Le Poidevin and Murray MacBeath, eds., *The Philosophy of Time,* Oxford Readings in Philosophy (Oxford: Oxford University Press, 1993).

10. Johannes Fabian, *Time and the Other: How Anthropology Makes Its Object* (New York: Columbia University Press, 1983); Nancy M. Farriss, "Remembering the Future, Anticipating the Past: History, Time, and Cosmology among the Maya of Yucatan," *Comparative Studies in Society and History* 29, no. 3 (1987): 566–93; Thomas M. Allen, *A Republic in Time: Temporality and Social Imagination in Nineteenth-Century America* (Chapel Hill:

University of North Carolina Press, 2008); Nancy D. Munn, "The Cultural Anthropology of Time: A Critical Essay," *Annual Review of Anthropology* 21 (1992): 93–123.

11. Nancy D. Munn, *The Fame of Gawa: A Symbolic Study of Value Transformation in a Massim (Papua New Guinea) Society* (Durham, NC: Duke University Press, 1992).

12. Lucas, *Archaeology of Time*, 43; Cornelius Holtorf, "The Presence of Pastness: Themed Environments and Beyond," in *Staging the Past: Themed Environments in Transcultural Perspectives*, ed. Judith Schlehe, Michiko Uike-Bormann, Carolyn Oesterle, and Wolfgang Hochbruck, Historische Lebenswelten in Populären Wissenskulturen, vol. 2 (Bielefeld: Transcript, 2010), 23–40, quote on 23.

13. The term *heterotemporality* is from the introduction to Alfredo González Ruibal, ed., *Reclaiming Archaeology: Beyond the Tropes of Modernity*, Archaeological Orientations (Milton Park, Abingdon, UK: Routledge, 2013). See also Richard Bradley, *The Past in Prehistoric Societies* (London: Routledge, 2002); Christopher Witmore, "Landscape, Time, Topology: An Archaeological Account of the Southern Argolid Greece," in *Envisioning Landscape: Situations and Standpoints in Archaeology and Heritage,* ed. Daniel Hicks, Laura McAtackney, and Graham J. Fairclough (Walnut Creek, CA: Left Coast Press, 2007), 194–225; Laurent Olivier, "The Past of the Present: Archaeological Memory and Time," *Archaeological Dialogues* 10, no. 2 (2004): 204–13; Laurent Olivier, *The Dark Abyss of Time: Archaeology and Memory,* Archaeology in Society Series (Lanham, MD: AltaMira Press, 2011).

14. Marcel Proust, *Remembrance of Things Past* (New York: Random House, 1981).

15. Walter Benjamin, *The Arcades Project*, ed. Rolf Tiedemann, trans. Howard Eiland (Cambridge, MA: Belknap Press, 1999), convolute N, p. 462.

16. Shannon Lee Dawdy, *Building the Devil's Empire: French Colonial New Orleans* (Chicago: University of Chicago Press, 2008).

17. Philip Pittman, *The Present State of the European Settlements on the Mississippi; with a Geographical Description of That River* (London: Printed for J. Nourse, 1770), 10–11.

18. James Pitot and Robert D. Bush, *Observations on the Colony of Louisiana, from 1796 to 1802* (Baton Rouge: Louisiana State University Press, 1979), 108.

19. Benjamin H. Latrobe, *The Journals of Benjamin Henry Latrobe, 1799–1820: From Philadelphia to New Orleans,* ed. E. C. Carter, J. C. Van Horne, L. W. Formwalt, and M. H. Society (New Haven, CT: Yale University Press, 1980), 3:171.

20. Ibid., 3:193–95, "old character," 266; Renato Rosaldo, *Culture & Truth: The Remaking of Social Analysis: With a New Introduction* (Boston: Beacon Press, 1993).

21. Latrobe, *Journals of Benjamin Henry Latrobe,* 3:255.

22. For details on the cathedral's history and our archaeological research, see Shannon Lee Dawdy, Kristen Gremillon, Susan Mulholland, and Jason Ramsey, *Archaeological Investigations at St. Anthony's Garden (160R443), New Orleans, Louisiana,* vol. 1, *2008 Fieldwork and Archaeobotanical Results* (Chicago: University of Chicago, Department of Anthropology, 2008); Shannon Lee Dawdy, Claire Bowman, Kristen Gremillon, Susan deFrance, and Lauren Zych, *Archaeological Investigations at St. Anthony's Garden (160R443), New Orleans, Louisiana,* vol. 2, *2009 Fieldwork and Final Laboratory Analysis for 2008 and 2009 Seasons* (Chicago: University of Chicago, Department of Anthropology, 2014); Shannon Lee Dawdy and Claire Bowman, *Archaeological Investigations at St. Anthony's Garden (160R443), New*

Orleans, Louisiana, vol. 3, *Artifact Inventory for 2008 and 2009 Seasons* (Chicago: University of Chicago, Department of Anthropology, 2013).

23. Thomas Metzinger, *Being No One: The Self-Model Theory of Subjectivity* (Cambridge, MA: MIT Press, 2003).

24. Nancy D. Munn, "Gawan Kula: Spatiotemporal Control and the Symbolism of Influence," in *The Kula: New Perspectives on Massim Exchange,* ed. E. Leach and J. Leach (Cambridge: Cambridge University Press, 1983), 277–308.

25. Shannon Lee Dawdy et al., *Archaeological Investigations at St. Anthony's Garden (160R443), New Orleans, Louisiana,* vol. 2, *2009 Fieldwork and Final Laboratory Analysis for 2008 and 2009 Seasons* (Chicago: University of Chicago, Department of Anthropology, 2014).

26. See chapter 5.

27. Shannon Lee Dawdy et al., *Archaeological Investigations at the Rising Sun Hotel Site, New Orleans, Louisiana* (Chicago: University of Chicago, Department of Anthropology, 2008).

28. Pierre Bourdieu, *Outline of a Theory of Practice,* Cambridge Studies in Social Anthropology, 16 (Cambridge: Cambridge University Press, 1977); Philip S. Gorski, ed., *Bourdieu and Historical Analysis,* Politics, History, and Culture (Durham, NC: Duke University Press, 2013). My points here are a variation on a theme Ann L. Stoler outlines in, "Imperial Debris: Reflections on Ruins and Ruination," *Cultural Anthropology* 23, no. 2 (2008): 191–219.

29. Emile Durkheim, *The Elementary Forms of Religious Life,* trans. Karen Fields (New York: Free Press, 1995), 214.

CHAPTER THREE

1. The story is "Tite Poulette," in George Washington Cable, *Old Creole Days* (New York: C. Scribner's, 1879). Inheritance by free women of color was a common pattern in historic New Orleans; see Emily Clark, *The Strange History of the American Quadroon: Free Women of Color in the Revolutionary Atlantic World* (Chapel Hill: University of North Carolina Press, 2013).

2. For details on property history and excavation, see Shannon Lee Dawdy, "Madame John's Legacy (160R51) Revisited: A Closer Look at the Archaeology of Colonial New Orleans," 1998, University of New Orleans. On Madame Real, Shannon Lee Dawdy, *Building the Devil's Empire: French Colonial New Orleans* (Chicago: University of Chicago Press, 2008).

3. Claude Lévi-Strauss, *The Way of the Masks,* trans. Sylvia Modelski (Seattle: University of Washington Press, 1982).

4. T. J. Jackson Lears, *No Place of Grace: Antimodernism and the Transformation of American Culture, 1880–1920* (Chicago: University of Chicago Press, 1994), quote on xv. See also Stephen Copley and Peter Garside, eds., *The Politics of the Picturesque: Literature, Landscape, and Aesthetics since 1770* (Cambridge: Cambridge University Press, 1994); John Macarthur, *The Picturesque: Architecture, Disgust and Other Irregularities,* Classical Tradition in Architecture (London: Routledge, 2007).

5. See, for example, William Kingsford, *Impressions of the West and South during a Six Weeks' Holiday* (Toronto: A. H. Armour, 1858); Frederick Law Olmstead, *A Journey in the Seaboard States: With Remarks on Their Economy* (New York: Dix and Edwards, 1856); George A. Sala, *America Revisited: From the Bay of New York to the Gulf of Mexico, and from Lake Michigan to the Pacific* (London: Vizetelly, 1885); and Arthur Singleton, *Letters from the South and West* (Boston: Richardson and Lord, 1824).

6. Cable, *Old Creole Days*, 1–2.

7. Ibid., 2.

8. Edward W. Said, *Orientalism*, vol. 1 (New York: Pantheon Books, 1978).

9. Lafcadio Hearn and S. Frederick Starr, *Inventing New Orleans: Writings of Lafcadio Hearn* (Jackson: University Press of Mississippi, 2001), quotes on 7, 13. See also Lafcadio Hearn, *Lafcadio Hearn's Japan: An Anthology of His Writings on the Country and Its People* (Rutland, VT: Charles E. Tuttle, 1997). On imperialist nostalgia, see Renato Rosaldo, *Culture & Truth: The Remaking of Social Analysis: With a New Introduction* (Boston: Beacon Press, 1993).

10. Henry C. Castellanos and George F. Reinecke, *New Orleans as It Was: Episodes of Louisiana Life* (Baton Rouge: Louisiana State University Press, 1978), ix–x. For other writers of this generation, see W. H. Coleman, *Historical Sketch Book and Guide to New Orleans and Environs . . .* (New York: W. H. Coleman, 1885); Alcée Fortier, *Louisiana Folk-Tales, in French Dialect and English Translation* (New York: Houghton Mifflin, 1895).

11. Strong studies of New Orleans's tourism complex have emerged in recent years, and each allocates space for an account of historic preservation in New Orleans, along with Mardi Gras and jazz. Kevin Fox Gotham, *Authentic New Orleans: Tourism, Culture, and Race in the Big Easy* (New York: New York University Press, 2007); Jonathan Mark Souther, *New Orleans on Parade: Tourism and the Transformation of the Crescent City*, Making the Modern South (Baton Rouge: Louisiana State University Press, 2006); Anthony J. Stanonis, *Creating the Big Easy: New Orleans and the Emergence of Modern Tourism, 1918–1945* (Athens: University of Georgia Press, 2006); Lynnell L. Thomas, *Desire & Disaster in New Orleans: Tourism, Race, and Historical Memory* (Durham, NC: Duke University Press, 2014).

12. Grace E. King, *New Orleans: The Place and the People* (New York: Macmillan, 1917); Lyle Saxon and E. H. Suydam, *Fabulous New Orleans* (New York: Century, 1928); Robert Tallant, *Voodoo in New Orleans* (New York: Macmillan, 1946); R. Tallant, *The Romantic New Orleanians*, vol. 1 (New York: Dutton, 1950); Harnett T. Kane, *Queen New Orleans, City by the River* (New York: W. Morrow, 1949). These writers bristled at the more popular, and in their eyes prurient, depiction by Herbert Asbury, *The French Quarter: An Informal History of the New Orleans Underworld* (New York: A. A. Knopf, 1936).

13. John Shelton Reed, *Dixie Bohemia: A French Quarter Circle in the 1920s* (Baton Rouge: Louisiana State University Press, 2012).

14. Cited in Souther, *New Orleans on Parade*, 6.

15. Stanonis, *Creating the Big Easy*, 28. On the architecture of the French Quarter, see Jay D. Edwards, "New Orleans Shotgun: An Historic Cultural Geography," in *Culture in the Wake: Rhetoric and Reinvention on the Gulf Coast*, ed. M. B. Hackler (Jackson: University Press of Mississippi, 2010); Malcolm Heard, *French Quarter Manual: An Architectural Guide to New Orleans' Vieux Carré* (New Orleans: Tulane School of Architecture, 1997).

16. Stanonis, *Creating the Big Easy*, 148–49.

17. Ibid., 26, 31, 74, Sherwood cited on 42. Locally the Depression resulted in an unemployment rate 40 percent higher than the rest of the country, exacerbated by Prohibition. Breweries were the city's second-largest revenue generator, after entertainment.

18. On the remarkable fluorescence of the women of Newcomb College, see David H. Conradsen, Newcomb Art Gallery, and Smithsonian Institution, *The Arts & Crafts of Newcomb Pottery* (New York: Skira Rizzoli; New Orleans: Tulane University, Newcomb Art Gallery, 2013).

19. William Faulkner, *Mosquitoes* (New York: Boni and Liveright, 1927).

20. Souther, *New Orleans on Parade*, 44.

21. City of New Orleans, Municipal Code. www.municode.com/library/la/new_orleans /codes/code_of_ordinances?nodeId=PTIICO_CH130SEGO (accessed April 11, 2015). See also Stanonis, *Creating the Big Easy*, 156.

22. Quoted in Stanonis, *Creating the Big Easy*, 164.

23. Souther, *New Orleans on Parade*, 44.

24. Randall Kenan, *Walking on Water: Black American Lives at the Turn of the Twenty-First Century* (New York: Knopf, 1999), 504–5.

25. Gotham, *Authentic New Orleans*, 195. See also John L. Comaroff and Jean Comaroff, eds., *Ethnicity, Inc.,* Chicago Studies in Practices of Meaning (Chicago: University of Chicago Press, 2009).

26. See especially Richard O. Baumbach, *The Second Battle of New Orleans: A History of the Vieux Carré Riverfront Expressway Controversy* (University: Published for the Preservation Press, National Trust for Historic Preservation in the United States, by the University of Alabama Press, 1981).

27. Samuel Wilson Jr. (1911–1993) was a major figure in this local architectural history as an architect, historian, teacher, and rare manuscript collector (his major essays are collected in Samuel Wilson Jr., *The Architecture of Colonial Louisiana: Collected Essays of Samuel Wilson, Jr.*, ed. Jean M. Farnsworth and Ann Masson [Lafayette: Center for Louisiana Studies, 1987]). He was the protégé of another architect and collector, Richard Koch (1889–1971). Together they formed the architectural firm of Koch and Wilson in 1955, a firm still in operation today that dominates the high-profile historic restoration projects in the French Quarter and across the Gulf states.

28. The Vieux Carré Survey is available digitally at www.hnoc.org/vcs/.

29. David Dillon, "Big Easy Faces Big Questions," *Dallas Morning News*, November 19, 2005. Gotham, *Authentic New Orleans*.

30. Danny Ryan Gray, "Effacing the 'Imagined Slum': Space, Subjectivity, and Sociality in the Margins of New Orleans" (PhD diss., University of Chicago, 2012); Jordan Flaherty, *Floodlines: Community and Resistance from Katrina to the Jena Six* (Chicago: Haymarket Books, 2010).

31. Jeremy Alford, "Public Housing's 'Legacy Buildings,'" *Gambit*, July 24, 2012. Public housing has been reduced 85 percent since Katrina.

32. Dell Upton, "Black and White Landscapes in Eighteenth-Century Virginia," *Places* 2, no. 2 (1984): 59–72.

33. For those unfamiliar, see Zada N. Johnson, "Walking the Post-disaster City: Race,

Space and the Politics of Tradition in the African-American Parading Practices of Post-Katrina New Orleans" (PhD diss., University of Chicago, 2010); Michael P. Smith, *Mardi Gras Indians* (Gretna, LA: Pelican, 1994).

34. From the Latin for "nod": "a spiritual force or influence often identified with a natural object, phenomenon, or place." *Merriam-Webster Dictionary*, online edition, www.merriam -webster.com/dictionary/numen (accessed May 9, 2015).

35. Militaryspeak for Meals Ready to Eat, distributed to remaining and returning residents after the storm.

36. Out of respect for J.J., I have decided to leave the transcript undoctored except for standardizing the spelling ("th," for example, is actually pronounced "d"), reflecting his thick New Orleans dialect, some version of which individuals from across the socioeconomic spectrum can drop into, depending on situational context (comfort level with listener, whether listener has local ties, the topic, etc.).

37. Emile Durkheim, *The Elementary Forms of Religious Life*, trans. Karen Fields (New York: Free Press, 1995), 280.

CHAPTER FOUR

1. Shannon Lee Dawdy et al., *Archaeological Investigations at the Rising Sun Hotel Site, New Orleans, Louisiana* (Chicago: University of Chicago, Department of Anthropology, 2008); Denis Diderot and Jean Le Rond d'Alembert, eds., *The Encyclopedia of Diderot and d'Alembert Collaborative Translation Project* (Ann Arbor: Scholarly Publishing Office of the University of Michigan and DLXS, 2002).

2. Scott Gold, "New Orleans Legend May Prove to Be Reputable," *Los Angeles Times*, March 20, 2005, A1.

3. Lafcadio Hearn and S. Frederick Starr, *Inventing New Orleans: Writings of Lafcadio Hearn* (Jackson: University Press of Mississippi, 2001), 173–74.

4. William Faulkner, *Mosquitoes* (New York: Boni and Liveright, 1927), 10.

5. Ibid., 15.

6. Edward W. Said, *Orientalism*, vol. 1 (New York: Pantheon Books, 1978); Ussama Makdisi, "Ottoman Orientalism," *American Historical Review* 107, no. 3 (2002): 768–96, quote on 768; Erik Camayd-Freixas, ed., *Orientalism and Identity in Latin America: Fashioning Self and Other from the (Post)colonial Margin* (Tucson: University of Arizona Press, 2013); Elisabeth Oxfeldt *Nordic Orientalism: Paris and the Cosmopolitan Imagination, 1800–1900* (Copenhagen: Museum Tusculanum, 2005).

7. Said, *Orientalism*, 103. Although "the other" was a term used by Hegel, Said purposely identifies his genealogy as feminist, through Simone de Beauvoir, who popularized the term for social criticism from the viewpoint of the excluded and objectified.

8. Ibid., 89, 91.

9. Makdisi, "Ottoman Orientalism," 771; Johannes Fabian, *Time and the Other: How Anthropology Makes Its Object* (New York: Columbia University Press, 1983).

10. On French colonialism and medinas see Paul Rabinow, *French Modern: Norms and*

Forms of the Social Environment (Cambridge, MA: MIT Press, 1989); Gwendolyn Wright, *The Politics of Design in French Colonial Urbanism* (Chicago: University of Chicago Press, 1991).

11. Alan Lomax, *The Folk Songs of North America* (Garden City, NY: Double Day, 1960), 280; Dawdy et al., *Investigations at Rising Sun Site;* Ted Anthony, *Chasing the Rising Sun: The Journey of an American Song* (New York: Simon & Schuster, 2007).

12. Shannon Lee Dawdy, "Sexualizing Space: The Colonial Leer and the Genealogy of Storyville," in *The Archaeology of Colonialism: Intimate Encounters and Sexual Effects,* ed. Barbara Voss and Eleanor Casella (New York: Cambridge University Press, 2011), 271–89.

13. Kevin Fox Gotham, *Authentic New Orleans: Tourism, Culture, and Race in the Big Easy* (New York: New York University Press, 2007); Julie Scott and Tom Selwyn, *Thinking through Tourism* (Oxford: Berg, 2010); George Paul Meiu, "Ethno-Erotic Economies: Crafting Samburu Futures in Postcolonial Kenya" (PhD diss., University of Chicago, 2013).

14. Frank A. De Caro and Rosen A. Jordan, eds., *Louisiana Sojourns: Travelers' Tales and Literary Journeys* (Baton Rouge: Louisiana State University Press, 1998); Timothy Flint, *Recollections of the Last Ten Years Passed in Occasional Residences and Journeyings in the Valley of the Mississippi . . .* (Boston: Cummings, Hilliard, 1826).

15. The Pitot House was moved to the site in 1964 to save it from the wrecking ball for the expansion of a Catholic school next door. We knew this, but we expected that the lot would yield information on the longer occupation of Bayou St. John.

16. *New Orleans Louisiana Gazette,* July 4, 1806, New Orleans Public Library microfilm; Al Rose, *Storyville, New Orleans: Being an Authentic, Illustrated Account of the Notorious Red-Light District* (University: University of Alabama Press, 1974), 65.

17. *New Orleans Louisiana Gazette,* March 22, 1808, *Courrier de la Louisiane* (New Orleans, LA), March 14, 1821.

18. Marc-Antoine Caillot, "Relation du Voyage de la Louisianne ou Nouvelle France fait par Sr. Caillot en l'Annee 1730," manuscript, Historic New Orleans Collection, MSS 596, fols. 105–6; Dumont de Montigny, "Mémoire de Lxx Dxx officier ingénieur, contenant les evenements qui se sont passés à la Louisiane depuis 1715 jusqu'à present," manuscript, Newberry Library, Ayer MS 257, fol. 170. I have provided here my own translations of the original texts, but recent English translations of these remarkable accounts are now available. See Marc-Antoine Caillot, *A Company Man: The Remarkable French-Atlantic Voyage of a Clerk for the Company of the Indies: A Memoir,* ed. Erin M. Greenwald, trans. Teri F. Chalmers (New Orleans, Louisiana: Historic New Orleans Collection, 2013); Dumont de Montigny, *The Memoir of Lieutenant Dumont, 1715–1747: A Sojourner in the French Atlantic,* trans. Gordon M. Sayre (Chapel Hill: University of North Carolina Press; Williamsburg, VA: Omohundro Institute of Early American History and Culture, 2012).

19. Daniel H. Usner, *Indians, Settlers, & Slaves in a Frontier Exchange Economy: The Lower Mississippi Valley before 1783* (Chapel Hill: Published for the Institute of Early American History and Culture, Williamsburg, VA, by University of North Carolina Press, 1992); Shannon Lee Dawdy et al., *Archaeological Investigations at St. Anthony's Garden (160R443), New Orleans, Louisiana,* vol. 2, *2009 Fieldwork and Final Laboratory Analysis for 2008 and 2009 Seasons* (Chicago: University of Chicago, Department of Anthropology, 2014).

20. Caillot, *Relation du Voyage,* fols. 133 (quote), 159.

21. Ibid., fols. 160–63.

22. Dawdy, "Sexualizing Space."

23. Nathalie Dessens, *From Saint-Domingue to New Orleans: Migration and Influences*, Southern Dissent (Gainesville: University Press of Florida, 2007); Samuel C. Shepherd, ed., *New Orleans and Urban Louisiana*, Louisiana Purchase Bicentennial Series in Louisiana History, vol. 14 (Lafayette: Center for Louisiana Studies, University of Louisiana at Lafayette, 2005); Carl A. Brasseaux and University of Southwestern Louisiana, eds., *A Refuge for All Ages: Immigration in Louisiana History*, Louisiana Purchase Bicentennial Series, vol. 10 (Lafayette: Center for Louisiana Studies, University of Southwestern Louisiana, 1996); Jay Gitlin, *The Bourgeois Frontier: French Towns, French Traders, and American Expansion* (New Haven, CT: Yale University Press, 2010).

24. Quoted in De Caro and Jordan, *Louisiana Sojourns*, 86.

25. Fragments from a minimum of thirteen rouge pots were found in a small sample from the Rising Sun Hotel stratum. For more on the history of French cosmetics, see Shannon Lee Dawdy and Richard Weyhing, "Beneath the Rising Sun: 'Frenchness' and the Archaeology of Desire," *International Journal of Historical Archaeology* 11, no. 3 (2008): 370–87.

26. Ibid.; Paul Manning and Ann Uplisashviliu, "'Our Beer': Ethnographic Brands in Postsocialist Georgia," *American Anthropologist* 109, no. 4 (December 1, 2007): 626–41; Elliott Weiss, "Packaging Jewishness: Novelty and Tradition in Kosher Food Packaging," *Design Issues* 20, no. 1 (2004): 48–61; Joseph Tregle, "Creoles and Americans," in *Creole New Orleans: Race and Americanization*, ed. Arnold R. Hirsch and Joseph Logsdon (Baton Rouge: Louisiana State University Press, 1992), 131–85.

27. Ivor Noël Hume, *A Guide to Artifacts of Colonial America* (Philadelphia: University of Pennsylvania Press, 2001); Jean-Robert Pitte, *La bouteille de vin: Histoire d'une révolution* (Paris: Tallandier, 2013).

28. Anne-Marie E. Cantwell and Diana diZerega Wall, *Unearthing Gotham: The Archaeology of New York City* (New Haven, CT: Yale University Press, 2001); Charles Ludington, *The Politics of Wine in Britain: A New Cultural History* (Basingstoke, UK: Palgrave Macmillan, 2013).

29. Dawdy et al., *Investigations at Rising Sun Site*; Dawdy et al., *Investigations at St. Anthony's Garden*, vol. 2. In France *caves* would have been small cellars, but in low-lying New Orleans, such excavations quickly fill with groundwater, so the switch was soon made to above-ground cabinets.

30. Shannon Lee Dawdy and Juana L. C. Ibáñez, *Beneath the Surface of New Orleans's Warehouse District: Archaeological Investigations at the Maginnis Cotton Mill Site* (New Orleans: University of New Orleans, College of Urban and Public Affairs, 1997); chant cited in Liliane Crété, *Daily Life in Louisiana, 1815–1830* (Baton Rouge: Louisiana State University Press, 1981), 14.

31. Both shops include histories of the business on their websites, www.neworleansperfume.com/about.htm and www.hoveparfumeur.com/HistoryPage.htm (quote) (both accessed September 22, 2014).

32. E. Bruce Goldstein, *Sensation and Perception*, 6th ed. (Pacific Grove, CA: Wadsworth-Thomson Learning, 2002); Tanya M. Luhrmann, "Can't Place That Smell? You Must Be American: How Culture Shapes Our Senses," *New York Times*, September 5, 2014; Donald A.

Wilson, *Learning to Smell: Olfactory Perception from Neurobiology to Behavior* (Baltimore: Johns Hopkins University Press, 2006).

33. For example, Shadows on the Teche plantation and Longue Vue House and Gardens.

34. The literature on Storyville remains uneven, but see Emily Epstein Landau, *Spectacular Wickedness: Sex, Race, and Memory in Storyville, New Orleans* (Baton Rouge: Louisiana State University Press, 2013); Alecia P. Long, *The Great Southern Babylon: Sex, Race, and Respectability in New Orleans, 1865–1920* (Baton Rouge: Louisiana State University Press, 2004); Rose, *Storyville, New Orleans;* Judith Kelleher Schafer, *Brothels, Depravity, and Abandoned Women: Illegal Sex in Antebellum New Orleans* (Baton Rouge: Louisiana State University Press, 2009).

35. Dawdy and Weyhing, "Beneath the Rising Sun"; Abigail Solomon-Godeau, "The Other Side of Venus: The Visual Economy of Female Display," in *The Sex of Things: Gender and Consumption in Historical Perspective,* ed. Victoria de Grazia and Ellen Furlough (Berkeley: University of California Press, 1996), 113–50; Rose, *Storyville, New Orleans,* 60.

36. Timothy J. Gilfoyle, *City of Eros: New York City, Prostitution, and the Commercialization of Sex, 1820–1920* (New York: Norton, 1992), 176, 234; Kellor quote on 176.

37. Rose, *Storyville, New Orleans,* 22–24, 56, 77, 84, 98.

38. *New Orleans Daily Picayune,* February 7, 1869.

39. Ibid., November 4, 1883; Rose, *Storyville, New Orleans,* 12; Pierre Bourdieu, *Distinction: A Social Critique of the Judgement of Taste* (Cambridge, MA: Harvard University Press, 1984).

40. Rose, *Storyville, New Orleans,* 11–12, 19, 30, 32, 80, Arlington quote on 48, Williams quote on 75; Schafer, *Brothels, Depravity, and Abandoned Women,* 73.

41. A large sample of Storyville Blue Book advertisements (rare ephemera) are photographically reproduced in Rose, *Storyville, New Orleans,* 136–45; Irwin appears on 138, Meeker on 139.

42. Alan Lomax, *Mister Jelly Roll: The Fortunes of Jelly Roll Morton, New Orleans Creole and "Inventor of Jazz"* (Berkeley: University of California Press, 2001); Donna J. Seifert and Joseph Balicki, "Mary Ann Hall's House," *Historical Archaeology* 39, no. 1 (January 1, 2005): 59–73. Quote from the *New Orleans Mascot,* January 5, 1889. The *Mascot* (1882–91) was a sensational New Orleans newspaper based in the red-light community that became Storyville. Copies are available on microfilm at the New Orleans Public Library. Working women (or writers posing as them) contributed to the gossip and advice columns.

43. On sexual exploitation under slavery, see National Humanities Center, "On Slaveholders' Sexual Abuse of Slaves: Selections from 19th-20th-Century Slave Narratives," in *The Making of African American Identity,* vol. 1, *1500–1865;* Jennifer M. Spear, *Race, Sex, and Social Order in Early New Orleans,* Early America (Baltimore: Johns Hopkins University Press, 2008).

44. Rose, *Storyville, New Orleans,* 9.

45. Ibid., ix–x.

46. Ibid., 172.

47. Walter Benjamin, *The Arcades Project,* ed. Rolf Tiedemann, trans. Howard Eiland (Cambridge, MA: Belknap Press, 1999), convolute O, p. 511.

48. Cited in Rose, *Storyville, New Orleans,* 127.

49. Schafer, *Brothels, Depravity, and Abandoned Women,* 133.

CHAPTER FIVE

1. Shannon Lee Dawdy et al., *Archaeological Investigations at Ursuline Convent (160R49), New Orleans, Louisiana* (Chicago: University of Chicago, 2015).

2. Emily Umberger, "Antiques, Revivals, and References to the Past in Aztec Art," *RES* 13 (1987).

3. Annette Weiner, *Inalienable Possessions: The Paradox of Keeping-While-Giving* (Berkeley: University of California Press, 1992).

4. For a definition and brief description of qualia, see chapter 1.

5. I am greatly indebted to the dissertation research of Lauren Zych on these ceramics. A preliminary report on her work can be found in Appendix E of Shannon Lee Dawdy et al., *Archaeological Investigations at St. Anthony's Garden (160R443), New Orleans, Louisiana*, vol. 2, *2009 Fieldwork and Final Laboratory Analysis for 2008 and 2009 Seasons* (Chicago: University of Chicago, Department of Anthropology, 2014). It should be added that the sherds also do not suggest Choctaw manufacture, though members of that group were active in the outdoor markets of nineteenth-century New Orleans.

6. On Creole interiors, see Liliane Crété, *Daily Life in Louisiana, 1815–1830* (Baton Rouge: Louisiana State University Press, 1981); Jack D. Holden, *Furnishing Louisiana: Creole and Acadian Furniture, 1735–1835*, ed. Jessica Dorman and Sarah Doerries (New Orleans: Historic New Orleans Collection, 2010). The size and lavishness of Dorman and Doerries's book is testimony itself to the local obsession with antiques.

7. For an overview of American Indians in historic Louisiana, see Fred Bowerman Kniffen, *The Historic Indian Tribes of Louisiana: From 1542 to the Present* (Baton Rouge: Louisiana State University Press, 1987); Daniel H. Usner, *Indians, Settlers, & Slaves in a Frontier Exchange Economy: The Lower Mississippi Valley before 1783* (Chapel Hill: University of North Carolina Press, 1992); Daniel H. Usner, *American Indians in the Lower Mississippi Valley: Social and Economic Histories*, Indians of the Southeast (Lincoln: University of Nebraska Press, 1998).

8. Bronislaw Malinowski, *Argonauts of the Western Pacific: An Account of Native Enterprise and Adventure in the Archipelagos of Melanesian New Guinea* (1922; repr., Prospect Heights, IL: Waveland Press, 1984), 90.

9. Anthony J. Stanonis, *Creating the Big Easy: New Orleans and the Emergence of Modern Tourism, 1918–1945* (Athens: University of Georgia Press, 2006), 18.

10. Lissa Capo, "'Throw Me Something, Mister': The History of Carnival Throws in New Orleans" (Master's thesis, University of New Orleans, 2011); Laurie A. Wilkie, *Strung Out on Archaeology* (Walnut Creek, CA: Left Coast Press, 2014). For those not familiar with New Orleans's Mardi Gras, "throws" are tossed to street crowds from masked riders on parade floats. These "gifts" are usually thrown anonymously and broadly, although individuals can be singled out and rewarded with special throws in appreciation for their costumes, for yelling something humorous, or for something else about their appearance that attracts the attention of the rider. Krewe members will also sometimes reward friends and family with special throws when they can identify them on the crowded parade route, but too much of this direct gifting would be frowned upon, as it goes against the general Mardi Gras ethos of generosity toward strangers.

11. Cf. chapter 2.

12. Michael T. Taussig, *Mimesis and Alterity: A Particular History of the Senses* (New York: Routledge, 1993).

13. The two best-known scholarly sources for this reputation still deserve respect: Mikhail Bakhtin, *Rabelais and His World* (Bloomington: Indiana University Press, 1941); Natalie Zemon Davis, *Society and Culture in Early Modern France* (Stanford, CA: Stanford University Press, 1985).

14. Grant David McCracken, *Culture and Consumption: New Approaches to the Symbolic Character of Consumer Goods and Activities* (Bloomington: Indiana University Press, 1988).

15. Kevin Fox Gotham, *Authentic New Orleans: Tourism, Culture, and Race in the Big Easy* (New York: New York University Press, 2007), 152.

16. I am here gesturing to a huge field in anthropology on exchange and value. For the essentials grounded in Melanesia, see Malinowski, *Argonauts of the Western Pacific*; Marcel Mauss, *The Gift: Forms and Functions of Exchange in Archaic Societies,* Norton Library (New York: W. W. Norton, 1967); Nancy D. Munn, *The Fame of Gawa: A Symbolic Study of Value Transformation in a Massim (Papua New Guinea) Society* (Durham, NC: Duke University Press, 1992); Marilyn Strathern, *The Gender of the Gift: Problems with Women and Problems with Society in Melanesia,* Studies in Melanesian Anthropology 6 (Berkeley: University of California Press, 1988); Weiner, *Inalienable Possessions.* See also Arjun Appadurai's introduction to *The Social Life of Things: Commodities in Cultural Perspective* (New York: Cambridge University Press, 1986).

17. Orange Grove Plantation, located in Plaquemines Parish, was abandoned and vandalized in the 1970s and 1980s.

18. What is meant by the ontological in anthropology can range from Deleuzian efforts to validate alternate worlds and unthink Cartesian categories to STS and multispecies interactions. For recent overviews, see B. Alberti et al., "Archaeology, Anthropology, and Ontological Difference Forum," *Current Anthropology* 52, no. 6 (2011): 896–912; Eduardo Kohn, *How Forests Think: Toward an Anthropology beyond the Human* (Berkeley: University of California Press, 2013); Soumhya Venkatesan, ed., "Ontology Is Just Another Word for Culture: Motion Tabled at the 2008 Meeting of the Group for Debates in Anthropological Theory, University of Manchester," with Matei Candea, Michael Carrithers, Martin Holbraad, and Karen Sykes, *Critique of Anthropology* 30, no. 2 (2010): 152–200. The branch that touches on my work is what we could call the "things" interest group. Bruno Latour is the best-known member; his attention to hybrids, assemblages, and actants emphasizes the agency and materiality of physical things as they constrain and/or shape human thought and action (e.g., Bruno Latour, *Reassembling the Social: An Introduction to Actor-Network-Theory* [Oxford: Oxford University Press, 2005]). He is not the only thinker concerned, though, nor is science the only realm in which to question the hoary old Western dualism of subject-object. Alfred Gell's *Art and Agency: An Anthropological Theory* (Oxford: Clarendon Press, 1998) was an important early contributor, and Bill Brown coined "thing theory" as a Heideggerian approach to material culture within and via literature. Bill Brown, "Thing Theory," *Critical Inquiry* 28, no. 1 (2001): 1–22; Bill Brown, *A Sense of Things: The Object Matter of American Literature* (Chicago: University of Chicago Press, 2003). While I have chosen not to engage the elaborate lexicon of the literature, I expect that fluent readers will recognize the nature

of my intervention, which is in part to say that the ontological turn is really a *return* to some fundamental themes in anthropological theory.

19. Patricia Spyer, ed., *Border Fetishisms: Material Objects in Unstable Spaces*. Zones of Religion (New York: Routledge, 1998), introduction.

20. Alfred Binet, *Le fétichisme dans l'amour: La vie psychique des micro-organismes, l'intensité des images mentales, etc.*, Collection Psychanalyse (1887; repr., Paris: Claude Tchou pour la Bibliothèque des Introuvables, 2000); Sigmund Freud, "Fetishism," in *The Complete Psychological Works of Sigmund Freud* (London: Hogarth and the Institute of Psychoanalysis, 1927), 21:147–57; Karl Marx, *Capital: A Critique of Political Economy* (London: Electric Book, 2001).

21. Freud, "Fetishism."

22. Robert J. Stoller, *Observing the Erotic Imagination* (New Haven, CT: Yale University Press, 1985), 155. Collecting itself could be seen as the activity of a fetishist. Baudrillard analyzes it as an extreme form of capitalist consumption. I believe that collecting, like nostalgic practices, can both critique and participate in dominant ideologies. Sometimes at the same time. Jean Baudrillard, "The System of Collecting," in *The Cultures of Collecting*, ed. John Elsner and Roger Cardinal (Cambridge, MA: Harvard University Press, 1994): 7–24.

23. William Pietz, "The Problem of the Fetish, I," *RES* 9 (1985): 5–17.; William Pietz, "The Problem of the Fetish, II: The Origin of the Fetish," *RES* 13 (1987): 23–45, quote on 24; William Pietz, "The Problem of the Fetish, IIIa: Bosman's Guinea and the Enlightenment Theory of Fetishism," *RES* 16 (1988): 105–24. A classic example is the well-known Kongo power figures. In fifteenth-century Portuguese, *feitiço* referred to objects used in witchcraft—or "false sacramental objects of superstition." It derived from the Latin root *factitius,* meaning simply manufactured or man-made (an oracular foreshadowing of Marx's use of the term).

24. Gilles Deleuze, *Difference and Repetition*, European Perspectives (New York: Columbia University Press, 1994), 259.

25. Pietz, "Problem of the Fetish, I."

26. Emile Durkheim, *The Elementary Forms of Religious Life*, trans. Karen Fields (New York: Free Press, 1995), 122.

27. Igor Kopytoff, "The Cultural Biography of Things: Commoditization as Process," in Appadurai, *Social Life of Things*, 64–91.

28. Brown, *Sense of Things*, 124.

CHAPTER SIX

1. Susan Stewart, *On Longing: Narratives of the Miniature, the Gigantic, the Souvenir, the Collection* (Durham, NC: Duke University Press, 1993), 65, 145. On melancholia and preservation, see also David Lowenthal, *The Past Is a Foreign Country* (Cambridge: Cambridge University Press, 1985).

2. Mary Douglas, *Purity and Danger: An Analysis of Concepts of Pollution and Taboo*, Routledge Classics (London: Routledge, 2002); Diana Eastop, "Conservation as Material

Culture," in *Handbook of Material Culture*, ed. Chris Tilley et al. (Thousand Oaks, CA: SAGE, 2006), 516–33, quote on 521.

3. Stewart, *On Longing*, 23.

4. Michael T. Taussig, *The Devil and Commodity Fetishism in South America* (Chapel Hill: University of North Carolina Press, 1980), 7, 123.

5. Georg Simmel, "The Metropolis and Mental Life (1903)," in *The Nineteenth-Century Visual Culture Reader*, ed. J. M. Przyblyski and V. R. Schwartz (New York: Routledge, 2004), 51–55; Bill Brown, *A Sense of Things: The Object Matter of American Literature* (Chicago: University of Chicago Press, 2003), 76.

6. Pierre Bourdieu, *Distinction: A Social Critique of the Judgement of Taste* (Cambridge, MA: Harvard University Press, 1984); Emile Durkheim, *The Elementary Forms of Religious Life*, trans. Karen Fields (New York: Free Press, 1995), 425.

7. Michel Foucault, "Of Other Spaces, Heterotopias," *Architecture, Mouvement, Continuité* 5 (1984); Anthony Shelton, "Museum and Museum Displays," in Tilley et al., *Handbook of Material Culture*, 480–99; Robert Harbison, *Eccentric Spaces* (Cambridge, MA: MIT Press, 2000).

8. Peter Stallybrass, "Marx's Coat," in *Border Fetishisms: Material Objects in Unstable Spaces*, ed. Patricia Spyer (New York: Routledge, 1997), 183–207.

9. Igor Kopytoff, "The Cultural Biography of Things: Commoditization as Process," in *The Social Life of Things*, ed. Arjun Appadurai (New York: Cambridge University Press, 1986), 64–91; Sigmund Freud, *Beyond the Pleasure Principle*, trans. James Strachey, standard ed. (New York: Norton, 1989).

10. Walter Johnson, *Soul by Soul: Life inside the Antebellum Slave Market* (Cambridge, MA: Harvard University Press, 1999).

11. Appadurai, *Social Life of Things*, introduction, quote on 15.

12. At the same time, without any circulation at all, there would be no collective act of valuation. Thus it is likely that the antique market works to renew the value of heirlooms as well as other patinated objects (such as reproductions). In parallel, "the value of the relic had to be renewed periodically through a repetition of transferral or discovery, which would then begin the cycle anew." Most anthropologists would recognize saints' relics, with their sacred dirt of blood and bones, rather unproblematically as an instance of the magico-religious fetish. They are presumed to contain some spiritual essence of the saint or religious person with whom they were associated. This did not mean that relics were inalienable. They could be, and were, bought and sold, as well as stolen and traded on the black market. And this process of the transformation of the fetish illuminates temporal and spatial contours of social belonging: "The transformations of relics from persons to commodities and in some cases back to persons [was] through a process of social and cultural transition." Patrick Geary, "Sacred Commodities: The Circulation of Medieval Relics," in Appadurai, *Social Life of Things*, 169–94, quotes on 188.

13. Stewart, *On Longing*, 136.

14. Kopytoff, "Cultural Biography of Things," 79. As Hoskins expresses it, "In relation to time, the biographical object grows old, and may become worn and tattered along the life span of its owner, while the public commodity is eternally youthful and not used up but

replaced." Janet Hoskins, "Agency, Biography, Objects," in Tilley et al., *Handbook of Material Culture*, 78.

15. Even Appadurai, in his authoritative introduction to *The Social Life of Things*, admitted that the commodity phase of any one object is extremely short. He nevertheless opined, "From a *theoretical* point of view human actors encode things with significance[;] from a *methodological* point of view it is the things-in-motion that illuminate their human and social context." Appadurai, *Social Life of Things*, 5. This is a very strange claim, because if objects are moving between different social worlds, they are without any meaning at all during that period of transport. It seems more reasonable to presume that the relationship between objects and people postpurchase is *at least* as meaningful as the periods of production and exchange. Contra Appadurai, understanding this system of value requires studying objects that are spatially at rest. For another post-Appadurai view, see Harvey Luskin Molotch, *Where Stuff Comes from: How Toasters, Toilets, Cars, Computers, and Many Others Things Come to Be as They Are* (New York: Routledge, 2003).

16. Patricia Spyer, ed., *Border Fetishisms: Material Objects in Unstable Spaces*, Zones of Religion (New York: Routledge, 1998), introduction, 3.

17. Peter Pels, "The Spirit of Matter: On Fetish, Rarity, Fact, and Fancy," in Spyer, *Border Fetishisms*, 91–121, quote on 101.

18. Susanne Kuchler, "Process and Transformation," in Tilley et al., *Handbook of Material Culture*, 328.

19. Pels, "Spirit of Matter," 101.

20. Jacques Derrida, *Specters of Marx: The State of the Debt, the Work of Mourning, and the New International* (New York: Routledge, 1994); Bill Maurer, "In the Matter of Marxism," in Tilley et al., *Handbook of Material Culture*, 23.

21. Stewart, *On Longing*, 139. One thing that is fascinating about this rarely discussed dialogue with the dead through objects is that the temporal sensibility it provokes is twisted— the present is infused not only with the anxiety of having only a quite partial notion of what has gone before, but an anxiety about the subject's future death and the unfair way in which our objects may persist without us. As Harriet Beecher Stowe wrote, "You are living your daily life among trifles that one death-stroke may make relics." Quoted in Brown, *Sense of Things*, 123. Likewise, one can inherit objects that take on the charge of a dead person, altering their meaning and place within our domestic assemblages. Or, through the antique market, the unnamed dead may come to play the role of adopted ancestors.

22. Durkheim, *Elementary Forms of Religious Life*, 191.

23. R. R. Marett, *The Threshold of Religion* (London: Methuen, 1914), 12.

BIBLIOGRAPHY

Adorno, Theodor W., Henri Lonitz, and Walter Benjamin. *The Complete Correspondence, 1928–1940*. Cambridge, MA: Harvard University Press, 1999.

Albertan-Coppola, Sylviane. *Abbé Prévost: Manon Lescaut*. Etudes Littéraires 52. Paris: Presses universitaires de France, 1995.

Alberti, B., S. Fowles, M. Holbraad, Y. Marshall, and C. Witmore. "Archaeology, Anthropology, and Ontological Difference Forum." *Current Anthropology* 52, no. 6 (2001): 896–912.

Alford, Jeremy. "Public Housing's 'Legacy Buildings.'" *Gambit*, July 24, 2012. www.bestof neworleans.com/gambit/legacy-buildings/Content?oid=2045710.

Allen, Thomas M. *A Republic in Time: Temporality and Social Imagination in Nineteenth-Century America*. Chapel Hill: University of North Carolina Press, 2008.

Anderson, Benedict R. *Imagined Communities: Reflections on the Origin and Spread of Nationalism*. Rev. ed. London: Verso, 2006.

Anthony, Ted. *Chasing the Rising Sun: The Journey of an American Song*. New York: Simon & Schuster, 2007.

Appadurai, Arjun. *The Social Life of Things: Commodities in Cultural Perspective*. Cambridge: Cambridge University Press, 1986.

Arendt, Hannah. *The Human Condition*. 2nd ed. Chicago: University of Chicago Press, 1998.

Arnesen, Eric. *Waterfront Workers of New Orleans: Race, Class, and Politics, 1863–1923*. New York: Oxford University Press, 1991.

Asbury, Herbert. *The French Quarter: An Informal History of the New Orleans Underworld*. New York: A. A. Knopf, 1936.

Bakhtin, Mikhail. *Rabelais and His World*. Bloomington: Indiana University Press, 1941.

Baldinucci, Filipe. *Vocabolario Toscano dell'arte del disegno*. Firenze, Italy: Santi Franchi, 1681.

Baudrillard, Jean. "The System of Collecting." In *The Cultures of Collecting*, edited by John Elsner and Roger Cardinal, 7–24. Cambridge, MA: Harvard University Press, 1994.

Baumbach, Richard O. *The Second Battle of New Orleans: A History of the Vieux Carré Riverfront Expressway Controversy*. University: Published for the Preservation Press, National Trust for Historic Preservation in the United States, by the University of Alabama Press, 1981.

Benjamin, Walter. *The Arcades Project*. Edited by Rolf Tiedemann, translated by Howard Eiland. Cambridge, MA: Belknap Press, 1999.

————. "Excavation and Memory." In *Selected Writings, 1931–1934*, edited by Michael W. Jennings, Howard Eiland, and Gary Smith, 576. Cambridge, MA: Belknap Press, 1999.

————. "On the Concept of History." In *Selected Writings, 1938–1940*. Cambridge, MA: Belknap Press, 2006.

————. "Surrealism: The Last Snapshot of the European Intelligentsia." In *Walter Benjamin: Selected Writings*, 2:207–21. Cambridge, MA: Belknap, 2004.

————. "The Work of Art in the Age of Mechanical Reproduction." In *Illuminations*, edited by Hannah Arendt, translated by Harry Zohn, 217–51. New York: Schocken Books, 1986.

Binet, Alfred. *Le fétichisme dans l'amour: La vie psychique des micro-organismes, l'intensité des images mentales, etc.* Collection Psychanalyse. 1887. Reprint, Paris: Claude Tchou pour la Bibliothèque des Introuvables, 2000.

Bourdieu, Pierre. *Distinction: A Social Critique of the Judgement of Taste.* Cambridge, MA: Harvard University Press, 1984.

————. *Outline of a Theory of Practice.* Cambridge Studies in Social Anthropology, 16. Cambridge: Cambridge University Press, 1977.

Boym, Svetlana. *The Future of Nostalgia.* New York: Basic Books, 2001.

Bradley, Richard. *The Past in Prehistoric Societies.* London: Routledge, 2002.

Brasseaux, Carl A., and University of Southwestern Louisiana, eds. *A Refuge for All Ages: Immigration in Louisiana History.* Louisiana Purchase Bicentennial Series in Louisiana History, vol. 10. Lafayette: Center for Louisiana Studies, University of Southwestern Louisiana, 1996.

Brown, Bill. *A Sense of Things: The Object Matter of American Literature.* Chicago: University of Chicago Press, 2003.

————. "Thing Theory." *Critical Inquiry* 28, no. 1 (2001): 1–22.

Brumann, Christoph. "Outside the Glass Case: The Social Life of Urban Heritage in Kyoto." *American Ethnologist* 36, no. 2 (May 1, 2009): 276–99. doi:10.2307/27667562.

Brunsma, David L., David Overfelt, and J. Steven Picou, eds. *The Sociology of Katrina: Perspectives on a Modern Catastrophe.* Lanham, MD: Rowman & Littlefield, 2007.

Buchli, V., G. Lucas, and M. Cox. *Archaeologies of the Contemporary Past.* London: Routledge, 2001.

Buck-Morss, Susan. *The Dialectics of Seeing: Walter Benjamin and the Arcades Project.* Cambridge, MA: MIT Press, 1989.

Butler, Beverly. "Heritage and Present Past." In Tilley et al., *Handbook of Material Culture*, 463–79.

Cable, George Washington. *Old Creole Days.* New York: C. Scribner's, 1879.

Caillot, Marc-Antoine. *A Company Man: The Remarkable French-Atlantic Voyage of a Clerk for the Company of the Indies: A Memoir.* Edited by Erin M. Greenwald, translated by Teri F. Chalmers. New Orleans: Historic New Orleans Collection, 2013.

————. "Relation du Voyage de la Louisianne ou Nouvelle France fait par Sr. Caillot en l'Annee 1730." Manuscript, Historic New Orleans Collection, MSS 596.

Camayd-Freixas, Erik, ed. *Orientalism and Identity in Latin America: Fashioning Self and Other from the (Post)colonial Margin.* Tucson: University of Arizona Press, 2013.

Campanella, Richard. *Geographies of New Orleans: Urban Fabrics before the Storm.* Lafayette: Center for Louisiana Studies, 2006.

Cantwell, Anne-Marie E., and Diana diZerega Wall. *Unearthing Gotham: The Archaeology of New York City*. New Haven, CT: Yale University Press, 2001.

Capo, Lissa. "'Throw Me Something, Mister': The History of Carnival Throws in New Orleans." Master's thesis, University of New Orleans, 2011.

Carlson, Allen. *Nature and Landscape: An Introduction to Environmental Aesthetics*. New York: Columbia University Press, 2009.

Castellanos, Henry C., and George F. Reinecke. *New Orleans as It Was: Episodes of Louisiana Life*. Baton Rouge: Louisiana State University Press, 1978.

Clark, Emily. *The Strange History of the American Quadroon: Free Women of Color in the Revolutionary Atlantic World*. Chapel Hill: University of North Carolina Press, 2013.

Cleere, Eileen. "Dirty Pictures: John Ruskin, 'Modern Painters,' and the Victorian Sanitation of Fine Art." *Representations* 78 (2002): 116–39.

Coleman, W. H. *Historical Sketch Book and Guide to New Orleans and Environs, with Map. Illustrated with Many Original Engravings; and Containing Exhaustive Accounts of the Traditions, Historical Legends, and Remarkable Localities of the Creole City*. New York: W. H. Coleman, 1885.

Collingwood, R. G. *The Idea of History*. Rev. ed., with lectures 1926–1928. Oxford: Oxford University Press, 1994.

Comaroff, John L., and Jean Comaroff, eds. *Ethnicity, Inc*. Chicago Studies in Practices of Meaning. Chicago: University of Chicago Press, 2009.

Connerton, Paul. *How Societies Remember*. Themes in the Social Sciences. Cambridge: Cambridge University Press, 1989.

Conradsen, David H., Newcomb Art Gallery, and Smithsonian Institution. *The Arts & Crafts of Newcomb Pottery*. New York: Skira Rizzoli; New Orleans: Tulane University, Newcomb Art Gallery, 2013.

Copley, Stephen, and Peter Garside, eds. *The Politics of the Picturesque: Literature, Landscape, and Aesthetics since 1770*. Cambridge: Cambridge University Press, 1994.

Crété, Liliane. *Daily Life in Louisiana, 1815–1830*. Baton Rouge: Louisiana State University Press, 1981.

Davis, Natalie Zemon. *Society and Culture in Early Modern France*. Stanford, CA: Stanford University Press, 1985.

Dawdy, Shannon Lee. *Building the Devil's Empire: French Colonial New Orleans*. Chicago: University of Chicago Press, 2008.

———. "Clockpunk Anthropology and the Ruins of Modernity." *Current Anthropology* 51, no. 6 (December 1, 2010): 761–93.

———. "Madame John's Legacy (160R51) Revisited: A Closer Look at the Archaeology of Colonial New Orleans." College of Urban and Public Affairs, University of New Orleans, 1998.

———. "Sexualizing Space: The Colonial Leer and the Genealogy of Storyville." In *The Archaeology of Colonialism: Intimate Encounters and Sexual Effects*, edited by Barbara Voss and Eleanor Casella, 271–89. New York: Cambridge University Press, 2011.

Dawdy, Shannon Lee, and Claire Bowman. *Archaeological Investigations at St. Anthony's Garden (160R443), New Orleans, Louisiana*. Vol. 3, *Artifact Inventory for 2008 and 2009 Seasons*. Chicago: University of Chicago, Department of Anthropology, 2013.

Dawdy, Shannon Lee, Claire Bowman, Christopher Grant, Kristen Gremillon, Susan de-France, and Lauren Zych. *Archaeological Investigations at Ursuline Convent (160R49), New Orleans, Louisiana.* Chicago: University of Chicago, 2015.

Dawdy, Shannon Lee, Claire Bowman, Kristen Gremillon, Susan deFrance, and Lauren Zych. *Archaeological Investigations at St. Anthony's Garden (160R443), New Orleans, Louisiana.* Vol. 2, *2009 Fieldwork and Final Laboratory Analysis for 2008 and 2009 Seasons.* Chicago: University of Chicago, Department of Anthropology, 2014.

Dawdy, Shannon Lee, D. Ryan Gray, Jill-Karen Yakubik, and Rebecca Graff. *Archaeological Investigations at the Rising Sun Hotel Site, New Orleans, Louisiana.* Chicago: University of Chicago, Department of Anthropology, 2008.

Dawdy, Shannon Lee, Kristen Gremillon, Susan Mulholland, and Jason Ramsey. *Archaeological Investigations at St. Anthony's Garden (160R443), New Orleans, Louisiana.* Vol. 1, *2008 Fieldwork and Archaeobotanical Results.* Chicago: University of Chicago, Department of Anthropology, 2008.

Dawdy, Shannon Lee, and Juana L. C. Ibáñez. *Beneath the Surface of New Orleans's Warehouse District: Archaeological Investigations at the Maginnis Cotton Mill Site.* New Orleans: University of New Orleans, College of Urban and Public Affairs, 1997.

Dawdy, Shannon Lee, and Richard Weyhing. "Beneath the Rising Sun: 'Frenchness' and the Archaeology of Desire." *International Journal of Historical Archaeology* 11, no. 3 (2008): 370–87.

De Caro, F. A., and R. A. Jordan, eds. *Louisiana Sojourns: Travelers' Tales and Literary Journeys.* Baton Rouge: Louisiana State University Press, 1998.

Deleuze, Gilles. *Difference and Repetition.* European Perspectives. New York: Columbia University Press, 1994. http://site.ebrary.com/lib/uchicago/Top?id=10333125.

Derrida, Jacques. *Specters of Marx: The State of the Debt, the Work of Mourning, and the New International.* New York: Routledge, 1994.

Dessens, Nathalie. *From Saint-Domingue to New Orleans: Migration and Influences.* Southern Dissent. Gainesville: University Press of Florida, 2007.

Diaconu, Madalina. "Patina—Atmosphere—Aroma: Towards an Aesthetics of Fine Differences." In *Logos of Phenomenology and Phenomenology of the Logos: The Creative Logos: Aesthetic Ciphering in Fine Arts, Literature and Aesthetics,* edited by A. T. Tyminiecka, 131–48. Dordrecht, Netherlands: Kluwer, 2006.

Diderot, Denis, and Jean Le Rond d'Alembert, eds. *The Encyclopedia of Diderot and d'Alembert Collaborative Translation Project.* Ann Arbor: Scholarly Publishing Office of the University of Michigan and DLXS, 2002. http://bibpurl.oclc.org/web/9406.

Dillon, David. "Big Easy Faces Big Questions." *Dallas Morning News,* November 19, 2005. www.dallasnews.com/sharedcontent/dws/news/nation/stories/112005dntexkaturban.25adb252.html.

Douglas, Mary. *Purity and Danger: An Analysis of Concepts of Pollution and Taboo.* Routledge Classics. London: Routledge, 2002.

Drenthen, Martinus Antonius Maria, and Jozef Keulartz, eds. *Environmental Aesthetics: Crossing Divides and Breaking Ground.* Groundworks: Ecological Issues in Philosophy and Theology. New York: Fordham University Press, 2014.

Dumont de Montigny. "Mémoire de Lxx Dxx officier ingénieur, contenant les evenements qui se sont passés à la Louisiane depuis 1715 jusqu'à present." Manuscript, Newberry Library, Ayer MS 257.

———. *The Memoir of Lieutenant Dumont, 1715–1747: A Sojourner in the French Atlantic.* Translated by Gordon M. Sayre. Chapel Hill: University of North Carolina Press; Williamsburg, VA: Omohundro Institute of Early American History and Culture, 2012.

Durkheim, Emile. *The Elementary Forms of Religious Life.* Translated by Karen Fields. New York: Free Press, 1995.

Dyson, Michael Eric. *Come Hell or High Water: Hurricane Katrina and the Color of Disaster.* New York: Basic Civitas, 2006.

Eagleton, Terry. *The Ideology of the Aesthetic.* Cambridge, MA: Basil Blackwell, 1990.

Eastop, Diana. "Conservation as Material Culture." In Tilley et al., *Handbook of Material Culture*, 516–33.

Edwards, Jay D. "New Orleans Shotgun: An Historic Cultural Geography." In *Culture in the Wake: Rhetoric and Reinvention on the Gulf Coast*, edited by M. B. Hackler. Jackson: University Press of Mississippi, 2010.

El-Habashi, Alaa, and Ihab Elzeyadi. "Consuming Built Patrimony: Social Perspectives and Preservation Strategies in Modern Cairo." *Traditional Dwellings and Settlements Review* 10, no. 1 (October 1, 1998): 18. doi:10.2307/41757420.

Fabian, Johannes. *Time and the Other: How Anthropology Makes Its Object.* New York: Columbia University Press, 1983.

Farriss, Nancy M. "Remembering the Future, Anticipating the Past: History, Time, and Cosmology among the Maya of Yucatan." *Comparative Studies in Society and History* 29, no. 3 (1987): 566–93.

Faulkner, William. *Mosquitoes.* New York: Boni and Liveright, 1927.

Flaherty, Jordan. *Floodlines: Community and Resistance from Katrina to the Jena Six.* Chicago: Haymarket Books, 2010.

Flint, Timothy. *Recollections of the Last Ten Years Passed in Occasional Residences and Journeyings in the Valley of the Mississippi, from Pittsburg and the Missouri to the Gulf of Mexico, and from Florida to the Spanish Frontier: In a Series of Letters to the Rev. James Flint, of Salem, Massachusetts.* Boston: Cummings, Hilliard, 1826.

Fortier, Alcée. *Louisiana Folk-Tales, in French Dialect and English Translation.* Boston: Houghton Mifflin, 1895.

Foucault, Michel. "Of Other Spaces, Heterotopias." *Architecture, Mouvement, Continuité* 5 (1984): 46–49.

French, Brigittine M. "The Semiotics of Collective Memories." *Annual Review of Anthropology* 41 (2012): 337–53.

Freud, Sigmund. *Beyond the Pleasure Principle.* Translated by James Strachey. Standard ed. New York: Norton, 1989.

———. "Fetishism." In *The Complete Psychological Works of Sigmund Freud.* London: Hogarth and the Institute of Psychoanalysis, 1927.

Geary, Patrick. "Sacred Commodities: The Circulation of Medieval Relics." In Appadurai, *Social Life of Things*, 169–94.

Gell, Alfred. *Art and Agency: An Anthropological Theory.* Oxford: Clarendon Press, 1998.

Gilfoyle, Timothy J. *City of Eros: New York City, Prostitution, and the Commercialization of Sex, 1820–1920.* New York: Norton, 1992.

Gilloch, Graeme. *Walter Benjamin: Critical Constellations.* Cambridge, UK: Polity Press; Malden, MA: Blackwell, 2002.

Gitlin, Jay. *The Bourgeois Frontier: French Towns, French Traders, and American Expansion.* New Haven, CT: Yale University Press, 2010.

Gold, Scott. "New Orleans Legend May Prove to Be Reputable." *Los Angeles Times,* March 20, 2005.

Goldstein, E. Bruce. *Sensation and Perception.* 6th ed. Pacific Grove, CA: Wadsworth-Thomson Learning, 2002.

Gombrich, E. H. *The Heritage of Apelles.* Ithaca, NY: Cornell University Press, 1976.

González Ruibal, Alfredo, ed. *Reclaiming Archaeology: Beyond the Tropes of Modernity.* Archaeological Orientations. Milton Park, Abingdon, UK: Routledge, 2013.

Gordon, Lori K. *The Katrina Collection,* 2008. http://thekatrinacollectionbylorikgordon .blogspot.com/.

Gorski, Philip S., ed. *Bourdieu and Historical Analysis.* Politics, History, and Culture. Durham, NC: Duke University Press, 2013.

Gotham, Kevin Fox. *Authentic New Orleans: Tourism, Culture, and Race in the Big Easy.* New York: New York University Press, 2007.

Graves-Brown, Paul. *Matter, Materiality, and Modern Culture.* London: Routledge, 2000.

———, ed. *The Oxford Handbook of the Archaeology of the Contemporary World.* Oxford Handbooks. Oxford: Oxford University Press, 2013.

Gray, Danny Ryan. "Effacing the 'Imagined Slum': Space, Subjectivity, and Sociality in the Margins of New Orleans." PhD diss., University of Chicago, 2012.

Grigsby, Darcy Grimaldo. "Patina, Painting, and Portentous Somethings." *Representations* 78 (2002): 140–44.

Gubser, Mike. *Time's Visible Surface: Alois Riegl and the Discourse on History and Temporality in Fin-de-Siècle Vienna.* Kritik: German Literary Theory and Cultural Studies. Detroit: Wayne State University Press, 2006.

Halbwachs, Maurice. *On Collective Memory.* Heritage of Sociology. Chicago: University of Chicago Press, 1992.

Hansen, Miriam. *Cinema and Experience: Siegfried Kracauer, Walter Benjamin, and Theodor W. Adorno.* Berkeley: University of California Press, 2012.

Harbison, Robert. *Eccentric Spaces.* Cambridge, MA: MIT Press, 2000.

Harkness, Nicolas, and Lily Hope Chumley, eds. "Qualia." Special issue, *Anthropological Theory* 13 (March–June 2013).

Harrison, Rodney. *Heritage: Critical Approaches.* Milton Park, Abingdon, UK: Routledge, 2013.

Harrison, Rodney, and A. J. Schofield. *After Modernity: Archaeological Approaches to the Contemporary Past.* Oxford: Oxford University Press, 2010.

Haug, Wolfgang Fritz. *Critique of Commodity Aesthetics: Appearance, Sexuality, and Advertising in Capitalist Society.* Minneapolis: University of Minnesota Press, 1986.

Heard, Malcolm. *French Quarter Manual: An Architectural Guide to New Orleans' Vieux Carré*. New Orleans: Tulane School of Architecture, 1997.

Hearn, Lafcadio. *Lafcadio Hearn's Japan: An Anthology of His Writings on the Country and Its People*. Rutland, VT: Charles E. Tuttle, 1997.

Hearn, Lafcadio, and S. Frederick Starr. *Inventing New Orleans: Writings of Lafcadio Hearn*. Jackson: University Press of Mississippi, 2001.

Heidegger, Martin. *Poetry, Language, Thought*. New York: Harper & Row, 1971.

Hicks, Daniel, Laura McAtackney, and Graham J. Fairclough. *Envisioning Landscape: Situations and Standpoints in Archaeology and Heritage*. Walnut Creek, CA: Left Coast Press, 2007.

Highmore, Ben. *Everyday Life and Cultural Theory: An Introduction*. London: Routledge, 2002.

Hobsbawm, Eric J., and Terence O. Ranger. *The Invention of Tradition*. Cambridge: Cambridge University Press, 1983.

Holden, Jack D. *Furnishing Louisiana: Creole and Acadian Furniture, 1735–1835*. Edited by Jessica Dorman and Sarah Doerries. New Orleans: Historic New Orleans Collection, 2010.

Holmes, Jack D. L. "Indigo in Colonial Louisiana and the Floridas." *Louisiana History* 8, no. 4 (1967): 329–49.

Holtorf, Cornelius. "The Presence of Pastness: Themed Environments and Beyond." In *Staging the Past: Themed Environments in Transcultural Perspectives*, edited by Judith Schlehe, Michiko Uike-Bormann, Carolyn Oesterle, and Wolfgang Hochbruck, 23–40. Historische Lebenswelten in Populären Wissenskulturen, vol. 2. Bielefeld, Germany: Transcript, 2010.

Hoskins, Janet. "Agency, Biography, Objects." In Tilley et al., *Handbook of Material Culture*, 74–84.

Hume, Ivor Noël. *A Guide to Artifacts of Colonial America*. Philadelphia: University of Pennsylvania Press, 2001.

Husserl, Edmund. *On the Phenomenology of the Consciousness of Internal Time (1893–1917)*. In *Collected Works*, vol. 4. Dordrecht, Netherlands: Kluwer Academic, 1991.

Johnson, Walter. *Soul by Soul: Life inside the Antebellum Slave Market*. Cambridge, MA: Harvard University Press, 1999.

Johnson, Zada N. "Walking the Post-disaster City: Race, Space and the Politics of Tradition in the African-American Parading Practices of Post-Katrina New Orleans." PhD diss., University of Chicago, 2010.

Kane, Harnett. *Queen New Orleans, City by the River*. New York: W. Morrow, 1949.

Kenan, Randall. *Walking on Water: Black American Lives at the Turn of the Twenty-First Century*. New York: Knopf, 1999.

Kepecs, Susan. "Saving Old Havana." *Archaeology* 55, no. 2 (March 1, 2002): 42–47. doi:10.2307/41779657.

King, Grace E. *New Orleans: The Place and the People*. New York: Macmillan, 1926.

Kingsford, William. *Impressions of the West and South during a Six Weeks' Holiday*. Toronto: A. H. Armour, 1858.

Kniffen, Fred Bowerman. *The Historic Indian Tribes of Louisiana: From 1542 to the Present.* Baton Rouge: Louisiana State University Press, 1987.

Kohn, Eduardo. *How Forests Think: Toward an Anthropology beyond the Human.* Berkeley: University of California Press, 2013.

Kopytoff, Igor. "The Cultural Biography of Things: Commoditization as Process." In Appadurai, *Social Life of Things*, 64–91.

Koselleck, Reinhart. *Futures Past: On the Semantics of Historical Time.* Cambridge, MA: MIT Press, 1985.

Kuchler, Susanne. "Process and Transformation." In Tilley et al., *Handbook of Material Culture*, 325–29.

Landau, Emily Epstein. *Spectacular Wickedness: Sex, Race, and Memory in Storyville, New Orleans.* Baton Rouge: Louisiana State University Press, 2013.

Latour, Bruno. *Reassembling the Social: An Introduction to Actor-Network-Theory.* Clarendon Lectures in Management Studies. Oxford: Oxford University Press, 2005.

Latrobe, Benjamin. *The Journals of Benjamin Henry Latrobe, 1799–1820: From Philadelphia to New Orleans.* Edited by E. C. Carter, J. C. Van Horne, L. W. Formwalt, and M. H. Society. New Haven, CT: Yale University Press, 1980.

Leach, Edmund Ronald. *Political Systems of Highland Burma: A Study of Kachin Social Structure.* Boston: Beacon Press, 1967.

Leach, Neil, ed. *Rethinking Architecture: A Reader in Cultural Theory.* New York: Routledge, 1997.

Lears, T. J. Jackson. *No Place of Grace: Antimodernism and the Transformation of American Culture, 1880–1920.* Chicago: University of Chicago Press, 1994.

Le Poidevin, Robin, and Murray MacBeath, eds. *The Philosophy of Time.* Oxford Readings in Philosophy. Oxford: Oxford University Press, 1993.

Lévi-Strauss, Claude. *The Way of the Masks.* Translated by Sylvia Modelski. Seattle: University of Washington Press, 1982.

Lewis, Peirce F. *New Orleans: The Making of an Urban Landscape.* 2nd ed. Charlottesville: University of Virginia Press, 2003.

Livingston, Morna. "Houses That Dream in Cuban: The Crumbling of Old Havana," *Traditional Dwellings and Settlements Review* 6, no. 1 (October 1, 1994): 69–70. doi:10.2307 /23565891.

Lomax, Alan. *The Folk Songs of North America.* Garden City, NY: Doubleday, 1960.

———. *Mister Jelly Roll: The Fortunes of Jelly Roll Morton, New Orleans Creole and "Inventor of Jazz."* Berkeley: University of California Press, 2001.

Long, Alecia P. *The Great Southern Babylon: Sex, Race, and Respectability in New Orleans, 1865–1920.* Baton Rouge: Louisiana State University Press, 2004.

Lowenthal, David. *The Past Is a Foreign Country.* Cambridge: Cambridge University Press, 1985.

Lucas, Gavin. *The Archaeology of Time.* London: Routledge, 2005.

Ludington, Charles. *The Politics of Wine in Britain: A New Cultural History.* Basingstoke, UK: Palgrave Macmillan, 2013.

Luhrmann, Tanya M. "Can't Place That Smell? You Must Be American: How Culture Shapes

Our Senses." *New York Times,* September 5, 2014. www.nytimes.com/2014/09/07/opinion/sunday/how-culture-shapes-our-senses.html?_r=0.

Macarthur, John. *The Picturesque: Architecture, Disgust and Other Irregularities.* Classical Tradition in Architecture. London: Routledge, 2007.

Makdisi, Ussama. "Ottoman Orientalism." *American Historical Review* 107, no. 3 (2002): 768–96.

Malinowski, Bronislaw. *Argonauts of the Western Pacific: An Account of Native Enterprise and Adventure in the Archipelagos of Melanesian New Guinea.* 1922. Reprint, Prospect Heights, IL: Waveland Press, 1984. Citations refer to the 1984 edition.

Manning, Paul, and Ann Uplisashviliu. "'Our Beer': Ethnographic Brands in Postsocialist Georgia." *American Anthropologist* 109, no. 4 (December 1, 2007): 626–41. doi:10.1525/aa.2007.109.4.626.

Marett, R. R. *The Threshold of Religion.* London: Methuen, 1914.

Marx, Karl. *Capital: A Critique of Political Economy.* London: Electric Book, 2001

Maurer, Bill. "In the Matter of Marxism." In Tilley et al., *Handbook of Material Culture,* 13–28.

Mauss, Marcel. *The Gift: Forms and Functions of Exchange in Archaic Societies.* Norton Library. New York: W. W. Norton, 1967.

McCracken, Grant David. *Culture and Consumption: New Approaches to the Symbolic Character of Consumer Goods and Activities.* Bloomington: Indiana University Press, 1988.

Meiu, George Paul. "Ethno-Erotic Economies: Crafting Samburu Futures in Postcolonial Kenya." PhD diss., University of Chicago, 2013.

Meskell, Lynn, *The Nature of Heritage: The New South Africa.* Hoboken, NJ: Wiley, 2011.

Metzinger, Thomas. *Being No One: The Self-Model Theory of Subjectivity.* Cambridge, MA: MIT Press, 2003.

Mitchell, W. J. T. "Romanticism and the Life of Things: Fossils, Totems, and Images." *Critical Inquiry* 28, no. 1 (2001): 167–84.

Molotch, Harvey Luskin. *Where Stuff Comes from: How Toasters, Toilets, Cars, Computers, and Many Others Things Come to Be as They Are.* New York: Routledge, 2003.

Moore, Leonard N. *Black Rage in New Orleans: Police Brutality and African American Activism from World War II to Hurricane Katrina.* Baton Rouge: Louisiana State University Press, 2010.

Munn, Nancy D. "The Cultural Anthropology of Time: A Critical Essay." *Annual Review of Anthropology* 21 (1992): 93–123.

———. *The Fame of Gawa: A Symbolic Study of Value Transformation in a Massim (Papua New Guinea) Society.* Durham, NC: Duke University Press, 1992.

———. "Gawan Kula: Spatiotemporal Control and the Symbolism of Influence." In *The Kula: New Perspectives on Massim Exchange,* edited by E. Leach and J. Leach, 277–308. Cambridge: Cambridge University Press, 1983.

Nasar, Jack L., ed. *Environmental Aesthetics: Theory, Research, and Applications.* Cambridge: Cambridge University Press, 1988.

National Humanities Center. "On Slaveholders' Sexual Abuse of Slaves: Selections from 19th-20th-Century Slave Narratives." In *The Making of African American Identity,* vol. 1,

1500–1865. http://nationalhumanitiescenter.org/pds/maai/enslavement/text6/master slavesexualabuse.pdf (accessed September 22, 2014).

Nichols, Henry W. *Restoration of Ancient Bronzes and Cure of Malignant Patina.* Chicago: Field Museum of Natural History, 1930.

Nora, Pierre. "Between Memory and History: Les Lieux de Mémoire." *Representations* 26 (1989): 7–24.

Olivier, Laurent. *The Dark Abyss of Time: Archaeology and Memory.* Translated by Arthur Greenspan. Archaeology in Society Series. Lanham, MD: AltaMira Press, 2011.

———. "The Past of the Present: Archaeological Memory and Time." *Archaeological Dialogues* 10, no. 2 (2004): 204–13.

Olmstead, Frederick Law. *A Journey in the Seaboard States: With Remarks on Their Economy.* New York: Dix and Edwards, 1856.

Oxfeldt, Elisabeth. *Nordic Orientalism: Paris and the Cosmopolitan Imagination, 1800–1900.* Copenhagen: Museum Tusculanum, 2005.

Peirce, Charles S. *Writings of Charles S. Peirce: A Chronological Edition.* Bloomington: Indiana University Press, 1982.

Pels, Peter. "The Spirit of Matter: On Fetish, Rarity, Fact, and Fancy." In Spyer, *Border Fetishisms*, 91–121.

Pensky, Max. "Method and Time: Benjamin's Dialectical Images." In *The Cambridge Companion to Walter Benjamin*, edited by David S. Ferris, 177–98. Cambridge Companions to Literature. Cambridge: Cambridge University Press, 2004.

Pietz, William. "The Problem of the Fetish, I." *RES* 9 (1985): 5–17.

———. "The Problem of the Fetish, II: The Origin of the Fetish." *RES* 13 (1987): 23–45.

———. "The Problem of the Fetish, IIIa: Bosman's Guinea and the Enlightenment Theory of Fetishism." *RES* 16 (1988): 105–24.

Pitot, James, and Robert D. Bush. *Observations on the Colony of Louisiana, from 1796 to 1802.* Baton Rouge: Louisiana State University Press, 1979.

Pitte, Jean-Robert. *La bouteille de vin: Histoire d'une révolution.* Paris: Tallandier, 2013.

Pittman, Philip. *The Present State of the European Settlements on the Mississippi; with a Geographical Description of That River.* London: Printed for J. Nourse, 1770.

Powell, Lawrence N. *The Accidental City: Improvising New Orleans.* Cambridge, MA: Harvard University Press, 2012.

Proust, Marcel. *Remembrance of Things Past.* New York: Random House, 1981.

Rabinow, Paul. *French Modern: Norms and Forms of the Social Environment.* Cambridge, MA: MIT Press, 1989.

Reed, John Shelton. *Dixie Bohemia: A French Quarter Circle in the 1920s.* Baton Rouge: Louisiana State University Press, 2012.

Riegl, Alois. "The Modern Cult of Monuments: Its Character and Its Origin." In *The Nineteenth-Century Visual Culture Reader*, edited by J. M. Przyblyski and V. R. Schwartz, 56–59. New York: Routledge, 2004.

Rosaldo, Renato. *Culture & Truth: The Remaking of Social Analysis: With a New Introduction.* Boston: Beacon Press, 1993.

Rose, Al. *Storyville, New Orleans: Being an Authentic, Illustrated Account of the Notorious Red-Light District.* Birmingham: University of Alabama Press, 1974.

Ruskin, John. *The Seven Lamps of Architecture*. London: Smith Elder, 1849.

Said, Edward W. *Orientalism*. Vol. 1. New York: Pantheon Books, 1978.

Saito, Yuriko. *Everyday Aesthetics*. London: Oxford University Press, 2008.

Sala, George A. *America Revisited: From the Bay of New York to the Gulf of Mexico, and from Lake Michigan to the Pacific*. London: Vizetelly, 1885.

Saxon, Lyle, and E. H. Suydam. *Fabulous New Orleans*. New York: Century, 1928.

Schafer, Judith Kelleher. *Brothels, Depravity, and Abandoned Women: Illegal Sex in Antebellum New Orleans*. Baton Rouge: Louisiana State University Press, 2009.

Schnapp, Jeffrey, Michael Shanks, and Matthew Tiews. "Editor's Introduction." *Modernism/Modernity* 11 (2004): 1–16.

Scott, Julie, and Tom Selwyn. *Thinking through Tourism*. Oxford: Berg, 2010.

Seifert, Donna J., and Joseph Balicki. "Mary Ann Hall's House." *Historical Archaeology* 39, no. 1 (January 1, 2005): 59–73. doi:10.2307/25617236.

Shapiro, Nat. *Hear Me Talkin' to Ya: The Story of Jazz as Told by the Men Who Made It*. New York: Dover, 1966.

Shelton, Anthony. "Museum and Museum Displays." In Tilley et al., *Handbook of Material Culture*, 480–99.

Shepherd, Samuel C., ed. *New Orleans and Urban Louisiana*. Louisiana Purchase Bicentennial Series in Louisiana History, vol. 14. Lafayette: Center for Louisiana Studies, University of Louisiana at Lafayette, 2005.

Sieberg, Daniel, and Soledad O'Brien. "Preserving New Orleans' Military History," *CNN American Morning*, November 11, 2005. http://transcripts.cnn.com/TRANSCRIPTS/0511/11/ltm.02.html.

Simmel, Georg. "The Metropolis and Mental Life (1903)." In *The Nineteenth-Century Visual Culture Reader*, edited by J. M. Przyblyski and V. R. Schwartz, 51–55. New York: Routledge, 2004.

Singleton, Arthur. *Letters from the South and West*. Boston: Richardson and Lord, 1824.

Smith, Michael P. *Mardi Gras Indians*. Gretna, LA: Pelican, 1994.

Solomon-Godeau, Abigail. "The Other Side of Venus: The Visual Economy of Female Display." In *The Sex of Things: Gender and Consumption in Historical Perspective*, edited by Victoria de Grazia and Ellen Furlough, 113–50. Berkeley: University of California Press, 1996.

Sørensen, Marie Louise Stig. *Heritage Studies: Methods and Approaches*. London: Routledge, 2009.

Souther, Jonathan Mark. "The Disneyfication of New Orleans: The French Quarter as Facade in a Divided City." *Journal of American History* 94 (2007): 804–11.

———. *New Orleans on Parade: Tourism and the Transformation of the Crescent City*. Making the Modern South. Baton Rouge: Louisiana State University Press, 2006.

Spear, Jennifer M. *Race, Sex, and Social Order in Early New Orleans*. Early America. Baltimore: Johns Hopkins University Press, 2008.

Spyer, Patricia, ed. *Border Fetishisms: Material Objects in Unstable Spaces*. Zones of Religion. New York: Routledge, 1998.

Stallybrass, Peter. "Marx's Coat." In *Border Fetishisms: Material Objects in Unstable Spaces*, edited by Patricia Spyer. New York: Routledge, 1997.

Stanonis, Anthony J. *Creating the Big Easy: New Orleans and the Emergence of Modern Tourism, 1918–1945*. Athens: University of Georgia Press, 2006.

Starn, Randolph. "Three Ages of 'Patina' in Painting." *Representations* 78 (2002): 86–115.

Stewart, Susan. *On Longing: Narratives of the Miniature, the Gigantic, the Souvenir, the Collection*. Durham, NC: Duke University Press, 1993.

Stoler, Ann L. "Imperial Debris: Reflections on Ruins and Ruination." *Cultural Anthropology* 23, no. 2 (2008): 191–219.

Stoller, Robert J. *Observing the Erotic Imagination*. New Haven, CT: Yale University Press, 1985.

Stoppani, Teresa. "Venice, Time, and the Meander." *Log* 12 (April 1, 2008): 131–43. doi:10.2307/41765626.

Strathern, Marilyn. *The Gender of the Gift: Problems with Women and Problems with Society in Melanesia*. Studies in Melanesian Anthropology 6. Berkeley: University of California Press, 1988.

Tallant, Robert. *The Romantic New Orleanians*. Vol. 1. New York: Dutton, 1950.

———. *Voodoo in New Orleans*. New York,: Macmillan, 1946.

Taussig, Michael T. *The Devil and Commodity Fetishism in South America*. Chapel Hill: University of North Carolina Press, 1980.

———. *Mimesis and Alterity: A Particular History of the Senses*. New York: Routledge, 1993.

Thomas, Lynnell L. *Desire & Disaster in New Orleans: Tourism, Race, and Historical Memory*. Durham, NC: Duke University Press, 2014.

Tilley, Christopher, Webb Keane, Susanne Kuechler-Fogden, Mike Rowlands, and Patricia Spyer, eds. *Handbook of Material Culture*. Thousand Oaks, CA.: SAGE, 2006.

Tregle, Joseph. "Creoles and Americans." In *Creole New Orleans: Race and Americanization*, edited by Arnold R. Hirsch and Joseph Logsdon, 131–85. Baton Rouge: Louisiana State University Press, 1992.

Umberger, Emily. "Antiques, Revivals, and References to the Past in Aztec Art." *RES* 13 (1987).

Upton, Dell. "Black and White Landscapes in Eighteenth-Century Virginia." *Places* 2, no. 2 (1984): 59–72.

Usner, Daniel H. *American Indians in the Lower Mississippi Valley: Social and Economic Histories*. Indians of the Southeast. Lincoln: University of Nebraska Press, 1998.

———. *Indians, Settlers, & Slaves in a Frontier Exchange Economy: The Lower Mississippi Valley before 1783*. Chapel Hill: Published for the Omohundro Institute of Early American History and Culture, Williamsburg, VA, by University of North Carolina Press, 1992.

Venkatesan, Soumhya, ed. "Ontology Is Just Another Word for Culture: Motion Tabled at the 2008 Meeting of the Group for Debates in Anthropological Theory, University of Manchester." With Matei Candea, Michael Carrithers, Martin Holbraad, and Karen Sykes. *Critique of Anthropology* 30, no. 2 (2010): 152–200.

Weiner, Annette. *Inalienable Possessions: The Paradox of Keeping-While-Giving*. Berkeley: University of California Press, 1992.

———. "Inalienable Wealth." *American Ethnologist* 12 (1985): 210–27.

Weiss, Elliott. "Packaging Jewishness: Novelty and Tradition in Kosher Food Packaging." *Design Issues* 20, no. 1 (2004): 48–61.

Wilkie, Laurie A. *Strung Out on Archaeology*. Walnut Creek, CA: Left Coast Press, 2014.

Wilson, Donald A. *Learning to Smell: Olfactory Perception from Neurobiology to Behavior*. Baltimore: Johns Hopkins University Press, 2006.

Wilson, Samuel, Jr. *The Architecture of Colonial Louisiana: Collected Essays of Samuel Wilson, Jr.* Edited by Jean M. Farnsworth and Ann Masson. Lafayette: Center for Louisiana Studies, 1987.

Witmore, Christopher. "Landscape, Time, Topology: An Archaeological Account of the Southern Argolid Greece." In Hicks, McAtackney, and Fairclough, *Envisioning Landscape*, 194–225.

Wright, Gwendolyn. *The Politics of Design in French Colonial Urbanism*. Chicago: University of Chicago Press, 1991.

INDEX

aesthetics, 4–7, 11–17, 29, 133, 141; of architecture, 33, 59–60, 62, 64, 66, 73; Creole, 118, 130, 132; everyday aesthetics, 16; of gardens, 99, 109; of modernism and modernity, 64, 123, 155; and nostalgia, 143–45; and orientalism, 87. *See also* patina: aesthetic of

African Americans, 45–46, 49, 55, 64, 135–36

Africans, 90–91, 138

age value, 15. *See also* look of age

alienation, 6–7, 15, 27, 114, 146, 149; of commodities, 127–29, 140, 152, 159n9

Allen, Thomas, 29

American Indians (Native Americans), 7, 79, 89–91, 114, 170n7, 158n12; Appalachee, 117; Chickasaw, 119; Choctaw, 170n5; Creek, 117; Natchez, 117, 119

Americans, 6–7, 22, 29, 33–34, 56–61, 91; and sexuality, 102–3, 106. *See also* Creoles: tensions with Americans

Anderson, Sherwood, 56–57

anomie, 6, 145, 155

antebellum period, 34, 43, 71, 103, 107, 119, 149; literature of, 52, 57; New Orleans society in, 23, 45, 48, 87–88, 96–97, 151

antimodernism, 6, 51, 144

antique cities, 1, 4, 6, 141, 145, 157n6

antique fetish, 114, 137–42, 152–53

antiques, 123–36, 139–41, 151–55; antique shops, 74, 113, 117, 126–27. *See also* collecting; markets: antique

Apelles of Kos, 12

Appadurai, Arjun, 151, 174n15

archaeology of the contemporary, 9, 158n15

architecture, 48–51, 53–55, 59–65, 112, 134, 148; aging and longevity of, 31–34, 77–80; connoisseurship of, 16, 76; and Frenchness, 92; mana of, 72–73; and romanticism, 13–14; of Storyville, 102, 105–7. *See also* historic preservation

Arendt, Hannah, 28

art, 4, 10, 13–16, 38, 104–5, 147, 154

arts and crafts style, 51, 120

atramentum, 12

auctions, 126, 128, 131–32, 140–41, 151–52

aura, 18, 26, 79, 86, 119, 139; Benjamin's aura of art, 9–11, 151, 154; Benjamin's aura of the habitual, 10–11, 149

authenticity, 27, 71–72, 76, 145–46, 149, 151; and aura, 10; authentication, 11–12, 41, 44, 51, 66, 151; and the fetish, 139; of objects, 93, 114, 121–22, 146, 154

Aztecs, 114

Baldinucci, Filippo, 12

balls (dances), 40, 88, 103, 110, 119

Baudelaire, Charles, 146, 149